Selected Works of C.J. DENNIS

With illustrations by Hal Gye
and
an introduction by Barry Watts

ANGUS
& ROBERTSON
PUBLISHERS

ACKNOWLEDGEMENTS

With the exception of the caricature of C. J. Dennis, which is used with permission of Fisher Library, University of Sydney, all the colour plates appear courtesy of the Mitchell Library and the artist's estate.

The black and white illustrations accompanying the children's poems are by the author and are from the Angus & Robertson archives.

ANGUS & ROBERTSON PUBLISHERS

Unit 4, Eden Park, 31 Waterloo Road,
North Ryde, NSW, Australia 2113, and
16 Golden Square, London W1R 4BN,
United Kingdom

First published in Australia
by Angus & Robertson Publishers in 1988

National Library of Australia
Cataloguing-in-publication data.
Dennis, C. J. (Clarence James), 1876-1938.
C. J. Dennis selected works.
ISBN 0 207 15744 8.
I. Gye, Hal, 1888-1967. II. Title.
A821'.2

Typeset in 10/11pt Goudy Old Style
Printed in Australia by Australian Print Group

CONTENTS

CONTENTS

INTRODUCTION

The Australian poet C. J. Dennis was at times very vague about his early background. Even his friend and biographer, Alec Chisholm, admitted to being confused when he tried to establish the truth about Dennis's childhood and youth. Chisholm's book, *C. J. Dennis — His Remarkable Career*, first published in 1946, notes the gaps in Dennis's life story which occur primarily in his teenage years and in his early twenties. Dennis was vague about these periods himself, even with his friends. When he was in his mid-thirties he told his mentor and friend, Robert Croll, a man of letters and author of several books, that he did not know the year of his birth. Dennis's biographical note which he gave to Croll in 1913 says, "Born in Auburn, SA, some time in late seventies — don't know exact year, say '77 or '78 . . ." He was actually born in 1876, on 7 September, to James Dennis and his second wife Katherine, and was baptised three days later as Clarence Michael James.

As Clarence Michael grew to maturity, he styled his name differently, dropping his given middle name altogether until eventually he was known as "C. J. Dennis" or in his later years, somewhat affectionately, as "Den".

A second son, Francis Albert (known as Bert), was born into the Dennis family in 1880 and, after a gap of six years, their third and final child, Claude Leo, arrived.

The death of Kate Dennis when she was thirty-seven years old caused a major upheaval in the family. She died in Adelaide on 16 August 1890 and was buried there in the West Terrace Cemetery. At this time Clarrie was a fourteen-year-old adolescent, Bert was ten and young Claude just four and a half. Their father was himself fifty-four and now fully occupied in running the Gladstone Hotel at Gladstone and hardly keen to tend to the upbringing of his growing family. A quick solution to this situation became imperative.

Two spinster sisters of the late Kate Dennis came to the family's rescue. Mary Ann and Sarah Tobin moved into the Dennis establishment and provided the comfort and direction their three Dennis nephews needed.

The sisters brought to their task some quaint attitudes of gentility which now seem to be at odds with the hotel environment into which their charges had been born. The aunts pampered the lads and dressed them in starched suits and patent leather shoes, setting them apart from their mates by being over-protective, strict and decidedly old-fashioned.

Due to his Little Lord Fauntleroy appearance, young Clarrie became subjected to much teasing and ridicule from other young men of his age. At school Clarrie Dennis had mostly played with the girls and was considered to be effeminate.

It has since been propounded by Chisholm and others that the "tough guys" in C. J. Dennis's subsequent literary career were created as deliberate contrasts to the "lavender and lace" of his adolescent upbringing.

These years of Dennis's youth were marked by a number of moves from town to town. His father, either due to financial success or wanderlust, was licensee of a succession of hotels in South Australia. The family moved from Watervale, to Gladstone, to Laura.

At fourteen, Master Clarrie Dennis was sent off to a boarding school in Adelaide — to the Christian Brothers' College in Wakefield Street. This was a major change in his life, and one to which he seemingly adapted well. "I have never ceased to remember the good old days at CBC," Dennis recalled much later, "and the great times I had there."

A Literary Society at the college published a journal called *Interesting Scraps*. Thanks to the keen bibliographic research undertaken by a more recent Dennis biographer, Ian F. McLaren of Melbourne, we know that "Clarence Dennis of Gladstone" contributed a serial story and a satiric interpretation of a well-known poem to this publication in 1891.

Dennis left school in December 1892, three months after his sixteenth birthday, and gained employment with an Adelaide stock and station agency and wool store. It proved a short engagement as Dennis was, in his own words, "sacked for reading Dickens and Rider Haggard in business hours".

From Dennis's own biographical note, we learn a little of his whereabouts and activities during the next few years:

Went North. Became Auctioneer's Clerk and knocked about Wheat and Sheep Country for three or four years. While there wrote some bush verse of which I was very much ashamed. Local doctor collared it and sent it to Critic. *They printed it and asked for more. Month or two later was astounded on being hailed as only decent versifier in SA.*

The local *Laura Standard* also published some verse by C. J. Dennis in 1895. The poet and five of his friends became lost in the Beetaloo Hills while on a shooting expedition, and Dennis, describing himself as "the best of the six", wrote a skit on their experience. Chisholm correctly observed that "the verses are brisk and saucy, with some foretaste of the clever rhyming that afterwards developed".

Dennis was at this time a dashing local figure who participated fully in local sporting and theatrical activities. He expressed a reforming zest in his ideas, and developed a liking for the works of Charles Dickens. He was working intermittently behind the bar of his father's hotel, and as Humphrey McQueen, social historian, commented, this work "apprenticed him to alcoholism".

At about this time C. J. Dennis went to Adelaide on holidays and visited the *Critic's* editor, Alfred McCain, who, as Dennis put it, "snared me for a position on the staff". Dennis remained on this "sedate social weekly" for twelve months before he "got sick of it and went to Broken Hill". Before leaving, he telegraphed his father in Laura: "Send ten pounds. Going to Broken Hill." Back came the prompt reply: "Sending nothing. Go to hell." As Dennis soon found out, that's precisely where he was going!

Dennis's terse biographical note speaks volumes:

Hell! Worked in mines, starved, travelled for photographer, carpenter's mate, station-hand, coal forger [?], starved some more, kangaroo shooter, canvasser.

Walking from Broken Hill to a homestead some fifty kilometres distant, C. J. Dennis almost perished in the harsh and barren country. He survived, but only just; his health and spirit were broken and it is likely that he had been drinking too much. He promptly returned to South Australia and to his accommodating aunts. They studiously nursed and fed him, and his health and disposition gradually improved.

This outback period had left him scarred, however. It is reflected in a later verse he wrote called "The Silver City". It starts:

> *Come sing us a song of the city of sand,*
> *Silver, sin, and sixpenny ale;*
> *Dumped in a desolate, drought-struck land,*
> *Where the dead-beat pitches his pitiful tale . . .*

Back in Adelaide, Dennis again pursued his literary ambitions. He rejoined the staff of the *Critic* and commenced writing and submitting material to other publications as well. He wrote a regular weekly prose column for the *Critic* called "The Curbstone Club". It ran for eighteen months, finishing around Christmas 1903.

Alf McCain was founder and editor of the *Critic* and on his retirement from that journal, C. J. Dennis was appointed editor. It was a great opportunity for him to build an interstate reputation as the *Critic* circulated beyond his home state. Further, it provided him with the unexpected chance to appoint a youthful contributor to a staff position. Sixteen-year-old Archie Martin was to shortly conceive the idea for a new, cheeky weekly magazine that would provide a stark contrast to the staid *Critic*.

In August 1905, Dennis and Martin called together a group of literary friends for the purpose of forming the "Gadfly Syndicate" to publish their new brainchild. Their difficulty in raising capital was counterbalanced by the enthusiastic group who undertook to supply contributions for the *Gadfly*, as the publication was to be named.

The *Gadfly* was first published on 14 February 1906. The editor, one C. J. Dennis, announced the paper's aims:

> *Our chief objective in coming out is to make money, which money we desire, with much fervency, to earn honestly, by giving our subscribers fair value ... The* Gadfly *is run by Australians in the interests of things Australian. It is our intention to encourage, so far as in our power, Australian literature and art ...*

The financial structure of the *Gadfly* was perilous from the outset; the advertising revenue was insufficient to pay the staff, contributors and printers. According to tales told since, Percy Bird, the magazine's secretary, was obliged to pawn his gold watch every Saturday morning in order to pay the staff. Early the following week, once the advertisers had paid their accounts, he would redeem it. The printers simply had to hope that sufficient funds remained to cover their bills!

Dennis summed up their situation in verse:

> *Sing a song of sixpence*
> *A pocket full of hope;*
> *Four and twenty printer's bills*
> *In an envelope.*
> *When the bills were opened*
> *The staff began to cry:*
> *Wasn't that an awful thing*
> *To set before the "Fly"!*

Lightheartedness and immodesty characterised the overall editorial approach ... bohemia had arrived in Adelaide!

To keep contributors' costs down, staff members wrote under a variety of psuedonyms and it was common to have several pieces of prose or verse appearing in a single issue emanating from a single person, but attributed to many. C. J. Dennis used a wide variety of signatures for his work — C.J.D., Den, Klariden, Ded, Terence O'Ruddy, T. O'R. and O'R. being just a few of them. (For a detailed account see "C. J. Dennis: A Chronological Checklist" by Ian F. McLaren.)

The "Gadfly Family" contributors were of a very high standard. They included Ruby Lindsay (sister of Norman and Lionel) who was married to Will Dyson, who himself was a contributor as, too, were his brothers, Edward and Ambrose. Illustrator Hal Gye, who later enhanced C. J. Dennis's best-known books, was yet another talented contributor.

But when the money runs out and the bills remain unpaid, the variety and standard of the contributors account for little. At the end of November 1907, the editor called it quits.

C. J. Dennis moved to Melbourne to live, leaving behind a supply of verse for the *Gadfly* to draw on. His twenty-one months there had tested his creative talents and not found him lacking. Now he sought broader horizons.

Dennis's meagre savings were exhausted soon after his arrival in Melbourne. He met, and drank with, many writers, artists, journalists and sculptors. He was introduced to politicians and businessmen, and although everyone was pleased to speak and drink with him, there was little prospect of obtaining gainful work.

The wild city life of bohemian Melbourne, with its drinking parties and boisterous company, was fine, but it began effecting Dennis's always-suspect health. One weekend he was taken to Toolangi for a camping holiday by a newly acquired artist friend, Hal Waugh.

Toolangi is a small timber-milling and potato-growing community on the southern edges of the Great Dividing Range, about seventy-five kilometres north-east of Melbourne. This part of the country was very different to any Dennis had experienced, the very antithesis of the arid areas around Broken Hill. The towering mountain ashes and the verdant fern gullies were home to countless carolling birds; the richness of the soil generated a vast variety of greenness; the crisp, clean air had about it the permanent spirit of rejuvenation. For a poet depleted of energy and money, this was an ideal place to rest up and consider his position.

In his biographical note addressed to Robert Croll, Dennis says, "Came to Toolangi to spend fortnight with Hal Waugh and you know the rest." The "rest" was that Dennis chose to settle in this mountain township and call it home for most of his life thereafter.

In 1908, with simply nowhere else to go, Dennis moved into a vacant weatherboard cottage, formerly occupied by a timber-cutter, and began concentrating on freelance journalism and verse writing.

One of the first things he wrote was submitted, tongue-in-cheek, to a national song competition being conducted by the *Bulletin* magazine. It was a four-verse poem which Dennis called "The Austra—laise". Dennis's submission was awarded a special prize of one guinea and the judge hailed it as "the only satisfactory battle-song submitted", predicting that it would "win its way to every heart in the backblocks".

An extended version of this poem was released by Dennis a few years later and incorporated into his first book. He suggested that it should be sung to the tune of "Onward Christian Soldiers" and that the missing words, which characterise it, should be replaced with the adjective "blessed" or for greater emphasis, "blooming". Readers can reasonably assume that most people used the "great Australian adjective", "bloody", to fill the gaps in Dennis's verse, but its author certainly never gave that possibility any written currency.

Dennis worked spasmodically as a freelance writer, mixed freely with the local denizens (who doubtless thought him a little strange), sending contributions to newspapers and magazines around Australia and by the following year his verse was receiving greater acceptance. Publications like the

Bulletin, Lone Hand and even the Adelaide *Critic* were pleased to publish him, even if they paid poorly.

An insight into Dennis's life at this time is provided by Florence Mitchell, schoolteacher at Toolangi from 1911 to 1913, who became a close friend.

> *Dennis came across from his hut, about a quarter of a mile from the Smedley house, arrayed in pink shirt and green tie. It was a bit much for Toolangi. The men dressed very conservatively there . . .*
>
> *Mr Dennis took me climbing Mt St Leonard [the highest local mountain, about 1000 metres high] and up Tanglefoot to Fiddler's Hill. That was the first time I saw a lyrebird, and he showed me my first platypus in the river behind Smedley's . . .*
>
> *Mr and Mrs Smedley were wonderfully good to Dennis; they deserve a plaque for what they did for him. He would stay talking by their fire until late at night — too long, I felt, when he should be getting on with his writing. Eventually I told him so . . . I told him he was apathetic.*

Nineteen thirteen was to become a watershed year for the poet. It was the year he met Robert Henderson Croll, and subsequently some of Croll's influential friends, and it was also the year his first book was published.

Robert Croll was a public servant in the Victorian Department of Education, an author and a dedicated bushwalker who had met Dennis by accident as he trekked through the bush near the hut Dennis had usurped.

Croll knew Dennis's work. They fell into lively conversation, probably over a billy of tea, and commenced a friendship that helped stimulate the poet and revive his creative instincts and ambitions.

Soon Croll introduced Dennis to a man who proved to be the kind of father figure Dennis required, one who provided incentive, succour and reassurance. His name was John Garibaldi Roberts, known as "Garry". Roberts was manager of Melbourne's original horse-drawn and cable tram operators, the Melbourne Tramway and Omnibus Company. He was not only a successful businessman, but a person of diverse intellectual interests as well. He held a special affection for Australian arts and literature. His wife, Roberta, shared these inclinations and proved an enormous ally to C. J. Dennis, a debt he fully acknowledged.

Dennis hoped to interest a publisher in producing a book of his work. By this time he had a collection of material which had appeared in the *Bulletin* and other journals around the country, sufficient in variety and style to appeal to a wider public. Dennis spoke with bookseller – publisher E. W. Cole of Cole's Book Arcade and *Cole's Funny Picture Book* fame about the book idea, and was delighted when the white-bearded eccentric agreed to publish it.

When he was next in Melbourne, Dennis was introduced to the New Zealand—born caricaturist David Low, who had joined the Melbourne office of the *Bulletin*. They became friends and Dennis was invited to share studio rooms Low had with Hal Gye. Dennis knew of Gye's work which he had published in the *Gadfly* years before.

David Low was impressed with Hal Gye's watercolour technique too. "He painted symphonies with a dreamy effect which he produced by losing his temper with them and putting them under the tap."

The trio got on extremely well. "Here were a couple of characters in whose company I found rest and understanding," Low wrote later. "We could laugh, shout, sing, exult, mourn, curse . . . as we wrestled with our work."

In his autobiography, published forty-three years later, David Low wrote of a weekend visit to Den's "home" in the bush.

We three would shut up shop, assemble some tins of beans and walk over the hills and far away to Den's broken-down house at Toolangi.

In those days we had to light the fire carefully in the old range because a snake lived there, and the only chance of a bath was in an ice-cold water-hole with crayfish [yabbies] on the bottom of it.

Young, romantic, sitting in congenial company on top of the wooded wilderness in the open clear blue Australian night . . . that was a taste of happiness.

Dennis's first book was called *Backblock Ballads and Other Verses*. Its front cover was designed by David Low and showed a dandified city poet sitting on a stool playing a lyre and singing to an uninterested farmer who is sitting on a billy can and smoking his pipe. "It was a modest association between a poet who was to become Australia's most famous writer of his day," wrote Alec Chisholm, "and an artist who was to become the most famous cartoonist of his time in Britain."

The book contained Dennis's complete version of "The Austra–laise", with seven stanzas and chorus. It also had a group of four rhymes with the overall title "The Sentimental Bloke", a set that Dennis felt had great potential for development.

The major local reviews of the book had been favourable. The *Weekly Times* said "Mr Dennis is very much at home when writing of the love affairs of the young people", and " . . . they are skillfully rhymed".

The *Age*, however, complained of the author, ". . . he does not take himself seriously enough; he dissipates his undoubted talents on unpromising themes".

Dennis's use of the vernacular along with his mastery of rhyme are the essence of his unique style of writing. Some have said it is also why his work is neglected for academic study, despite his ongoing popularity. The poet himself wrote: "Someone has said that slang is the illegitimate sister of poetry, and if an illegitimate relationship is the nearest I can get, I am content."

But *Backblock Ballads* was a failure. Like most authors, Dennis put considerable blame for this on his publisher for producing such a shoddy work. He resolved to follow through his own judgement on these matters in future. It was a bitter, disappointing affair.

Dennis sent inscribed copies of *Backblock Ballads and Other Verses* to his friends, including his new acquaintances Croll and Roberts. Croll's copy, with photographs added, marginal notes, pasted-in reviews and Dennis's biographical note, is now lodged in the Mitchell Library, Sydney.

The Robertses owned a weekend bungalow overlooking Sassafras Gully in an area now known as Kallista, thirty kilometres to the east of Melbourne. This property was called "Sunnyside".

Garry Roberts offered his patronage to struggling writers and artists, not only providing "Sunnyside" as a meeting place where they could exchange ideas and enjoy good company, but sometimes offering temporary accommodation, meals and financial incentives. C. J. Dennis became a recipient of this hospitality. He shared his time between Toolangi and "Sunnyside", often calling in on the Robertses' home in Melbourne too.

At Toolangi Dennis's only regular company was his fox terrier dog, Bloke, which, according to its master, was often sent into the scrub to fetch a word that rhymed! It is not surprising therefore to read in a letter Dennis sent to Croll from Toolangi:

> The loneliness of life in this humpy has never hit me quite so badly before, and I have to work like blazes to fend off the blues . . . When I think of the kindness of Roberts and yourself and the others I feel somewhat swinish — like a fat pig at a banquet.

Among others who enjoyed the hospitality of "Sunnyside" were etcher John Shirlow, illustrator and writer Hal Gye, artist Tom Roberts, Robert Croll and his wife, Grace, sculptor Charles Web Gilbert, art critic Harold Herbert, barrister David Wright and writer Mrs Aeneas Gunn. They enjoyed long walks through the countryside, impromptu evening concerts, during which Dennis entertained with his banjo, and stimulating conversation.

There were several old tram carriages on the property, brought up from Melbourne when their usefulness for transport had ended. They provided excellent accommodation for the weekend guests.

On one visit to "Sunnyside", Dennis talked with Garry Roberts, John Shirlow and Robert Croll about a novel he was going to write, tentatively called *Peter*. He confessed to a lack of concentration in starting the project. Garry Roberts suggested that Dennis stay on at "Sunnyside" with his eldest son, Frank, so that Dennis would not be distracted from his work.

Gwen, the Robertses' daughter, takes up the story.

> My father used to read aloud splendidly and often entertained our guests reading to them, as we sat around the fire.
>
> On one weekend he read to the guests — comprising Dennis, Shirlow and Croll — some verses he had cut out of the Bulletin, entitled or rather commencing — "I wish yer meant it, Bill", which Den had written at Toolangi previously, together with two or three other similar verses.
>
> Den then decided to write other sets of verses to complete the series and thus The Sentimental Bloke was written instead of the novel Peter.
>
> My father made Den a financial allowance on condition that he did a certain amount of writing weekly.

During this period Dennis noted to Croll, "If only I can get a damned publisher to produce the 'Bloke' as I want it, I am confident it will go!"

He was back living in Toolangi, feeling "just like flat soda water". Again he confided in Croll: "My poor old abused system [is] fretting for a little drug-induced excitement. My nerves have been suddenly reminded of the buck-up they used to get in bygone days." Whether he was seeking adrenalin or alcohol to stimulate him is not clear. He opted to visit Sydney and seek work there — making himself available to both stimulants in doing so.

Dennis obtained work on the *Australian Worker*, which suited his political leanings and brought him in contact with other local writers. He also worked on *Labour Call*, a trades hall journal, and mixed with Sydney politicians. Mostly, though, he drank (usually too much) with Henry Lawson, Rod Quinn, Bert Stevens and Randolph Bedford. These friendships were later to be quite helpful to him as a rising literary light. Lawson wrote the foreword to his next book and Stevens recommended him to George Robertson, publisher.

Dennis was still in Sydney and drinking more than was wise when the First World War broke out in August 1914. He was described at the time as being "a very seedy, unkempt, and generally forlorn little figure".

By the end of August, he was writing to Mrs Roberts:

I know that Dad and yourself will be glad to know that I am gradually getting over my silly weaknesses. Being wise in my generation, I am not so foolish as to try to pull up all at once.
That would mean I would be very ill and not be able to get back to Melbourne and my friends.

Within a month he was back in Melbourne, decidedly the worse for wear. He had wanted to join the services but was ruled ineligible because he suffered from asthma and had flat feet. (The Sentimental Bloke, Bill, was refused enlistment for the same reason.) Mrs Roberts packed him off to "Sunnyside" with instructions to rest and relax.

The poet finalised the publication of the remaining "Bloke" verses with the *Bulletin* and approached a Melbourne publisher with his book idea. He was rejected, and so approached another, with the same response. Both Thomas Lothian's and George Robertson of Robertson & Mullens failed to recognise the potential of the work ... the "most eloquent example of publisher's indiscretion", as Alec Chisholm expressed it.

Dennis realised, at this stage, that he needed to obtain employment to support himself. His paltry income from writing was insufficient, and his self-esteem was most likely suffering from his acceptance of charity from the Robertses.

He obtained work as a clerk in the Navy Department at a salary of three pounds a week, and joined the Clerks' Union. In a letter to Mrs Roberts on 30 January 1915 describing his situation, Dennis wrote:

... started work this morning. I am in the Navy Office, and Dad is not likely to let me forget it. He insists on calling me "Admiral", and will talk to me only in an unintelligible gibberish which he calls sea talk, and he salutes every time he meets me.

Towards the end of February 1915 , he moved out of the protection offered by "Sunnyside", and took up lodgings in Burke Road, Camberwell, less than ten kilometres from the centre of Melbourne.

Dennis's impish humour pervades his correspondence of the time in an unusual manner. He commenced writing on departmental letterheads to friends and business acquaintances. An inspection of some of his letters held in the Mitchell Library reveals Dennis's distinctive rounded hand expressing itself in green ink on Commonwealth Treasury, Navy Office, Attorney General and, on one occasion, even Prime Ministerial stationery.

During 1915, the great Australian soprano, Dame Nellie Melba, decided to contribute to the war effort by persuading leading artists, writers and sculptors to contribute, without cost, to a book she would sponsor to raise funds for the Belgium Relief Fund. Her book, *Melba's Gift Book of Australian Art and Literature*, was packed with the notables of the era: Henry Lawson, Mrs Aeneas Gunn, Dorothea Mackellar, Edward Dyson, Julian Ashton and dozens of others. C. J. Dennis contributed a prose piece he called "The Year Around in Timber Land", an impressive discourse on the effect of seasonal changes on the people living in the mountains. It was illustrated by Hal Gye. This became the first time the pair had appeared in print together and marked the beginning of a partnership that spanned a further eight adult books over a decade.

On 23 March 1915, Dennis wrote two significant letters, each pursuing his desire to have his latest poems published as a book. He did not use stolen letterheads for these.

Dennis's first letter was a request directed to his new friend, Henry Lawson, whom he had met and drank and talked with in Sydney the previous year.

> By this mail I am sending you a complete copy of the "Sentimental Bloke", in manuscript ... Now, I am going to ask you a pretty big thing, and I am quite sensible of the cheek of it. Will you write a brief introduction for the first edition ...
>
> I have tried to tell a common but very beautiful story in coarse language, to prove, among other things, that life and love can be just as real and splendid to the "common" bloke as to the "cultured" ...
>
> I'm pretty sure you will grasp what I have tried to convey in the verse that appears to the average reader (I fear) merely as humorous rhymes in slang ...

Henry Lawson's reply, containing all the good news Dennis could justly expect, was sent by return post:

> Dear Den,
> I dips me lid. Of course I will you old fule. By a coincidence (which does not seem strange to me) I showed the last of yours (Sentimental Bloke) to Mr Robertson the other Saturday morning when he was in a bad temper and it tickled him immensely ... I will see Mr Robertson gets parcel himself.
>
> Yours ever,
> Henry Lawson

Lawson was as good as his word. An envelope is extant, marked in Lawson's distinctive scrawl:

> 'The Sentimental Bloke' Mr. Robertson,
> [signed] H.L.

Dennis's second letter written from his Camberwell lodgings on that day was to the same George Robertson, head of the publishing and bookselling company, Angus & Robertson Limited. He enclosed his "series of rhymes entitled 'The Sentimental Bloke' (wishing) to have them published in book form".

Dennis then explained, in precise detail, how he expected Robertson to handle the work ... a subscription edition first followed by a cheaper edition; what royalties he required; how Lawson had been approached to write the foreword; the quality of paper he wanted; that he had approached Hal Gye to prepare some drawings for it, and that he was undecided about the binding and would come back to Robertson after he had made up his mind.

Robertson replied with equal forthrightness: "Sir, we like your stuff, but we don't like your letter." He continued: "We are publishers, not printers and binders, and we do not take instructions from authors as to the get-up of a book which is going to bear our imprint." But the shrewd Scot, having issued this rebuke, promptly detailed for the poet some counter-proposals on royalties, stock, size and quantities to consider.

"Your chastening letter to hand," Dennis wrote back to the publisher on 8 April, "I am glad you like my stuff but grieved that you do not like my letter. I cannot say I am overjoyed at the tone of yours." Dennis explained that they were basically suggestions in his first letter and that he had been tripped up by a publisher before. He certainly was not trying to teach Australia's leading publisher his job, he implied.

"The fact that I don't resent it [Robertson's rebuke]," Dennis wrote, "seems to say a lot for my good temper ... or sense of humour, or something of the sort."

In response, Robertson wrote on 13 April: "We like your second letter much better. At this rate we'll soon be able to swear eternal friendship!" He told Dennis that a publishing agreement for *The Sentimental Bloke* was being forwarded shortly.

The slowest part of the publishing process of *The Sentimental Bloke* was getting the foreword from Henry Lawson. After three months it arrived and C. J. Dennis found it, in parts, unacceptable. Dennis thought it patronising, and was surprised to note that Lawson had used direct extracts from Dennis's letter to him. When the galley proofs of the typesetting arrived, Dennis edited this out. Then he became dissatisfied with his own corrections and wrote again to Lawson. "Would you mind writing one or two sentences of your own ... to oblige a pal further?" the poet asked. Lawson acquiesced.

The Sentimental Bloke was published in an edition of 2450 copies on 9 October 1915. George Robertson, a shrewd marketer by today's values, despatched 250 review copies to newspapers and magazines in Australia and New Zealand and to notable writers and opinion-leaders of the day. Even before the first edition had left the bindery, George Robertson had ordered a second printing, this time of 5000 copies.

Dennis had dedicated *The Sentimental Bloke* "To Mr and Mrs J. G. Roberts", and as soon as he received two early copies of the book, showed one to Hal Gye and sent the other by Bob Croll to Garry Roberts:

I am sending you, by the strong right hand of Bob, one of the two advance copies of "The Bloke" which I have received. This for your perusal. My special copies are to arrive early next week.
I think you will be pleased with the general get-up. Both Hal and myself are delighted.

The book was outstandingly well received. The *Bulletin*, in the issue of 14 October, said in a review over two columns, "The Sentimental Bloke ... is the most typical Australian that has ever mooched into Australian literature." But, as the poet himself had noted when sending an advance copy to Roberts:

The one thing I regret about the "Bully" review is their curt treatment of Hal. His work certainly deserved a warmer word of praise, and honestly, I would have been more pleased if they had thrown him a few flowers at the expense of my own bouquet.
I think he feels it more than he admits, because I know he expected something good from the "B".

Towards the end of 1915, Dennis caught the train to Sydney to meet his publisher face to face. They discussed a further book which Dennis proposed, one about Ginger Mick, the Bloke's friend. Robertson was pleased to meet in person the author of the firm's latest success. Yes, he was certainly interested in a follow-up book.

In the meantime, *The Bloke* was winning greater popular acclaim. It was recited on stage by several performers and a silent movie was mooted. Within ninety days, *The Sentimental Bloke* had outsold every previous book of Australian verse. "We are proceeding at once to print another 5000 copies," his publishers told him in February 1916.

After its first year, *The Sentimental Bloke* had sold 55,370 copies — a remarkable confirmation of it being "the right book at the right time". Bibliographer Ian McLaren estimated that 300,000 copies had been sold up until 1980, and there has been further reprinting since.

All of a sudden, the impoverished poet was not just a celebrity but a man of increasing means.

C. J. Dennis as portrayed by Hal Gye

He did not give up his job, however, and continued to write in the evenings and at weekends.

C. J. Dennis, or "Den" as he was now known to the public at large, was naturally delighted with the success of his book. "This success is becoming monotonous," he wrote to his publisher, revelling in his new-found popularity. A few months later, after glowing reviews in two English magazines, he wrote again:

> It is all more than half a dream to me. Things are materialising now that I fondly dreamed of years ago, and it is all so strangely like my dreams that I can only half convince myself that it is reality ... You write about godfathers! Strike a light! I'm beginning to believe in them — fairy ones, brothers of the original old lady who interviewed Cinderella.

In October 1916, just twelve months after *The Bloke*, Dennis's next book was published. It was *The Moods of Ginger Mick* also illustrated by Hal Gye.

It was intended by both Dennis and Robertson that *The Moods of Ginger Mick* should include a poem called "The Battle of the Wazzir". It is a graphic account based on an actual event that occurred in 1915, involving Australian and New Zealand troops in Cairo. The soldiers, perhaps inflamed by liquor, decided to wreak vengeance on the occupants of the city's red-light district. They set the area on fire and clashed with the British military police and the Egyptian fire brigades.

Dennis's plans were thwarted by the intervention of the military censor in Australia. He considered the subject potentially offensive and *The Moods of Ginger Mick* was published without it.

Within six months, it had sold 42,349 copies; it was another runaway success!

Robertson produced a special smaller-sized edition of *Ginger Mick*, known as the "Pocket Edition for the Trenches", intended for the Australian troops fighting in Europe and the Middle East.

In four years, *Ginger Mick* sold over 70,000 copies. In November 1916, Dennis resigned trom his safe job to concentrate on his writing at Toolangi, where he had just acquired the property he'd been illegally occupying for years.

It was David Low who had introduced C. J. Dennis to his future wife in 1915. The dark-eyed beauty was the former Mrs Olive Price of Tasmania, a daughter of John Herron of Melbourne. Dennis, aged thirty-nine at the time, met her in the studio shared by David Low and Hal Gye. Little is known about her background, age or status other than that she was probably a widow who had previously lived in Victoria.

Their wedding took place in July 1917. The Toolangi property was extensively renovated and given the name "Arden" — soon to appear as part of the address on Dennis's embossed stationery.

Even in 1917 there was considerable newspaper interest in the couple, not dissimilar to that accorded media personalities today. Around the wedding date, the *Bulletin* featured separate photographs of the couple, and reported that they were off to Cairns for their honeymoon. Three consecutive issues carried gossip items about them.

Dennis had tapped a deep vein in the Australian imagination with his pen, an acceptable balance between reality and fantasy, wit and wisdom, and city and country living. He had touched the swelling pride of nationalism and the ethos of "fair go".

In the following two years, C. J. Dennis produced three books. The first of these, *The Glugs of Gosh*, was being printed in Sydney when the new Mr and Mrs Dennis were heading north to Cairns.

Naturally the couple visited George Robertson, who made them particularly welcome.

When asked by Norman Lindsay if she had met C. J. Dennis, Robertson's secretary, Rebecca Wiley, described her impressions:

> *The first time I saw him was just after* The Bloke *was published, and I thought he looked like a working plumber . . . on the second occasion he was on his honeymoon, had his hair well brushed back, and I thought he looked just like the Church of England curate one sees on the stage.*

Lindsay enjoyed these observations because he held Dennis in low esteem. His distaste was influenced by his belief that Bill, the central character in *The Sentimental Bloke*, was derived from a larrikin character in Louis Stone's book, *Jonah*. Stone was Norman Lindsay's friend, and Lindsay felt that *Jonah* had not received the acclaim it deserved. Dennis's success, he thought, should have gone to Lou Stone.

Lindsay had refused to read a copy of *The Glugs of Gosh* sent to him by George Robertson; and, to a great extent, the general public did too.

In this book Dennis had moved from his vernacular mode into a work of conventional satire on the social system. Some people, including the poet himself, considered it his best work, a view still held by many. In it Dennis expresses his political conscience, urging through his characters that the citizens should expand their minds and not be unthinkingly led by politicians and bureaucrats.

It is easy to envisage Dennis as Sym, the poet in the tale, and to substitute Australians for Glugs and Australia for Gosh. Dennis's railing against petty authority in *Glugs*, those "coldly distant, sub-assistant under-Swanks, galore", could conceivably have struck another responsive Australian chord; but it didn't.

The lukewarm reaction to *The Glugs of Gosh* sent the poet scurrying back to the type of verse he had built his reputation on. For Christmas 1917, he had a small twenty-four–page booklet, *Doreen*, with two Hal Gye watercolour plates, in the bookstores. Robertson, perhaps eager to keep his best-selling author before the public, printed an enormous run of 100,000 copies.

Doreen had been a character in Dennis's *Bulletin* verses back in 1909 and became Bill's bride in *The Sentimental Bloke*. This charming gift book remained out of print for sixty-four years — it was reissued as a hardback with Hal Gye endpapers in 1981.

In the meantime, Dennis had pressed Robertson to reissue the book published by E. W. Cole, *Backblock Ballads*. Robertson agreed. The book's full title was changed from *Backblock Ballads and Other Verses*, the Cole name, to allow for some additions and revisions. It became *Backblock Ballads and Later Verses* in George Robertson's edition. It demonstrated Dennis's wide-ranging ability in both topic and wit, and includes his "A Guide for Poits", supposedly compiled by the Sentimental Bloke, in which he satirically belittles his own poetic achievements. The new *Backblock Ballads* was released early in 1918.

Two other significant things occurred during this time that affected C. J. Dennis materially. He sold the film rights to *The Sentimental Bloke* for a thousand pounds and, perhaps more importantly, his reading public moved its interest away from verse in slang. Poet and publisher had to learn that lesson the hard way.

Dennis had another book ready, *Digger Smith*. In it, he tried to tap onto the social changes that were obvious in the community, particularly the repatriation of ex-servicemen. His character this time was "little Smith uv Collin'wood" — a former Gallipoli digger.

Geoge Robertson was delighted with this manuscript. He wrote to Dennis when he received it,

"It is delightful, and would have put you where 'The Bloke' did if 'The Bloke' had not already put you there!"

Digger Smith did not quite live up to the publisher's expectations, and Robertson detected a change in the public mind about war, peace and nationalism. The book was reprinted three times, enough for some authors to be called a "success", but it fell significantly short of the standards of its precursors.

The film of *The Sentimental Bloke* burst onto the Australian cinema scene during 1918. It was a silent film produced by Raymond Longford. Archive copies of it are studied and admired even today. Joan Long, film historian and producer (*Caddie, The Picture Show Man, Puberty Blues*), says of it:

> It had more reviews, longer reviews, more enthusiastic and more consistent reviews, both here and in England, than any other Australian silent film . . .
>
> It was one of those films that just took off. It played to full houses, people queued in the streets to see it . . .
>
> The screenplay for the film was co-written by Longford himself with Lottie Lyell . . . she also played the leading role of Doreen.
>
> The Bloke himself was played by Arthur Tauchert, a Sydneysider born in The Rocks, who had been an entertainer for most of his life . . .

Although he went to see the film with "very solid doubts" about the likely result, Dennis said he came away "almost believing in miracles". "The fidelity with which the written story has been converted into what may be termed a visual narrative," he remarked, "is amazing to me."

A stage play of *The Bloke* was also on national tour. Like the silent film, it was sponsored by E. J. Carroll and his brother, Dan, together with Bert Bailey. According to reports, it played Melbourne for eleven weeks, then eight weeks in Sydney and for "healthy periods in other States and New Zealand".

But it wasn't all glitter and success for C. J. Dennis. One manuscript he submitted to George Robertson was rejected outright by the publisher. It was called *Limpy Ben*, and remains unpublished today. Dennis had considered it a better work than *Doreen* and said it would make a "good Christmas book". It must have been a shock for the poet to learn that Robertson only wanted "bright and happy stuff" in future.

This was one of several distractions to Dennis at the time. He had invested some of his new resources in a local timber mill and had purchased shares in an Australian motion picture company as well. Both activities were putting money back into things that interested him. They proved poor investments for him, however, and became a source of continuous problems.

Robertson had shrewdly proposed paying Dennis a fixed salary in return for all Dennis's literary output, but the poet demurred, a fact he later regretted.

During the following year, 1919, another Dennis book was published unsuccessfully. This was *Jim of the Hills*, a book dedicated to Robertson himself. *Jim* is a real bushman's book; as Alec Chisholm described it:

> The strength of the book was not in its sugary story but in . . . the axeman's joy in "swingin' Douglas", the menace of forest fires, the tragedy of a timber-getter's death, and, most of all, the revelry of wild birds.

In *Jim of the Hills*, Dennis moved from his vernacular style into verse ballads saluting Mother Nature. An interesting change it may have been, but his public wanted none of it.

But there was a new development ahead, one that George Robertson signalled to the bush poet in 1920. The publisher wanted to produce a collection of Australian nursery rhymes and asked Dennis to contribute to it. Dennis readily agreed. But when he sent them to Robertson in Sydney, he attached a note:

> *The rhymes I am sending because I promised them to your collection, but if A&R will favourably consider a book of kid rhymes by C. J. Dennis, I should like them to be kept for that.*
>
> *I find them rather easy to write, and I think they will go with the kids. I propose to do stories as well as verse. Let me know what you think of the suggestion.*

Robertson liked the idea, and told him so. "Good," Dennis reacted, "I'll illustrate them myself, too." The publisher became even more enthusiastic when he saw the poet's naive drawings. "We would not have your baker's wheel or his horse's hind feet improved on for worlds!" Robertson wrote back.

Dennis's poor financial management was nagging him throughout his preparation of the children's book. "There is money, money everywhere [referring to his investments], but not a bob to spend," he advised his publisher. The royalties from his book sales had dwindled to a trickle, so Robertson offered, "if a couple of hundred pounds will be of any use, let me know."

In August 1921, the poet-cum-illustrator had finished his work on the children's book and sent it off to George Robertson in Sydney. It was published as *A Book for Kids*.

Unfortunately, it was not spectacularly successful. It contained some good fun rhymes that still amuse and enthral children but it was not, as Robertson had hoped, the book "from which we'll garner many a harvest". Nonetheless, it was republished under the title *Roundabout* fourteen years later, and again under its original title and format in 1958. A third edition, intended in three parts with new illustrations, began in 1975.

Things were not going well for C. J. Dennis. In a letter to his publisher in Sydney written on New Year's Eve 1922, the poet painted a glum picture.

> *Have I written you a cheerful letter within the last six months? . . .*
>
> *A cable has come through to say that in four trial public showings of the film [The Sentimental Bloke] in America it has proved an utter failure, and the lessees refuse to handle it further.*
>
> *That is bad enough; but I find that, as a result, my picture shares — my chief assets — are now unsaleable.*
>
> *To cheer us further, the sawmill, which has been eating up piles of cash, shut down the other day as a hopeless proposition . . .*
>
> *In my usual businesslike manner I have built a fine house in a charming but remote spot where it is practically unsaleable. I doubt if I could even raise a mortgage on it . . .*

Robertson sent a cheque straightaway — whether as a loan or an advance against royalties is unclear. In his reply Dennis told him of his plans to take a flat in the city and of a job he had accepted on the Melbourne *Herald*.

In its issue of 22 May 1922, the *Herald* carried a front page item headed "Noted Writer's New Role: 'The Sentimental Bloke' will conduct daily *Herald* column".

For the next sixteen years, living at either Toolangi or in "digs" in Melbourne, Dennis contributed continuously to that paper, right up until his death. During this period, the Dennises had several apartments in Melbourne as domestic addresses, even a suite in the then-famous Menzies Hotel for a time. On other occasions, Mrs Dennis remained at Toolangi and tended her flower beds and he drove up on weekends, laden with goods from the city.

Often, especially when he was not under the supervision of his spouse, Dennis got involved in drinking bouts with some of his newspaper friends. He had many visitors in the city, mostly artists and theatrical people. Columnist Jim Macdougall once shared a city flat with Dennis on the insistence of *Herald* boss, Keith Murdoch. Macdougall wrote: "He drank much but I cannot remember him being drunk. [The considerations] of daily journalism pressed rather heavily upon him." Dennis became more morose and he also became more addicted to drink than ever before. Much of his subsequent writing dealt with the trivia of daily news which taxed his tired creative spirits.

Then, in March, 1924, Robertson received a letter from a distressed Olive (Biddy) Dennis from Toolangi:

I am in despair. Den is in hospital again. He has been drinking very badly this last two years. I seem to have lost all grip on him . . .

In justice to myself, though, I must say 'tis hard to live week after week with a drunken man and remain sweet and placid . . .

Den will be coming home next week and will be in his right mind and his brain will be clear. Will you write to him and suggest he gets busy on a book?

Even if it is a bad book and never published, it will give him something to think about. That beastly Herald job has ruined him . . .

George Robertson wrote back immediately. Waiting for Dennis when he arrived home "in his right mind" was an unopened letter:

Dear Dennis,

Don't you think it is quite time we had another book? How about "Rose"? Only that we have been so busy of late reprinting out-of-prints I should have been sitting on your doorstep — metaphorically speaking, of course, for it seems impossible for me to get away from Sydney . . .

Do let me here from you. With kind regards.

The scheme worked. "I have a dozen ideas simmering and a dimmed reputation to refurbish . . . through my very unwise excursion into daily journalism." Dennis undertook to write a long letter shortly.

A long two months later, he wrote to Robertson about his suggestion of "Rose" — she was Ginger Mick's old girlfriend from Spadgers Lane. "I am pretty confident I can have her finished in about six weeks," the revitalised poet advised. The publisher accepted, even offering an increased royalty on the new work, *Rose of Spadgers*. It was released in time for the 1924 Christmas market and met a lukewarm response. Fifty-eight years later, in 1982, Dennis's former publishers released the book for the second time.

In the early 1930s Dennis sold the "talking picture rights" of *The Sentimental Bloke* to Frank Thring's Efftee Film Productions of Melbourne. Dennis was keenly interested in converting his verse to the spoken word and was retained by Thring to adapt the book to a film script.

The premiere of the sound version of *The Bloke* was held on 26 March 1932, at the Hoyts Deluxe Theatre in Melbourne. Joan Long compared the two film versions of *The Bloke*:

The sound version seems unstable, artificial, self-conscious, badly-paced — everything that the Longford–Lyell version was not.

    Dennis himself had something to do with the Efftee script, perhaps another illustration of the often-proved rule that authors should not adapt their own works ...

    Incidentally, the sound film of The Sentimental Bloke *had nothing like the commercial success of its silent forerunner.*

There was something odd about the sound version of *The Bloke* film; here was the ideal opportunity for the wonderful rhyming "English as she is spoke" of Dennis's books to be presented to a public who could recite much of it word perfectly. Somehow, it didn't happen that way.

Another film historian, Susan Dermody, suggests a reason for its lack of success. She proffers that the class differences, which are fundamental to the progress of Dennis's *Bloke* narrative ("from street-gang to family, from itinerant city worker to small rural land-holder — in a gentrified working class marriage"), were "much grosser and more simplified" in Thring's sound version.

However the film did return Dennis some funds, sufficient for him to move back to Toolangi and wire his contributions to the newspaper each day.

He loved the country life and enjoyed his now-famous gardens, which were about to receive a distinguished visitor. The poet laureate, John Masefield, was visiting Melbourne in 1934 as part of Victoria's centenary celebrations. It was planned that Masefield and Dennis should meet, but Dennis was not well and was unable to be in Melbourne. A colleague from the Melbourne *Herald*, Roger Webb, arranged to drive the visitors up to Toolangi, as Masefield had expressed a keen desire to meet *The Bloke's* author.

It was a warm sunny day. The tall trees and Biddy Dennis's flowering gardens set a poetic scene for their introduction. The pair clicked from the start. They strolled around the carefully laid out grounds chatting quietly, inspecting shrubs, strolling beside the boundary creek, posing for commemorative photographs and sitting on the lawn by the dovecote in the sunshine. They exchanged stories of their youth, and the poet laureate, to mark the occasion of his visit, planted a Copper Beech tree (marked today with a plaque and sundial).

Angus & Robertson, the publishing house that had helped Dennis through his unproductive period and benefited from his most creative time, was to publish only one more book by C. J. Dennis. A decade after *Rose* and two years after the death of George Robertson himself, A&R published a selection of Dennis's verse and prose from the Melbourne *Herald*, with the title *The Singing Garden*. This time there were no Hal Gye watercolours (nor even his line drawings) to enliven the presentation. Dennis's old familiar style of vernacular verse was gone too.

Shortly after his last published book, Dennis began experiencing difficulty moving around. He kept a shooting stick handy and took things very quietly. He was in his early sixties. His frail body was now paying the toll for its previous neglect and abuse. The deterioration of his health did not, however, alter the regularity of his almost daily contributions to his employer's newspaper.

He was referred to a private hospital in St Kilda Road, Melbourne, and died there of asthma-induced heart failure on 22 June 1938.

When poet laureate Masefield heard the news in London, he cabled immediately to the *Herald* with the following recollection of his time with the poet:

I shall never forget the day I spent with C. J. Dennis at Toolangi. He and Mrs Dennis could not have been kinder to me, and their home, set among big trees, was one of the most beautiful places I have seen . . .

I saw him only once, but he left an ineffaceable impression on my mind. Poetry with such a universal appeal, reaching all classes of readers, must have great merits . . .

The *Bulletin* devoted half its next Red Page to his literary career, concluding with:

Bulletin *readers will have a particularly soft spot for "Den", for it was in these pages that he first dipped his lid to Australia; but there is no need for sentiment to keep his memory alive. His verse, unique in Australian literature, will do that for itself.*

THE SONGS
OF A
SENTIMENTAL BLOKE

A
SPRING
SONG

The world 'as got me snouted jist a treat;
   Crool Forchin's dirty left 'as smote me soul;
An' all them joys o' life I 'eld so sweet
   Is up the pole.
Fer, as the poit sex, me 'eart 'as got
The pip wiv yearnin' fer—I dunno wot.

I'm crook; me name is Mud; I've done me dash;
   Me flamin' spirit's got the flamin' 'ump!
I'm longin' to let loose on somethin' rash . . .
   Aw, I'm a chump!
I know it; but this blimed ole Springtime craze
Fair outs me, on these dilly, silly days.

The young green leaves is shootin' on the trees,
   The air is like a long, cool swig o' beer,
The bonzer smell o' flow'rs is on the breeze,
   An' 'ere's me, 'ere,
Jist moochin' round like some pore, barmy coot,
Of 'ope, an' joy, an' forchin destichoot.

I've lorst me former joy in gittin' shick,
   Or 'eadin' browns; I 'aven't got the 'eart
To word a tom; an', square an' all, I'm sick
   Of that cheap tart
'Oo chucks 'er carkis at a feller's 'ead
An' mauls 'im . . . Ar! I wisht that I wus dead!

What *is* the matter wiv me? . . . I dunno.
   I got a sorter yearnin' 'ere inside,
A dead-crook sorter thing that won't let go
   Or be denied—
A feelin' like I want to do a break,
An' stoush creation for some woman's sake.

The little birds is chirpin' in the nest,
   The parks an' gardings is a bosker sight,
Where smilin' tarts walks up an' down, all dressed
   In clobber white.
An', as their snowy forms goes steppin' by,
It seems I'm seekin' somethin' on the sly:

Somethin' or someone—I don't rightly know;
   But, seems to me, I'm kind er lookin' for
A tart I knoo a 'undred years ago,
   Or, maybe, more.

Wot's this I've 'eard them call that thing? ... Geewhizz
Me ideel bit o' skirt! That's wot it is!

Me ideel tart! ... An', bli'me, look at me!
  Jist take a squiz at this, an' tell me can
Some square an' honist tom take this to be .
   'Er own true man?
Aw, Gawd! I'd be as true to 'er, I would—
As straight an' stiddy as ... Ar, wot's the good?

Me, that 'as done me stretch fer stoushin' Johns,
  An' spen's me leisure gittin' on the shick,
An' 'arf me nights down there, in Little Lons.,
   Wiv Ginger Mick,
Jist 'eadin' 'em, an' doin' in me gilt.
Tough luck! I s'pose it's 'ow a man is built.

It's 'ow Gawd builds a bloke; but don't it 'urt
  When 'e gits yearnin's fer this 'igher life,
On these Spring mornin's, watchin' some sweet skirt—
   Some fucher wife—
Go sailin' by, an' turnin' on his phiz
The glarssy eye—fer bein' wot 'e is.

I've watched 'em walkin' in the gardings 'ere—
  Cliners from orfices an' shops an' such;
The sorter skirts I dursn't come too near,
   Or dare to touch.
An' when I see the kind er looks they carst ...
Gorstrooth! Wot is the *use* o'me, I arst?

The little winds is stirrin' in the trees,
  Where little birds is chantin' lovers' lays;
The music of the sorft an' barmy breeze ...
   Aw, spare me days!
If this 'ere dilly feelin' doesn't stop
I'll lose me block an' stoush some flamin' cop!

THE
INTRO

'Er name's Doreen ... Well, spare me bloomin' days!
You could 'a' knocked me down wiv 'arf a brick!
   Yes, me, that kids meself I know their ways,
   An' 'as a name for smoogin' in our click!
I jist lines up an' tips the saucy wink.
But strike! The way she piled on dawg! Yer'd think
   A bloke was givin' back-chat to the Queen ...
     'Er name's Doreen.

I seen 'er in the markit first uv all,
Inspectin' brums at Steeny Isaacs' stall.
   I backs me barrer in—the same ole way—
   An' sez, "Wot O! It's been a bonzer day.
'Ow is it fer a walk?" ... Oh, 'oly wars!
The sorter *look* she gimme! Jest becors
   I tried to chat'er, like you'd make a start
     Wiv *any* tart.

An' I kin take me oaf I wus perlite,
An' never said no word that wasn't right,
   An' never tried to maul 'er, or to do
   A thing yeh might call crook. Ter tell yeh true,
I didn't seem to 'ave the nerve—wiv 'er.
I felt as if I couldn't go that fur,
   An' start to sling off chiack like I used.
     Not intrajuiced!

Nex' time I sighted 'er in Little Bourke,
Where she wus in a job. I found 'er lurk
   Wus pastin' labels in a pickle joint,
   A game that—any'ow, that ain't the point.
Once more I tried ter chat 'er in the street,
But, bli'me! Did she turn me down a treat!
   The way she tossed 'er 'ead an' swished 'er skirt!
     Oh, it wus dirt!

A squarer tom, I swear, I never seen,
In all me natchril, than this 'ere Doreen.
   It wer'n't no guyver neither; fer I knoo
   That any other bloke 'ad Buckley's 'oo
Tried fer to pick 'er up. Yes, she wus square.
She jist sailed by an' lef' me standin' there
   Like any mug. Thinks I, "I'm out o' luck,"
     An' done a duck.

Well, I dunno. It's that way wiv a bloke.
If she'd ha' breasted up ter me an' spoke,
    I'd thort 'er jist a commin bit er fluff,
    An' then fergot about 'er, like enough.
It's just like this. The tarts that's 'ard ter get
Makes you all 'ot to chase 'em, an' to let
    The cove called Cupid get an 'ammer-lock,
      An' lose yer block.

I know a bloke 'oo knows a bloke 'oo toils
In that same pickle found-ery. ('E boils
    The cabbitch storks or somethink.) Anyway,
    I gives me pal the orfis fer to say
'E 'as a sister in the trade 'oo's been
Out uv a job, an' wants ter meet Doreen;
    Then we kin get an intro, if we've luck.
      'E sez, "Ribuck."

O' course we worked the oricle; you bet!
But, struth, I ain't recovered frum it yet!
    'T'was on a Saturdee, in Colluns Street,
    An'—quite be accident, o' course—we meet.
Me pal 'e trots 'er up an' does the toff—
    'E allus wus a bloke fer showin' off.
    "This 'ere's Doreen," 'e sez. "This 'ere's the Kid."
      I dips me lid.

"This 'ere's Doreen," 'e sez. I sez "Good day."
An', bli'me, I 'ad nothin' more ter say!
    I couldn't speak a word, or meet 'er eye.
    Clean done me block! I never been so shy
Not since I wus a tiny little cub,
An' run the rabbit to the corner pub—
    Wot time the Summer days wus dry an' 'ot—
      Fer my ole pot.

I dunno 'ow I done it in the end.
I reckerlect I arst ter be 'er friend;
    An' tried ter play at 'andies in the park,
    A thing she wouldn't sight. Aw, it's a nark!
I gotter swear when I think wot a mug
I must 'a' seemed to 'er. But still I 'ug
    That promise that she give me fer the beach.
      That bonzer peach!

Now, as the poit sez, the days drag by
On ledding feet. I wish't they'd do a guy.
  I dunno 'ow I 'ad the nerve ter speak
  An' make' that meet wiv 'er fer Sundee week!
But, strike! It's funny wot a bloke'll do
When 'e's all out ... She's gorn, when I come-to.
  I'm yappin' to me cobber uv me mash ...
    I've done me dash!

'Er name's Doreen ... An' me—that thort I knoo
  The ways uv tarts, an' all that smoogin' game!
An' so I ort; fer ain't I known a few?
  Yet some'ow ... I dunno. It ain't the same.
  I carn't tell *wot* it is; but, all I know,
I've dropped me bundle—an' I'm glad it's so.
  Fer when I come ter think uv wot I been ...
    'Er name's Doreen.

THE
STOUSH
O' DAY

Ar, these is 'appy days! An' 'ow they've flown—
  Flown like the smoke of some inchanted fag;
Since dear Doreen, the sweetest tart I've known,
  Passed me the jolt that made me sky the rag.
An' ev'ry golding day floats o'er a chap
  Like a glad dream of some celeschil scrap.

Refreshed wiv sleep Day to the mornin' mill
  Comes jauntily to out the nigger, Night.
Trained to the minute, confident in skill,
  'E swaggers in the east, chock-full o' skite;
Then spars a bit, an' plugs Night on the point.
  Out go the stars; an' Day 'as jumped the joint.

The sun looks up, an' wiv a cautious stare,
  Like some crook keekin' o'er a winder sill
To make dead cert'in everythink is square,
  'E shoves 'is boko o'er an Eastern 'ill,
Then rises, wiv 'is dial all a'grin,
  An' sez, "'Ooray! I knoo that we could win!"

Sure of 'is title then, the champeen Day
  Begins to put on dawg among 'is push,
An', as he mooches on 'is gaudy way,
  Drors tribute from each tree an' flow'r an' bush.
An', w'ile 'e swigs the dew in sylvan bars,
  The sun shouts insults at the sneakin' stars.

Then, lo! the push o' Day rise to applaud;
  An' all 'is creatures clamour at 'is feet
Until 'e thinks 'imself a little gawd,
  An' swaggers on an' kids 'imself a treat.
The w'ile the lurkin' barrackers o' Night
  Sneak in retreat an' plan another fight.

On thro' the hours, triumphant, proud an' fit,
  The champeen marches on 'is up'ard way,
Till, at the zenith, bli'me! 'e—is—IT!
  And all the world bows to the Boshter Day.
The jealous Night speeds messidges thro' space
  'Otly demandin' terms, an' time, an' place.

A w'ile the champeen scorns to make reply;
  'E's taken tickets on 'is own 'igh worth;
Puffed up wiv pride, an' livin' mighty 'igh,
  'E don't admit that Night is on the earth.

Hal Gye's original cover for
Songs of a Sentimental Bloke

But as the hours creep on 'e deigns to state
   'E'll fight for all the earth an' 'arf the gate.

Late afternoon ... Day feels 'is flabby arms,
   An' tells 'imself 'e don't seem quite the thing.
The 'omin' birds shriek clamorous alarms;
   An' Night creeps stealthily to gain the ring.
But see! The champeen backs an' fills, becos
   'E doesn't feel the Boshter Bloke 'e was.

Time does a bunk as us-u-al, nor stays
   A single instant, e'en at Day's be'est.
Alas, the 'eavy-weight's 'igh-livin' ways
   'As made 'im soft, an' large around the vest.
'E sez 'e's fat inside; 'e starts to whine;
   'E sez 'e wants to dror the colour line.

Relentless nigger Night crawls thro' the ropes,
   Advancin' grimly on the quakin' Day,
Whose noisy push, shorn of their 'igh-noon 'opes,
   Wait, 'ushed an' anxious, fer the comin' fray.
And many lusty barrackers of noon
   Desert 'im one by one—traitors so soon!

'E's out er form! 'E 'asn't trained enough!
   They mark their sickly champeen on the stage,
An' narked, the sun, 'is backer, in a huff,
   Sneaks outer sight, red in the face wiv rage.
W'ile gloomy roosters, they 'oo made the morn
   Ring wiv 'is praises, creep to bed ferlorn.

All faint an' groggy grows the beaten Day;
   'E staggers drunkenly about the ring;
An owl 'oots jeerin'ly across the way,
   An' bats come out to mock the fallin' King.
Now, wiv a jolt, Night spreads 'im on the floor,
   An' all the west grows ruddy wiv 'is gore.

A single, vulgar star leers from the sky
   An' in derision, rudely mutters, "Yah!"
The moon, Night's conkerbine, comes glidin' by
   An' laughs a 'eartless, silvery "Ha-ha!"
Scorned, beaten, Day gives up the 'opeless fight,
   An' drops 'is bundle in the lap o' Night.

* * * *

So goes each day, like some celeschil mill,
    E'er since I met that shyin' little peach.
'Er bonzer voice! I 'ear its music still,
    As when she guv that promise fer the beach.
An', square an' all, no matter 'ow yeh start,
    The commin end of most of us is—Tart.

THE PLAY

"Wot's in a name?" she sez ... And then she sighs,
An' clasps 'er little 'ands, an' rolls 'er eyes.
"A rose," she sez, "be any other name
Would smell the same.
Oh, w'erefore art you Romeo, young sir?
Chuck yer ole pot, an' change yer moniker!"

Doreen an' me, we bin to see a show—
The swell two-dollar touch. Bong tong, yeh know
A chair apiece wiv velvit on the seat;
A slap-up treat.
The drarmer's writ be Shakespeare, years ago,
About a barmy goat called Romeo.

"Lady, be yonder moon I swear!" sez 'e.
An then 'e climbs up on the balkiney;
An' there they smooge a treat, wiv pretty words,
Like two love-birds.
I nudge Doreen. She whispers, "Ain't it grand!"
'Er eyes is shinin'; an' I squeeze 'er 'and.

"Wot's in a name?" she sez. 'Struth, I dunno.
Billo is just as good as Romeo.
She may be Juli-er or Juliet—
'E loves 'er yet.
If she's the tart 'e wants, then she's 'is queen,
Names never count ... But ar, I like "Doreen!"

A sweeter, dearer sound I never 'eard;
Ther's music 'angs around that little word,
Doreen! ... But wot was this I starts to say
About the play?
I'm off me beat. But when a bloke's in love
'Is thorts turn 'er way, like a 'omin' dove.

This Romeo 'e's lurkin' wiv a crew—
A dead tough crowd o' crooks—called Montague.
'Is cliner's push—wot's nicknamed Capulet—
They 'as 'em set.
Fair narks they are, jist like them back-street clicks.
Ixcep' they fights wiv skewers 'stid o' bricks.

Wot's in a name? Wot's in a string o' words?
They scraps in ole Verona wiv the'r swords,
An' never give a bloke a stray dog's chance,
An' that's Romance.

But when they deals it out wiv bricks an' boots
In Little Lon., they're low, degraded broots.

Wot's jist plain stoush wiv us, right 'ere to-day,
Is "valler" if yer fur enough away.
Some time, some writer bloke will do the trick
Wiv Ginger Mick,
Of Spadger's Lane. 'E'll be a Romeo,
When 'e's bin dead five 'undred years or so.

Fair Juli-et, she gives 'er boy the tip.
Sez she: "Don't sling that crowd o' mine no lip;
An' if you run agin a Capulet,
Jist do a get,"
'E swears 'e's done wiv lash; 'e'll chuck it clean.
(Same as I done when I first met Doreen.)

They smooge some more at that. Ar, strike me blue!
It gimme Joes to sit an' watch them two!
'E'd break away an' start to say good-bye,
An' then she'd sigh
"Ow, Ro-me-o!" an' git a strangle-holt,
An' 'ang around 'im like she feared 'e'd bolt.

Nex' day 'e words a gorspil cove about
A secrit weddin'; an' they plan it out.
'E spouts a piece about 'ow 'e's bewitched:
Then they git 'itched . . .
Now, 'ere's the place where I fair git the pip:
She's 'is for keeps, an' yet 'e lets 'er slip!

Ar! but 'e makes me sick! A fair gazob!
'E's jist the glarsey on the soulful sob,
'E'll sigh and spruik, an' 'owl a love-sick vow—
(The silly cow!)
But when 'e's got 'er, spliced an' on the straight,
'E crools the pitch, an' tries to kid it's Fate.

Aw! Fate me foot! Instid of slopin' soon
As 'e was wed, off on 'is 'oneymoon,
'Im an' 'is cobber, called Mick Curio,
They 'ave to go
An' mix it wiv that push o' Capulets.
They look fer trouble; an' it's wot they gets.

A tug named Tyball (cousin to the skirt)
Sprags 'em an' makes a start to sling off dirt.

Nex' minnit there's a reel ole ding-dong go—
'Arf round or so.
Mick Curio, 'e gets it in the neck,
"Ar, rats!" 'e sez, an' passes in 'is check.

Quite natchril, Romeo gits wet as 'ell.
"It's me or you!" 'e 'owls, an' wiv a yell,
Plunks Tyball through the gizzard wiv 'is sword,
'Ow I ongcored!
"Put in the boot!" I sez. "Put in the boot!"
"Ush!" sez Doreen . . . "Shame!" sez some silly coot.

Then Romeo, 'e dunno wot to do.
The cops gits busy, like they allwiz do,
An' nose around until 'e gits blue funk
An' does a bunk.
They wants 'is tart to wed some other guy.
"Ah, strike!" she sez. "I wish that I could die!"

Now, this 'ere gorspil bloke's a fair shrewd 'ead.
Sez 'e, "I'll dope yeh, so they'll *think* yer dead."
(I tips 'e was a cunnin' sort, wot knoo
A thing or two).
She takes 'is knock-out drops, up in 'er room:
They think she's snuffed, an' plant 'er in 'er tomb.

Then things gits mixed a treat an' starts to whirl.
'Ere's Romeo comes back an' finds 'is girl
Tucked in 'er little coffing, cold an' stiff,
An' in a jiff
'E swallers lysol, throws a fancy fit,
'Ead over turkey, an' 'is soul 'as flit.

Then Juli-et wakes up an' sees 'im there,
Turns on the water-works an' tears 'er 'air,
"Dear love," she sez, "I cannot live alone!"
An', wif a moan,
She grabs 'is pockit knife, an' ends 'er cares . . .
"Peanuts or lollies!" sez a boy upstairs.

M A R

"'Er pore dear Par," she sez, "'e kept a store;"
An' then she weeps an' stares 'ard at the floor.
   "'Twas thro' 'is death," she sez, "we wus rejuiced
To this," she sez . . . An' then she weeps some more.

"'Er Par," she sez, "me poor late 'usband, kept
An 'ay an' corn store. 'E'd no faults ixcept
   'Im fallin' 'eavy orf a load o' charf
W'ich—killed 'im—on the—" 'Struth! But 'ow she wept.

She blows 'er nose an' sniffs. "'E would 'a' made,"
She sez, "a lot of money in the trade.
   But, 'im took orf so sudden-like, we found
'E 'adn't kept 'is life insurince paid.

"To think," she sez, "a child o'mine should be
Rejuiced to workin' in a factory!
   If 'er pore Par 'e 'adn't died," she sobs . . .
I sez, "It wus a bit o' luck for me."

Then I gits red as 'ell, "That is—I mean,"
I sez, "I mighter never met Doreen
   If 'e 'ad not"—an' 'ere I lose me block—
"I 'ope," I sez, "'e snuffed it quick and clean."

An' that wus 'ow I made me first deboo.
I'd dodged it cunnin' fer a month or two.
   Doreen she sez, "You'll 'ave to meet my Mar
Some day," she sez. An' so I seen it thro'.

I'd pictered some stern female in a cap
Wot puts the fear o' Gawd into a chap.
   An' 'ere she wus, aweepin' in 'er tea
An' drippin' moistcher like a leaky tap.

Two dilly sorter dawgs made outer delf
Stares 'ard at me frum orf the mantleshelf;
   I seemed to symperthise wiv them there pups;
I felt so stiff an' brittle-like meself.

Clobber? Me trosso, 'ead to foot, wus noo—
Got up regardless, fer this interview:
   Stiff shirt, a Yankee soot split up the back,
A tie wiv yeller spots an' stripes o' blue.

Me cuffs kep' playin' wiv me nervis fears,
Me patent leathers nearly brought the tears.

An' there I sits wiv, "Yes, mum. Thanks. Indeed?"
Me stand-up collar sorin' orf me ears.

"Life's 'ard," she sez, an' then she brightens up:
"Still, we 'ave alwus 'ad our bite and sup.
    Dorreen's been *sich* a help; she 'as indeed.
Some more tea, Willy? '*Ave* another cup."

Willy! O, 'ell! 'Ere wus a flamin' pill!
A moniker that alwus makes me ill.
    "If it's the same to you, mum," I replies,
"I answer quicker to the name of Bill."

Up goes 'er 'ands an' eyes, "That vulgar name!
No, Willy, but it isn't all the same;
    My fucher son must be respectable."
"Orright," I sez, "I s'pose it's in the game."

"Me fucher son," she sez, "right on frum this
Must not take anythink I say amiss.
    I know me jooty be me son-in-lor;
So, Willy, come an' give yer Mar a kiss."

I done it. Tho' I dunno 'ow I did.
"Dear boy," she sez, "to do as you are bid.
    Be kind to 'er," she sobs, "my little girl!"
An' then I kiss Doreen. Sez she, "Ah, Kid!"

Doreen! Ar 'ow 'er pretty eyes did shine.
No sight on earth or 'Eaven's 'arf so fine,
    An' as they looked at me she seemed to say
"I'm proud of 'im, I am, an' 'e is mine."

There wus a sorter glimmer in 'er eye,
An 'appy, nervis look, 'arf proud, 'arf shy;
    I seen 'er in me mind be'ind the cups
In our own little kipsie, bye an' bye.

An' then when Mar-in-lor an' me began
To tork of 'ouse'old things an' scheme an' plan,
    A sudden thort fair jolts me where I live:
"These is my wimmin folk! An' I'm a man!"

It's wot they calls responsibility.
All of a 'eap that feelin' come to me;
    An' somew'ere in me 'ead I seemed to feel
A sneakin' sort o' wish that I was free.

'Ere's me, 'oo never took no 'eed o' life,
Investin' in a mar-in-lor an' wife:
   Someone to battle fer besides meself,
Somethink to love an' shield frum care and strife.

"'Er pore dead Par," she sez, an' gulps a sob.
An' then I tells 'er 'ow I got a job
   As storeman down at Jones' printin' joint,
A decent sorter cop at fifty bob.

Then things get 'ome-like; an' we torks till late,
An' tries to tease Doreen to fix the date,
   An' she gits suddin soft and tender-like,
An' cries a bit, when we parts at the gate.

An', as I'm moochin' 'omeward frum the car,
A suddin notion stops me wiv a jar—
   Wot if Doreen, I thinks, should grow to be
A fat ole weepin' willer like 'er Mar!

O, 'struth! It won't bear thinkin' of! It's crook!
An' I'm a mean, unfeelin' dawg to look
   At things like that. Doreen's Doreen to me,
The sweetest peach on w'ich a man wus shook

'Er "pore dear Par" ... I s'pose 'e 'ad 'is day,
An' kissed an' smooged an' loved 'er in 'is way.
   An' wed an' took 'is chances like a man—
But, Gawd! this splicin' racket ain't all play.

Love is a gamble, an' there ain't no certs.
Some day, I s'pose, I'll git wise to the skirts,
   An' learn to take the bitter wiv the sweet ...
But, strike me purple! "Willie!" *That's* wot 'urts.

HITCHED

"An'—wilt—yeh—take—this—woman—fer—to be—
    Yer—weddid—wife?" . . . O, strike me! Will I wot?
Take 'er Doreen? 'E stan's there *arstin'* me!
    As if 'e thort per'aps I'd rather not!
    Take 'er? 'E seemed to think 'er kind was got
Like cigarette-cards, fer the arstin'. Still,
    I does me stunt in this 'ere hitchin' rot,
An' speaks me piece: "Righto!" I sez, "I will."

"I will," I sez. An' tho' a joyful shout
    Come from me bustin' 'eart—I know it did—
Me voice got sorter mangled comin' out,
    An' makes me whisper like a frightened kid.
    "I will," I squeaks. An' I'd 'a' give a quid
To 'ad it on the quite, wivout this fuss,
    An' orl the starin' crowd that Mar 'ad bid
To see this solim hitchin' up of us.

"Fer—rich-er—er—fer—poor-er." So 'e bleats.
    "In—sick-ness—an'—in—'ealth." . . . An' there I stands.
An' dunno 'arf the chatter I repeats,
    Nor wot the 'ell to do wiv my two 'ands.
    But 'e don't 'urry puttin' on our brands—
This white-'aired pilot-bloke—but gives it lip,
    Dressed in 'is little shirt, wiv frills an' bands.
"In sick-ness—an'—in—" Ar! I got the pip!

An' once I missed me turn; an' Ginger Mick,
    'Oo's my best-man, 'e ups an' beefs it out.
"I will!" 'e 'owls; an' fetches me a kick.
    "Your turn to chin!" 'e tips wiv a shout.
    An' there I'm standin' like a gawky lout.
(Aw, spare me! But I seemed to be *all* 'ands!)
    An' wonders wot 'e's goin' crook about,
Wiv 'arf a mind to crack 'im where 'e stands.

O, lumme! But ole Ginger was a trick!
    Got up regardless fer the solim rite
('E 'awks the bunnies when 'e toils, does Mick)
    An' twice I saw 'im feelin' fer a light
    To start a fag; an' trembles lest 'e might,
Thro' force o' habit like. 'E's nervis too;
    That's plain, fer orl 'is air o' bluff an' skite;
An' jist as keen as me to see it thro'.

But, 'struth, the wimmin! 'Ow they love this frill!
  Fer Auntie Liz, an' Mar, o' course, wus there;
An' Mar's two uncles' wives, an' Cousin Lil,
  An' 'arf a dozen more to grin and stare.
  I couldn't make me 'ands fit anywhere!
I felt like I wus up afore the Beak!
  But my Doreen she never turns a air,
Nor misses once when it's 'er turn to speak.

"To—be—yer—weddid—wife—" Aw, take a pull!
  Wot in the 'ell's 'e think I come there for?
An' so 'e drawls an' drones until I'm full,
  An' wants to do a duck clean out the door.
  An' yet, fer orl 'is 'igh-falutin' jor,
Ole Snowy wus a reel good-meanin' bloke;
  If 'twasn't fer the 'oly look 'e wore
Yeh'd think 'e piled it on jist fer a joke.

An', when at last 'e shuts 'is little book,
  I 'eaves a sigh that nearly bust me vest.
But, 'Eavens! Now 'ere's muvver goin' crook!
  An' sobbin' awful on me manly chest!
  (I wish sh'd give them water-works a rest.)
"My little girl!" she 'owls. "O, treat 'er well!
  She's young—too young to leave 'er muvver's nest!"
"Orright, ole chook," I nearly sez. O, 'ell!

An' then we 'as a beano up at Mar's—
  A slap-up feed, wiv wine an' two big geese.
Doreen sits next ter me, 'er eyes like stars.
  O, 'ow I wished their blessed yap would cease!
  The Parson-bloke 'e speaks a little piece,
That makes me blush an' 'ang me silly 'ead.
  'E sez 'e 'opes our lovin' will increase—
I *likes* that pilot fer the things 'e said.

'E sez Doreen an' me is in a boat,
  An' sailin' on the matrimonial sea;
'E sez as 'ow 'e 'opes we'll allus float
  In peace an' joy, from storm an' danger free.
  Then muvver gits to weepin' in 'er tea;
An' Auntie Liz sobs like a winded colt;
  An' Cousin Lil comes 'round an' kisses me;
Until I feel I'll 'ave to do a bolt.

Then Ginger gits end-up an' makes a speech—
  ('E'd 'ad a couple, but 'e wasn't shick).
"My cobber 'ere," 'e sez, "'as copped a peach!
  Of orl the barrer-load she is the pick!
  I 'opes 'e won't fergit 'is pals too quick
As wus 'is frien's in olden days, becors,
  I'm trustin', later on," sez Ginger Mick,
"To celebrate the chris'nin'." . . . 'Oly wars!

At last Doreen an' me we gits away,
  An' leaves 'em doin' nothin' to the scran.
(We're honey-moonin' down beside the Bay.)
  I gives a 'arf a dollar to the man
  Wot drives the cab; an' like two kids we ran
To ketch the train—Ah, strike! I could 'a' flown!
  We gets the carridge right agen the van.
She whistles, jolts, an' starts . . . An' we're alone!

Doreen an' me! My precious bit o' fluff!
  Me own true weddid wife! . . . An' we're alone!
She seems to frail, an' me so big an' rough—
  I dunno wot this feelin' is that's grown
  Inside me 'ere that makes me feel I own
A think so tender like I fear to squeeze
  Too 'ard fer fear she'll break . . . Then, wiv a groan
I starts to 'ear a coot call, "Tickets, please!"

You could 'a' outed me right on the spot!
  I wus so rattled when that porter spoke;
Fer, 'struth! them tickets I 'ad fair forgot!
  But 'e jist laughs, an' takes it fer a joke.
  "We must ixcuse," 'e sez, "new-married folk."
An' I pays up, an' grins, an' blushes red . . .
  It shows 'ow married life improves a bloke:
If I'd bin single I'd 'a' punched 'is 'ead!

B E E F   T E A

She never magged; she never said no word;
But sat an' looked at me an' never stirred.
  I could 'a' bluffed it out if she 'ad been
Fair narked, an' let me 'ave it wiv 'er tongue;
But silence told me 'ow 'er 'eart wus wrung.
    Poor 'urt Doreen!
Gorstruth! I'd sooner fight wiv fifty men
Than git one look like that frum 'er agen!

She never moved; she never spoke no word;
That 'urt look in 'er eyes, like some scared bird:
  "'Ere is the man I loved," it seemed to say.
"'E's mine, this crawlin' thing, an' I'm 'is wife;
Tied up fer good; an' orl me joy in life
    Is chucked away!"
If she 'ad bashed me I'd 'a felt no 'urt!
But 'ere she treats me like—like I wus dirt.

'Ow is a man to guard agen that look?
Fer other wimmin, when the'r blokes go crook,
  An' lobs 'ome wiv the wages uv a jag,
They smashes things an' carries on a treat
An' 'owls an' scolds an' wakes the bloomin' street
    Wiv noisy mag.
But 'er—she never speaks; she never stirs ...
I drops me bundle ... An' the game is 'ers.

Jist two months wed! Eight weeks uv married bliss
Wiv my Doreen, an' now it's come to this!
  Wot wus I thinkin' uv? Gawd! I ain't fit
To kiss the place 'er little feet 'as been!
'Er that I called me wife, me own Doreen!
    Fond dreams 'as flit;
Love's done a bunk, an' joy is up the pole;
An' shame an' sorrer's roostin' in me soul.

'Twus orl becors uv Ginger Mick—the cow!
(I wish't I 'ad 'im 'ere to deal wiv now!
  I'd pass 'im one, I would! 'E ain't no man!)
I meets 'im Choosdee ev'nin' up the town.
"Wot O," 'e chips me. "Kin yeh keep one down?"
    I sez I can.
We 'as a couple; then meets three er four
Flash coves I useter know, an' 'as some more.

"'Ow are yeh on a little gamble, Kid?"

Sez Ginger Mick. "Lars' night I'm on four quid.
  Come 'round an' try yer luck at Steeny's school."
"No," sez me conscience. Then I thinks, "Why not?
An' buy 'er presents if I wins a pot?
    A blazin' fool
I wus. Fer 'arf a mo' I 'as a fight;
Then conscience skies the wipe ... Sez I "Orright."

Ten minutes later I was back once more,
Kip in me 'and, on Steeny Isaac's floor,
  Me luck was in an' I wus 'eadin' good.
Yes, back agen amongst the same old crew!
An' orl the time down in me 'eart I knew
    I never should ...
Nex' thing I knows it's after two o'clock—
Two in the mornin'! An' I've done me block!

"Wot odds?" I thinks. "I'm in fer it orright."
An' so I stops an' gambles orl the night;
  An' bribes me conscience wiv the gilt I wins.
But when I comes out in the cold, 'ard dawn
I know I've crooled me pitch; me soul's in pawn.
    My flamin' sins
They 'its me in a 'eap right where I live;
Fer I 'ave broke the solim vow I give.

She never magged; she never said no word.
An' when I speaks, it seems she never 'eard.
  I could 'a' sung a nim, I feels so gay!
If she 'ad only roused I might 'a' smiled.
She jist seems 'urt an' crushed; not even riled.
    I turns away,
An' yanks me carkis out into the yard,
Like some whipped pup; an' kicks meself reel 'ard.

An' then, I sneaks to bed, an' feels dead crook.
Fer golden quids I couldn't face that look—
  That trouble in the eyes uv my Doreen.
Aw, strike! Wot made me go an' do this thing?
I feel jist like a chewed up bit of string,
    An' rotten mean!
Fer 'arf an hour I lies there feelin' cheap;
An' then I 's'pose, I muster fell asleep ...

"'Ere, Kid, drink this" ... I wakes, an' lifts me 'ead,
An' sees 'er standin' there beside the bed;

A basin in 'er 'ands; an' in 'er eyes—
(Eyes that wiv unshed tears is shinin' wet)—
The sorter look I never shall ferget,
    Until I dies.
"'Ere, Kid, drink this," she sez, an' smiles at me.
I looks—an' spare me days! *It was beef tea!*

Beef tea! She treats me like a hinvaleed!
Me! that 'as caused 'er lovin' 'eart to bleed.
   It 'urts me worse than maggin' fer a week!
'Er! 'oo 'ad right to turn dead sour on me,
Fergives like that, an' feeds me wiv beef tea . . .
    I tries to speak;
An' then—I ain't ashamed o' wot I did—
I 'ides me face . . . an' blubbers like a kid.

UNCLE
JIM

"I got no time fer wasters, lad," sez 'e
    "Give me a man wiv grit," sez Uncle Jim.
'E bores 'is cute ole eyes right into me,
    While I stares 'ard an' gives it back to 'im.
Then orl at once 'e grips me 'and in 'is:
"Some'ow," 'e sez, "I likes yer ugly phiz."

"You got a look," 'e sez, "like you could stay;
    Altho' yeh mauls King's English when yeh yaps
An' 'angs flash frills on ev'rythink yeh say.
    I ain't no grammarist meself, per'aps,
But langwidge is a 'elp, I owns," sez Unk,
"When things is goin' crook." An' 'ere 'e wunk.

"Yeh'll find it tough," 'e sez, "to knuckle down.
    Good farmin' is a gift—like spoutin' slang.
Yeh'll 'ave to cut the luxuries o' town,
    An' chuck the manners of this back-street gang;
Fer country life ain't cigarettes and beer."
"I'm game," I sez. Sez Uncle, "Put it 'ere!"

Like that I took the plunge, an' slung the game.
    I've parted wiv them joys I 'eld most dear;
I've sent the leery bloke that bore me name
    Clean to the pack wivout one pearly tear;
An' frum the ashes of a ne'er-do-well
A bloomin' farmer's blossomin' like 'ell.

Farmer! That's me! Wiv this 'ere strong right 'and
    I've gripped the plough; and blistered jist a treat.
Doreen an' me 'as gone upon the land.
    Yours truly fer the burden an' the 'eat!
Yours truly for upendin' chunks o' soil!
The 'ealthy, 'ardy, 'appy son o' toil!

I owns I've 'ankered fer me former joys;
    I've 'ad me hours o' broodin' on me woes;
I've missed the comp'ny, an' I've missed the noise,
    The football matches an' the picter shows.
I've missed—but, say, it makes me feel fair mean
To whip the cat; an' then see my Doreen.

To see the colour comin' in 'er cheeks,
    To see 'er eyes grow brighter day be day,
The new, glad way she looks an' laughs an' speaks
    Is worf ten times the things I've chucked away.

An' there's a secret, whispered in the dark,
'As made me 'eart sing like a flamin' lark.

Jist let me tell yeh 'ow it come about.
 The things that I've been thro' 'ud fill a book.
Right frum me birf Fate played to knock me out;
 The 'and that I 'ad dealt to me was crook!
Then comes Doreen, an' patches up me parst;
Now Forchin's come to bunk wiv me at larst.

First orf, one night poor Mar gits suddin fits,
 An' floats wivout the time to wave "good-byes".
Doreen is orl broke up the day she flits;
 It tears me 'eart in two the way she cries.
To see 'er grief, it almost made me glad
I never knowed the mar I must 'ave 'ad.

We done poor Muvver proud when she went out—
 A slap-up send-orf, trimmed wiv tears an' crape.
An' then fer weeks Doreen she mopes about,
 An' life takes on a gloomy sorter shape.
I watch 'er face git pale, 'er eyes grow dim;
Till—like some 'airy angel—comes ole Jim.

A cherub togged in sunburn an' a beard
 An' duds that shouted "'Ayseed!" fer a mile:
Care took the count the minute 'e appeared,
 An' sorrer shrivelled up before 'is smile,
'E got the 'ammer-lock on my good-will
The minute that 'e sez, "So, this is Bill."

It's got me beat. Doreen's late Par, some way,
 Was second cousin to 'is bruvver's wife.
Somethin' like that. In less than 'arf a day
 It seemed 'e'd been my uncle orl me life.
'E takes me 'and: "I dunno 'ow it is,"
'E sez, "but, lad, I likes that ugly phiz."

An' when 'e'd stayed wiv us a little while
 The 'ouse begun to look like 'ome once more.
Doreen she brightens up beneath 'is smile,
 An' 'ugs 'im till I kids I'm gettin' sore.
Then, late one night, 'e opens up 'is scheme,
An' passed me wot looks like some fond dream.

'E 'as a little fruit-farm, doin' well;
 'E saved a tidy bit to see 'im thro';

Hitched

'E's gittin' old fer toil, an' wants a spell;
  An' 'ere's a 'ome jist waitin' fer us two.
"It's 'er's an' yours fer keeps when I am gone,"
Sez Uncle Jim. "Lad, will yeh take it on?"

So that's the strength of it. An' 'ere's me now
  A flamin' berry farmer, full o' toil;
Playin' joo-jitsoo wiv an 'orse an' plough,
  An' coaxin' fancy tucker frum the soil;
An' longin', while I wrestles with the rake,
Fer days when my poor back fergits to ache.

Me days an' nights is full of schemes an' plans
  To figger profits an' cut out the loss;
An' when the pickin's on, I 'ave me 'an's
  To take me orders while I act the boss;
It's sorter sweet to 'ave the right to rouse ...
An' my Doreen's the lady of the 'ouse.

To see 'er bustlin' 'round about the place,
  Full of the simple joy o' doin' things,
That thoughtful, 'appy look upon 'er face,
  That 'ope an' peace an' pride o' labour brings,
Is worth the crowd of joys I knoo one time,
An' makes regrettin' 'em seem like a crime.

An' ev'ry little while ole Uncle Jim
  Comes up to stay a bit an' pass a tip.
It gives us 'eart jist fer to look at 'im,
  An' feel the friendship in 'is warm 'and-grip.
'Im, wiv the sunburn on 'is kind ole dile;
'Im, wiv the sunbeams in 'is sweet ole smile.

"I got no time fer wasters, lad," sez 'e,
  "But that there ugly mug o' yourn I trust."
An' so I reckon that it's up to me
  To make a bloomin' do of it or bust.
I got to take the back-ache wiv the rest,
An' plug along, an' do me little best.

Luck ain't no steady visitor, I know;
  But now an' then it calls—fer look at me!
You wouldn't take me, 'bout a year ago,
  Free gratis wiv a shillin' pound o' tea;
Then, in a blessed 'eap, ole Forchin lands
A missus an' a farm fair in me 'ands.

THE KID

My son! ... Them words, jist like a blessed song,
Is singin' in me 'eart the 'ole day long;
 Over an' over; while I'm scared I'll wake
 Out of a dream, to find it all a fake.

My son! Two little words, that, yesterdee,
Wus jist two simple, senseless words to me;
 An' now—no man, not since the world begun,
 Made any better pray'r that ... My son!

A little while ago it was jist "me"—
A loney, longin' streak o' misery.
 An' then 'twas "'er an' me"—Doreen, my wife!
 An' now it's "'im an' us," an'—sich is life!

But, 'struth! 'E is king-pin! The 'ead serang!
I mustn't tramp about, or talk no slang;
 I mustn't pinch 'is nose, or make a face,
 I mustn't—Strike! 'E seems to own the place!

"Goog, goo," 'e sez, an' curls 'is cunnin' toes.
Yeh'd be su'prised the 'eaps o' things 'e knows.
 I'll swear 'e tumbles I'm 'is father, too;
 The way 'e squints at me, an' sez, "Goog, goo."

"Goog, goo," 'e sez. I'll swear yeh never did
In all yer natcheril see sich a kid.
 The cunnin' ways 'e's got; the knowin' stare—
 Ther' ain't a youngster like 'im *anywhere*!

An', when 'e gets a little pain inside,
'Is dead straight griffin ain't to be denied.
 I'm sent to talk sweet nuffin's to the fowls;
 While nurse turns 'and-springs ev'ry time 'e 'owls.

But, say, I tell yeh straight ... I been thro' 'ell!
The things I thort I wouldn't dare to tell
 Lest, in the tellin' I might feel again
 One little part of all that fear an' pain.

It come so sudden that I lorst me block.
First, it was 'ell-fer-leather to the doc.,
 'Oo took it all so calm 'e made me curse—
 An' then I sprints like mad to get the nurse.

By gum; that woman! But she beat me flat!
A man's jist putty in a game like that.

She owned me 'appy 'ome almost before
She fairly got 'er nose inside me door.

I wus too weak wiv funk to start an' rouse.
'Struth! Ain't a man the boss in 'is own 'ouse?
    "You go an' chase yerself!" she tips me straight.
    "There's nothin' now fer you to do but—wait."

Wait? ... Gawd! ... I never knoo wot waitin' meant
In all me life, till that day I was sent
    To loaf around, while there inside—Aw, strike!
    I couldn't tell yeh wot that hour was like!

Three times I comes to listen at the door;
Three times I drags meself away once more;
    'Arf dead wiv fear; 'arf filled wiv tremblin' joy ...
    An' then she beckons me, an' sez—"A boy!"

"A boy!" she sez. "An' bofe is doin' well!"
I drops into a chair, an' jist sez—"'Ell!"
    It was a pray'r. I feels bofe crook an' glad ...
    An' that's the strength of bein' made a dad.

I thinks of church when in that room I goes,
'Oldin' me breaf an' walkin' on me toes;
    Fer 'arf a mo' I feared me nerve 'ud fail
    To see 'er lying there so still an' pale.

She looks so frail, at first, I dursn't stir.
An' then, I leans acrost an' kisses 'er;
    An' all the room gits sorter blurred an' dim ...
    She smiles, an' moves 'er 'ead. "Dear lad! Kiss 'im."

Near smothered in a ton of snowy clothes,
First thing, I sees a bunch o' stubby toes,
    Bald 'ead, termater face, an' two big eyes.
    "Look, Kid," she smiles at me. "Ain't 'e a size?"

'E didn't seem no sorter size to me;
But yet, I speak no lie when I agree;
    "'E is," I sez, an' smiles back at Doreen,
    "The biggest nipper fer 'is age I've seen."

She turns away; 'er eyes is brimmin' wet.
"Our little son!" she sez. "Our precious pet!"
    An' then, I seen a great big drop roll down
    An' fall—kersplosh!—fair on 'is nibs's crown.

An' still she smiles. "A lucky sign," she said.
"Somewhere, in some ole book, one time I read,
  'The child will sure be blest all thro' the years
  Who's christened wiv 'is mother's 'appy tears.'"

                  * * * *

My wife an' fam'ly! Don't it sound all right!
That's wot I whispers to meself at night.
  Some day, I s'pose, I'll learn to say it loud
  An' careless—kiddin' that I don't feel proud.

My son!...If ther's a Gawd 'oo's leanin' near
To watch our dilly little lives down 'ere,
  'E smiles, I guess, if 'E's a lovin' one—
  Smiles, friendly-like, to 'ear them words—My son.

**THE
MOOCH
O' LIFE**

This ev'nin' I was sittin' wiv Doreen,
  Peaceful an' 'appy wiv the day's work done,
Watchin', be'ind the orchard's bonzer green,
  The flamin' wonder of the settin' sun.

Another day gone by; another night
Creepin' along to douse Day's golden light;
  Another dawnin', when the night is gone,
  To live an' love—an' so life mooches on.

Times I 'ave thought, when things was goin' crook,
  When 'Ope turned nark an' Love forgot to smile,
Of somethin' I once seen in some ole book
  Where an ole sore-'ead arsts, "Is life worf w'ile?"

But in that stillness, as the day grows dim,
An' I am sittin' there wiv 'er an' 'im—
  My wife, my son! an' strength in me to strive,
  I only know—it's good to be alive!

Yeh live, yeh love, yeh learn; an' when yeh come
  To square the ledger in some thortful hour,
The everlastin' answer to the sum
  Must allus be, "Where's sense in gittin' sour?"

Fer when yeh've come to weigh the good an' bad—
The gladness wiv the sadness you 'ave 'ad—
  Then 'im 'oo's faith in 'uman goodness fails
  Fergits to put 'is liver in the scales.

Livin' an' lovin'; learnin' day be day;
  Pausin' a minute in the barmy strife
To find that 'elpin' others on the way
  Is gold coined fer your profit—sich is life.

I've studied books wiv yearnin' to improve,
To 'eave meself out of me lowly groove,
  An' 'ere is orl the change I ever got:
  "'Ark at yer 'eart, an' you kin learn the lot."

I gives it in—that wisdom o' the mind—
  I wasn't built to play no lofty part.
Orl such is welkim to the joys they find;
  I only know the wisdom o' the 'eart.

An' ever it 'as taught me, day be day,
The one same lesson in the same ole way:

"Look fer yer profits in the 'earts o' friends,
Fer 'atin' never paid no dividends."

Life's wot yeh make it; an' the bloke 'oo tries
To grab the shinin' stars frum out the skies
　　Goes crook on life, an' calls the world a cheat,
　　An' tramples on the daisies at 'is feet.

But when the moon comes creepin' o'er the hill,
　　An' when the mopoke calls along the creek,
I takes me cup o' joy an' drinks me fill,
　　An' arsts meself wot better could I seek.

An' ev'ry song I 'ear the thrushes sing
That everlastin' message seems to bring;
　　An' ev'ry wind that whispers in the trees
　　Gives me the tip there ain't no joys like these.

Livin' an' lovin'; wand'rin' on yer way;
　　Reapin' the 'arvest of a kind deed done;
An' watchin', in the sundown of yer day,
　　Yerself again, grown nobler in yer son.

Knowin' that ev'ry coin o' kindness spent
Bears interest in yer 'eart at cent per cent;
　　Measurin' wisdom by the peace it brings
　　To simple minds that values simple things.

An' when I take a look along the way
　　That I 'ave trod, it seems the man knows best,
Who's met wiv slabs of sorrer in 'is day,
　　When 'e is truly rich an' truly blest.

An' I am rich, becos me eyes 'ave seen
The lovelight in the eyes of my Doreen;
　　An' I am blest, becos me feet 'ave trod
　　A land 'oo's fields reflect the smile o' God.

Livin' an' lovin'; learnin' to fergive
　　The deeds an' words of some un'appy bloke
Who's missed the bus—so 'ave I come to live,
　　An' take the 'ole mad world as 'arf a joke.

* * * *

Sittin' at ev'nin' in this sunset-land,
Wiv 'Er in all the World to 'old me 'and,
　　A son, to bear me name when I am gone ...
　　Livin' an' lovin'—so life mooches on.

THE MOODS
OF
GINGER MICK

DUCK
AN' FOWL

Now, when a bloke 'e cracks a bloke fer insults to a skirt,
   An' wrecks a joint to square a lady's name,
They used to call it chivalry, but now they calls it dirt,
   An' the end of it is cops an' quod an' shame.
Fer insults to fair Gwendoline they 'ad to be wiped out;
But Rosie's sort is jist fair game—when Ginger ain't about.

It was Jimmie Ah Foo's cook-shop, which is close be Spadger's Lane,
   Where a vari'gated comp'ny tears the scran,
An' there's some is "tup'ny coloured," an' some is "penny plain,"
   Frum a lawyer to a common lumper-man.
Or a writer fer the papers, or a slaver on the prowl,
An' noiseless Chows a-glidin' 'round wiv plates uv duck an' fowl.

But if yeh wanted juicy bits that 'ung around Foo's perch
   Yeh fetched 'em down an' wolfed 'em in yer place.
An' Foo sat sad an' solim, like an 'oly man in church,
   Wiv an early-martyr look upon 'is face;
Wot never changed, not even when a toff upon a jag
Tried to pick up Ginger's Rosie, an' collided wiv a snag.

Ginger Mick's bin at the races, an' 'e'd made a little rise,
   'Avin' knowed a bloke wot knowed the trainer's cook.
An' easy money's very sweet, as punters reckernise,
   An' sweetest when yeh've prized it orf a "book."
So Ginger calls fer Rosie, an' to celerbrate 'is win
'E trots 'er down to Ah Foo's joint to splash a bit uv tin.

There wus lights, an' smells of Asia, an' a strange, Chow-'aunted
      scene;
   Floatin' scraps of forrin lingo 'it the ear;
But Rose sails in an' takes 'er seat like any soshul queen
   Sich as stokes 'erself wiv foy grass orl the year.
"Duck an' Fowl" 's 'er nomination; so ole Ginger jerks 'is frame
'Cross to git some fancy pickin's, an' to give 'is choice a name.

While Ginger paws the tucker, an' 'as words about the price,
   There's a shickered toff slings Rosie goo-goo eyes.
'E's a mug 'oo thinks 'e's 'it a flamin' 'all uv scarlet vice
   An' 'e picks on gentle Rosie fer a prize.
Then 'e tries to play at 'andies, an' arrange about a meet;
But Rosie fetches 'im a welt that shifts 'im in 'is seat.

Ginger's busy makin' bargins, an' 'e never seen the clout;
   'E is 'agglin' wiv Ah Foo fer 'arf a duck;

But the toff's too shick or silly fer to 'eave 'is carkis out,
   An' to fade while goin's good an' 'e's in luck.
Then Ginger clinched 'is bargin, an', as down the room 'e came,
'E seen the toff jump frum 'is seat, an' call the girl a name.

That done it. Less than 'arf a mo, an' 'ell got orf the chain;
   An' the swell stopped 'arf a ducklin' wiv 'is neck,
As Ginger guv the war-cry that is dreaded in the Lane.
   An' the rest wus whirlin' toff an' sudden wreck.
Mick never reely stoushed 'im, but 'e used 'im fer a mop.
Then someone doused the bloomin' glim, an' Foo run fer a cop.

Down the stairs an' in the passidge come the shufflin' feet uv
      Chows,
   An' a crash, as Ah Foo's chiner found it's mark.
Fer more than Mick 'ad ancient scores left over frum ole rows,
   An' more than one stopped somethin' in the dark.
Then the tabbies took to screamin', an' a Chow remarked "Wha'
      for?"
While the live ducks quacked blue murder frum their corner uv the
      floor.

Fer full ten minutes it was joy, reel willin' an' to spare,
   Wiv noise uv tarts, an' Chows, an' ducks, an' lash;
An' plates uv fowl an' bird's-nest soup went whizzin' thro' the air,
   While 'arf-a-dozen fought to reach Foo's cash.
Then, thro' an open doorway, three Chows' 'eads is framed in
      light,
An' sudden in Mick's corner orl is gentle peace an' quite.

Up goes the lights; in comes the cops; an' there's a sudden rush;
   But the Johns 'as got 'em safe an' 'emmed 'em in;
An' ev'ryone looks innercent. Then thro' the anxious 'ush
   The toff's voice frum the floor calls fer a gin . . .
But Mick an' Rose, O where are they? Arst uv the silent night!
They 'ad a date about a dawg, an' vanished out o' sight.

Then Foo an' orl 'is cousins an' the ducks torks orl at once,
   An' the tabbies pitch the weary Johns a tale,
'Ow they orl is puffick ladies 'oo 'ave not bin pinched fer munce;
   An' the crooks does mental sums concernin' bail.
The cops they takes a name er two, then gathers in the toff,
An' lobs 'im in a cold, 'ard cell to sleep 'is love-quest off.

But down in Rosie's kipsie, at the end uv Spadger's Lane,
   'Er an' Mick is layin' supper out fer two.

"Now, I 'ate the game," sez Ginger, "an' it goes agin the grain;
   But wot's a 'elpless, 'ungry bloke to do?"
An' 'e yanks a cold roast chicken frum the bosom uv 'is shirt,
An' Rosie finds a ducklin' underneath 'er Sund'y skirt.

So, when a bloke fergits 'imself, an' soils a lady's name,
   Altho' Romance is dead an' in the dirt,
In ole Madrid or Little Bourke they treats 'im much the same,
   An' 'e collects wot's comin' fer a cert.
But, spite uv 'igh-falutin' tork, the fact is jist the same:
Ole Ginger Mick wus out fer loot, an' played a risky game.

To fight an' forage ... Spare me days! It's been man's leadin' soot
   Since 'e learned to word a tart an' make a date.
'E's been at it, good an' solid, since ole Adam bit the froot:
   To fight an' forage, an' pertect 'is mate.
But this story 'as no moral, an' it 'as a vulgar plot;
It is jist a small igzample uv a way ole Ginger's got.

WAR

'E sez to me, "Wot's orl this flamin' war?
  The papers torks uv nothin' else but scraps.
An' wot's ole England got snake-'eaded for?
  An' wot's the strength uv callin' out our chaps?"
'E sez to me, "Struth! Don't she rule the sea?
Wot does she want wiv us?" 'e sez to me.

Ole Ginger Mick is loadin' up 'is truck
  One mornin' in the markit feelin' sore.
'E sez to me, "Well, mate, I've done me luck;
  An' Rose is arstin', 'Wot about this war?'
I'm gone a tenner at the two-up school;
The game is crook, an' Rose is turnin' cool."

'E sez to me, "'Ow is it fer a beer?"
  I tips 'im 'ow I've told me wife, Doreen,
That when I comes down to the markit 'ere
  I dodges pubs, an' chucks the tipple, clean.
Wiv 'er an' kid alone up on the farm
She's full uv fancies that I'll come to 'arm.

"'Enpecked!" 'e sez. An' then, "Ar, I dunno.
  I wouldn't mind if I wus in yer place.
I've 'arf a mind to give cold tea a go—
  It's no game, pourin' snake-juice in yer face.
But, lad, I 'ave to, wiv the thirst I got:
I'm goin' over now to stop a pot."

'E goes acrost to find a pint a 'ome;
  An' meets a pal an' keeps another down.
Ten minutes later, when 'e starts to roam
  Back to the markit, wiv an ugly frown,
'E sprags a soljer bloke 'oo's passin' by,
An' sez 'e'd like to dot 'im in the eye.

"Your sort," sez Mick, "don't know yer silly mind!
  They lead yeh like a sheep; it's time yeh woke—
The 'eads is makin' piles out uv your kind!"
  "Aw, git yer 'ead read!" sez the soljer bloke.
'Struth! 'e wus willin' wus that Kharki chap;
I 'ad me work cut out to stop a scrap.

An' as the soljer fades acrost the street,
  Mick strikes a light an' sits down on 'is truck,
An' chews 'is fag—a sign 'is nerve is beat—
  An' swears a bit, an' sez 'e's done 'is luck.

'E grouches there ten minutes, maybe more,
Then sez quite sudden, *"Blarst the flamin' war!"*

Jist then a motor car goes glidin' by
  Wiv two fat toffs be'ind two fat cigars;
Mick twigs 'em frum the corner uv 'is eye—
  "I 'ope," 'e sez, "the 'Uns don't git *my* cars.
Me di'mon's, too, don't let me sleep a wink . . .
Ar, 'Struth! I'd fight fer that sort—I *don't* think."

          * * * *

Then Mick gits up an' starts another fag.
  "Ar, well," 'e sez, "it's no affair uv mine,
If I don't work they'd pinch me on the vag;
  But I'm not keen to fight so toffs kin dine
On pickled olives . . . *Blarst* the flamin' war!
I ain't got nothin' worth the fightin' for.

"So long," 'e sez. "I got ter trade me stock;
  An' when yeh 'ear I've took a soljer's job
I give yeh leave to say I've done me block
  An' got a flock uv weevils in me knob."
An' then, orf-'anded-like, 'e arsts me; "Say,
Wot are they slingin' soljers fer their pay?"

I tells 'im; an' 'e sez to me, "So long.
  Some day this rabbit trade will git me beat."
An' Ginger Mick shoves thro' the markit throng,
  An' gits 'is barrer out into the street.
An', as 'e goes, I 'ears 'is gentle roar:
'Rabbee! *Wile Rabbee!* . . . Blarst the flamin' war!"

**THE
CALL
OF
STOUSH**

Wot price ole Ginger Mick? 'E's done a break—
   Gone to the flamin' war to stoush the foe.
Wus it fer glory, or a woman's sake?
   Ar, arst me somethin' easy! I dunno.
'Is Kharki clobber set 'im off a treat,
That's all I know; 'is motive's got me beat.

Ole Mick 'e's trainin' up in Cairo now;
   An' all the cops in Spadger's Lane is sad.
They miss 'is music in the midnight row
   Wot time the pushes mix it good an' glad.
Fer 'e wus one o' them, you understand,
Wot "soils the soshul life uv this fair land."

'E wus a man uv vierlence, wus Mick,
   Coarse wiv 'is speech an' in 'is manner low,
Slick wiv 'is 'ands, an' 'andy wiv a brick
   When bricks wus needful to defeat a foe.
An' now 'e's gone an' mizzled to the war,
An' some blokes 'as the nerve to arst "Wot for?"

Why did 'e go? 'E 'ad a decent job,
   'Is tart an' 'im they could 'a' made it right.
Why does a wild bull fight to guard the mob?
   Why does a bloomin' bull-ant look fer fight?
Why does a rooster scrap an' flap an' crow?
'E went becos 'e dam well *'ad* to go.

'E never spouted no 'igh-soundin' stuff
   About stern jooty an' 'is country's call;
But, in 'is way, 'e 'eard it right enough
   A-callin' like the shout uv "On the Ball!"
Wot time the footer brings the clicks great joy,
An' Saints or Carlton roughs it up wiv 'Roy.

The call wot came to cave-men in the days
   When rocks wus stylish in the scrappin' line;
The call wot knights 'eard in the minstrel's lays,
   That sent 'em in tin soots to Palerstine;
The call wot draws all fighters to the fray
It come to Mick, an' Mick 'e must obey . . .

Be'ind that dile uv 'is, as 'ard as sin,
   Wus strange, soft thorts that never yet showed out;
An' down in Spadger's Lane, in dirt an' din,
   'E dreamed sich dreams as poits sing about.

'E's 'ad 'is visions uv the Bonzer Tart;
An' stoushed some coot to ease 'is swellin' 'eart.

Lovin' an' fightin' . . . when the tale is told,
   That's all there is to it; an' in their way
Them brave an' noble 'ero blokes uv old
   Wus Ginger Micks—the crook 'uns uv their day.
Jist let the Call uv Stoush give 'im 'is chance
An' Ginger Mick's the 'ero of Romance.

So Ginger Mick 'e's mizzled to the war;
   Joy in 'is 'eart, an' wild dreams in 'is brain;
Gawd 'elp the foe that 'e goes gunnin' for
   If tales is true they tell in Spadger's Lane—
Tales that ud fairly freeze the gentle 'earts
Uv them 'oo knits 'is socks—the Culchered Tarts.

**THE
PUSH**

Becos a crook done in a prince, an' narked an Emperor,
    An' struck a light that set the world aflame;
Becos the bugles East an' West sooled on the dawgs o' war,
    A bloke called Ginger Mick 'as found 'is game—
Found 'is game an' found 'is brothers, 'oo wus strangers in 'is sight,
Till they shed their silly clobber an' put on the duds fer fight.

'E 'as struck it fer a moral. Ginger's found 'is game at last,
    An' 'e's took to it like ducklin's take to drink;
An' 'is slouchin' an' 'is grouchin' an' 'is loafin' uv the past—
    'E's done wiv 'em, an' dumped 'em down the sink.
'E's a bright an' shinin' sample uv a the'ry that I 'old:
That ev'ry 'eart that ever pumped is good fer chunks o' gold.

Ev'ry feller is a gold mine if yeh take an' work 'im right:
    It is shinin' on the surface now an' then;
An' there's some is easy sinkin', but there's some wants dynermite,
    Fer they looks a 'opeless prospect—yet they're men.
An' Ginger—'ard-shell Ginger's showin' signs that 'e will pay;
But it took a flamin' world-war fer to blarst 'is crust away.

But they took 'im an' they drilled 'im an' they shipped 'im overseas
    Wiv a crowd uv blokes 'e never met before.
'E rowed wiv 'em, an' scrapped wiv 'em, an' done some tall C.B.'s,
    An' 'e lobbed wiv 'em on Egyp's sandy shore.
Then Pride o' Race lay 'olt on 'im, an' Mick shoves out 'is chest
To find 'imself Australian an' blood brothers wiv the rest.

So I gits some reel good readin' in the letter wot 'e sent—
    Tho' the spellin's pretty rotten now an' then.
'I 'ad the joes at first," 'e sez; "but now I'm glad I went,
    Fer it's fine to be among reel, livin' men.
An' it's grand to be Australian, an' to say it good an' loud
When yeh bump a forrin country wiv sich fellers as our crowd.

"'Struth! I've 'ung around me native land fer close on thirty year,
    An' I never knoo wot men me cobbers were:
Never knoo that toffs wus white men till I met 'em over 'ere—
    Blokes an' coves I sort o' snouted over there.
Yes, I loafed aroun' me country; an' I never knoo 'er then;
But the reel, ribuck Australia's 'ere, among the fightin' men.

"We've slung the swank fer good an' all; it don't fit in our plan;
    To skite uv birth an' boodle is a crime.
A man wiv us, why, 'e's a man becos 'e *is* a man,
    An' a reel red-'ot Australian ev'ry time.

Fer dawg an' side an' snobbery is down an' out fer keeps.
It's grit an' reel good feellership that gits yeh friends in 'eaps.

"There's a bloke 'oo shipped when I did; 'e wus lately frum 'is ma.
  'Oo 'ad filled 'im full uv notions uv 'is birth;
An' 'e overworked 'is aitches till 'e got the loud 'Ha-ha'
  Frum the fellers, but 'e wouldn't come to earth.
I bumped 'is lordship, name o' Keith, an' 'ad a little row,
An' 'e lost some chunks uv beauty; but 'e's good Australian now.

"There is Privit Snifty Thompson, 'oo wus once a Sydney rat,
  An' 'e 'ung around the Rocks when 'e wus young.
There's little Smith uv Collin'wood, wiv fags stuck in 'is 'at,
  An' a string uv dirty insults on 'is tongue.
A corperil took them in 'and—a lad frum Lameroo.
Now both is nearly gentlemen, an' good Australians too.

"There's one, 'e doesn't tork a lot, 'e sez 'is name is Trent,
  Jist a privit, but 'e knows 'is drill a treat;
A stand-orf bloke, but reel good pals wiv fellers in 'is tent,
  But 'is 'ome an' 'istoree 'as got 'em beat.
They reckon when 'e starts to bleed 'e'll stain 'is Kharki blue;
An' 'is lingo smells uv Oxford—but 'e's good Australian too.

"Then there's Lofty Craig uv Queensland, 'oo's a special pal uv mine;
  Slow an' shy, an' kind o' nervous uv 'is height;
An' Jupp, 'oo owns a copper show, an' arsts us out to dine
  When we're doo fer leave in Cairo uv a night.
An' there's Bills an' Jims an' Bennos, an' there's Roys an' 'Arolds too,
An' they're cobbers, an' they're brothers, an' Australians thro' an'
    thro'.

"There is farmers frum the Mallee, there is bushmen down frum
    Bourke,
  There's college men wiv letters to their name;
There is grafters, an' there's blokes 'oo never done a 'ard day's work
  Till they tumbled, wiv the rest, into the game—
An' they're drillin' 'ere together, men uv ev'ry creed an' kind
It's Australia! Solid! Dinkum! that 'as left the land be'ind.

"An' if yeh want a slushy, or a station overseer,
  Or a tinker, or a tailor, or a snob,
Or a 'andy bloke wiv 'orses, or a minin' ingineer,
  Why, we've got the very man to do yer job.
Butcher, baker, undertaker, or a Caf' de Pary chef,
'E is waitin', keen an' ready, in the little A.I.F.

"Rabbee! Wile Rabbee!"

"An' they've drilled us. Strike me lucky! but they've drilled us fer a
     cert!
  We 'ave trod around ole Egyp's burnin' sand
Till I tells meself at evenin', when I'm wringin' out me shirt,
    That we're built uv wire an' green-'ide in our land.
Strike! I thort I knoo 'ard yakker, w'ish I've tackled many ways,
But uv late I've took a tumble I bin dozin' orl me days.

"It's a game, lad," writes ole Ginger, "it's a game I'm likin' grand,
    An' I'm tryin' fer a stripe to fill in time;
I 'ave took a pull on shicker fer the honour uv me land,
    An' I'm umpty round the chest an' feelin' prime.
Yeh kin tell Rose, if yeh see 'er, I serloots 'er o'er the foam,
An' we'll 'ave a cray fer supper when I comes a'marchin' 'ome."

So ole Ginger sends a letter, an' 'is letter's good to read,
    Fer the things 'e sez, an' some things 'e leaves out;
An' when a bloke like 'im wakes up an' starts to take a 'eed,
    Well, it's sort o' worth the writin' 'ome about.
'E's one uv many little things Australia chanced to find
She never knoo she 'ad around till bugles cleared 'er mind.

Becos ole Europe lost 'er block an' started 'eavin' bricks,
    Becos the bugles wailed a song uv war,
We found reel gold down in the 'earts uv orl our Ginger Micks
    We never thort worth minin' fer before.
An' so, I'm tippin' we will pray, before our win is scored:
"Thank God for Mick, an' Bill an' Jim, an' little brother Clord."

GINGER'S
COBBER

"'E wears perjarmer soots an' cleans 'is teeth,"
    That's wot I reads. It fairly knocked me flat,
"Me soljer cobber, be the name o' Keith."
    Well, if that ain't the limit, strike me fat!
The sort that Ginger Mick would think beneath
'Is notice once. Perjarmers! Cleans 'is teeth?

Ole Ginger Mick 'as sent a billy-doo
    Frum somew'ere on the earth where fightin' thick.
The Censor wus a sport to let it thro',
    Considerin' the choice remarks o' Mick.
It wus that 'ot, I'm wond'rin' since it came
It didn't set the bloomin' mail aflame.

I'd love to let yeh 'ave it word fer word;
    But, strickly, it's a bit above the odds;
An' there's remarks that's 'ardly ever 'eard
    Amongst the company to w'ich we nods.
It seems they use the style in Ginger's trench
Wot's written out an' 'anded to the Bench.

I tones the langwidge down to soot the ears
    Of sich as me an' you resorts wiv now.
If I should give it jist as it appears
    Partic'lar folk might want ter make a row.
But say, yeh'd think ole Ginger wus a pote
If yeh could read some juicy bits 'e's wrote.

It's this noo pal uv 'is that tickles me;
    'E's got a mumma, an' 'is name is Keith.
A knut upon the Block 'e used to be,
    'Ome 'ere; the sort that flashes golden teeth,
An' wears 'ot socks, an' torks a lot o' guff;
But Ginger sez they're cobbers till they snuff.

It come about like this: Mick spragged 'im first
    Fer swankin' it too much abroad the ship.
'E 'ad nice manners an' 'e never cursed;
    Which set Mick's teeth on edge, as you may tip.
Likewise, 'e 'ad two silver brushes, w'ich
'Is mumma give 'im, 'cos 'e fancied sich.

Mick pinched 'em. Not, as you will understand,
    Becos uv any base desire fer loot,
But jist becos, in that rough soljer band,
    Them silver-backed arrangements didn't soot:

An' etiket must be observed always.
(They fetched ten drinks in Cairo, Ginger says.)

That satisfied Mick's honour fer a bit,
  But still 'e picks at Keith fer exercise,
An' all the other blokes near 'as a fit
  To see Mick squirm at Keith's perlite replies,
Till one day Keith 'owls back "You flamin' cow!"
Then Mick permotes 'im, an' they 'as a row.

I sez "permotes 'im," fer, yeh'll understand
  Ole Ginger 'as 'is pride o' class orl right;
'E's not the bloke to go an' soil 'is 'and
  Be stoushin' any coot that wants to fight.
'Im, that 'as 'ad 'is chances more'n once
Up at the Stajum, ain't no bloomin' dunce.

Yeh'll 'ave to guess wot sort o' fight took place.
  Keith learnt 'is boxin' at a "culcher" school.
The first three rounds, to save 'im frum disgrace,
  Mick kids 'im on an' plays the gentle fool.
An' then 'e outs 'im wiv a little tap,
An' tells 'im 'e's a reg'lar plucky chap.

They likes each other better after that,
  Fer Ginger alwus 'ad a reel soft spot
Fer blokes 'oo 'ad some man beneath their 'at,
  An' never whined about the jolts they got.
Still, pride o' class kept 'em frum gettin' thick.
It's 'ard to git right next to Ginger Mick.

Then comes Gallipoli an' wot Mick calls
  "An orl-in push fight multerplied be ten;"
An' one be one the orfficers they falls,
  Until there's no one left to lead the men.
Fer 'arf a mo' they 'esitates stock still;
Fer 'oo's to lead 'em up the flamin' 'ill?

'Oo is to lead 'em if it ain't the bloke
  'Oo's 'eaded pushes down in Spadger's Lane,
Since 'e first learnt to walk an' swear an' smoke,
  An' mixed it willin' both fer fun an' gain—
That narsty, ugly, vi'lent man, 'oo's got
Grip on the minds uv men when blood runs 'ot?

Mick led 'em; an' be'ind 'im up the rise,
  'Owlin' an' cursin', comes that mumma's boy,

'Is cobber, Keith, with that look in 'is eyes
   To give the 'eart uv any leader joy.
An' langwidge! If 'is mar at 'ome 'ad 'eard
She would 'a' threw a fit at ev'ry word.

Mick dunno much about wot 'appened then,
   Excep' 'e felt 'is Dream uv Stoush come true;
Fer 'im an' Keith they fought like fifty men,
   An' felt like gawds wiv ev'ry breath they drew.
Then Ginger gits it solid in the neck,
An' flops; an' counts on passin' in 'is check.

When 'e come to, the light wus gettin' dim,
   The ground wus cold an' sodden underneath,
Someone is lyin' right 'longside uv 'im.
   Groanin' wiv pain, 'e turns, an' sees it's Keith—
Keith, wiv 'is rifle cocked, an' starin' 'ard
Ahead. An' now 'e sez "'Ow is it, pard?"

Mick gently lifts 'is 'ead an' looks around.
   There ain't another flamin' soul in sight,
They're covered be a bit o' risin' ground,
   An' rifle-fire is cracklin' to the right.
"Down!" sez the mumma's joy. "Don't show yer 'ead!
Unless yeh want it loaded full o' lead."

Then, bit be bit, Mick gits the strength uv it.
   They wus so occupied wiv privit scraps,
They never noticed 'ow they come to git
   Right out ahead uv orl the other chaps.
They've bin cut orf, wiv jist one little chance
Uv gittin' back. Mick seen it at a glance.

"'Ere, Kid," 'e sez, "you sneak around that 'ill.
   I'm down an' out; an' you kin tell the boys;"
Keith don't reply to 'im but jist lies still,
   An' signs to Ginger not to make a noise.
"'Ere, you!" sez Mick, "I ain't the man to funk—
I won't feel 'ome-sick. Imshee! Do a bunk!"

Keith bites 'is lips; 'e never turns 'is 'ead.
   "Wot in the 'ell;" sez Mick, "'ere, wot's yer game?"
"I'm an Australian," that wus all 'e said,
   An' pride took 'old o' Mick to 'ear that name—
A noo, glad pride that ain't the pride o' class—
An' Mick's contempt, it took the count at lars'!

All night they stayed there, Mick near mad wiv pain,
  An' Keith jist lettin' up 'is watchful eye
To ease Mick's wounds an' bind 'em up again,
  An' give 'im water, w'ile 'imself went dry.
Brothers they wus, 'oo found their brother'ood
That night on Sari Bair, an' found it good.

Brothers they wus. I'm wond'rin', as I read
  This scrawl uv Mick's, an' git its meanin' plain,
If you, 'oo never give these things no 'eed,
  Ain't got some brothers down in Spadger's Lane—
Brothers you never 'ad the chance to meet
Becos they got no time fer Collins Street.

"I'm an Australian." Well, it takes the bun!
  It's got that soft spot in the 'eart o' Mick.
But don't make no mistake; 'e don't gush none,
  Or come them "brother'ood" remarks too thick.
'E only writes, *"This Keith's a decent coot,*
Cobber o' mine, an' white from cap to boot."

"'E wears perjarmers an' 'e cleans 'is teeth,"
  The sort o' bloke that Ginger once dispised!
But once a man shows metal underneath,
  Cobbers is found, an' brothers reckernised.
Fer, when a bloke's soul-clobber's shed in war,
'E looks the sort o' man Gawd meant 'im for.

IN
SPADGER'S
LANE

Ole Mother Moon 'oo yanks 'er beamin' dile
  Acrost the sky when we've grown sick o' day,
She's like some fat ole Jane 'oo loves to smile
  On all concerned, an' smooth our faults away;
An', like a woman, tries to 'ide again
The sores an' scars crool day 'as made too plain.

To all the earth she gives the soft glad-eye;
  She picks no fav'rits in this world o' men;
She peeps in nooks, where 'appy lovers sigh,
  To make their job more bonzer still; an' then,
O'er Spadger's Lane she waves a podgy 'and,
An' turns the scowlin' slums to Fairyland.

Aw, strike! I'm gettin' soft in my ole age!
  I'm growin' mushy wiv the passin' years.
Me! that 'as called it weakness to ingage
  In sloppy thorts that coax the pearly tears.
But say, me state o' mind I can't ixplain
When I seen Rose lars' night in Spadger's Lane.

'Twas Spadger's Lane where Ginger Mick 'ung out
  Before 'e took to follerin' the Flag;
The Lane that echoed to 'is drunken shout
  When 'e lobbed 'omeward on a gaudy jag.
Now Spadger's Lane knows Ginger Mick no more,
Fer 'e's become an 'ero at the War.

A flamin' 'ero at the War, that's Mick.
  An' Rose—'is Rise, is waitin' in the Lane,
Nursin' 'er achin' 'eart, an' lookin' sick
  As she crawls out to work an' 'ome again,
Givin' the bird to blokes 'oo'd be 'er "friend,"
An' prayin', wiv the rest, fer wars to end.

Quite right; I'm growin' sloppy fer a cert;
  But I must git it orf me chest or bust.
So 'ere's a song about a grievin' skirt,
  An' love, an' Ginger Mick, an' maiden trust!
The choky sort o' song that fetches tears
When blokes is full o' sentiment—or beers.

Lars' night, when I sneaks down to taste again
  The sights an' sounds I used to know so well,
The moon wus shinin' over Spadger's Lane,
  Sof'nin' the sorrer where 'er kind light fell:

Sof'nin' an' soothin', like it wus 'er plan
To make ixcuses fer the sins uv man.

Frum shadder inter shadder, up the street,
   A prowlin' moll sneaks by, wiv eyes all 'ate,
Dodgin' some unseen John, 'oo's sure, slow feet
   Comes tappin' after, certin as 'er fate;
In some back crib, a shicker's loud 'owled verse
Stops sudden, wiv a crash, an' then a curse.

Low down, a splotch o' red, where 'angs a blind
   Before the winder uv a Chow caboose,
Shines in the dead black wall, an' frum be'ind,
   Like all the cats o' Chinertown broke loose,
A mad Chow fiddle wails a two-note toon ...
An' then I seen 'er, underneath the moon.

A LETTER TO THE FRONT

I 'ave written Mick a letter in reply to one uv 'is,
Where 'e arsts 'ow things is goin' where the gums an' wattles is.
So I tries to buck 'im up a bit; to go fer Abdul's fez;
An' I ain't no nob at litrachure; but this is wot I sez:

I suppose you fellers dream, Mick, in between the scraps out there,
Uv the land yeh left be'ind yeh when yeh sailed to do yer share:
Uv Collins Street, or Rundle Street, or Pitt, or George, or Hay,
Uv the land beyond the Murray or along the Castlereagh.
An' I guess yeh dream of old days an' the things yeh used to do,
An' yeh wonder 'ow 'twill strike yeh when yeh've seen this
      business thro';
An' yeh try to count yer chances when yeh've finished wiv the Turk
An' swap the gaudy war game fer a spell o' plain, drab work.

Well, Mick, yeh know jist 'ow it is these early days o' Spring,
When the gildin' o' the wattle chucks a glow on ev'rything:
Them olden days, the golden days that you remember well,
In spite o' war an' worry, Mick, are wiv us fer a spell.
Fer the green is on the paddicks, an' the sap is in the trees.
An' the bush birds in the gullies sing the ole, sweet melerdies;
An' we're 'opin', as we 'ear 'em, that, when next the Springtime
      comes,
You'll be wiv us 'ere to listen to that bird-tork in the gums.

It's much the same ole Springtime, Mick, yeh reckerlect uv yore;
Boronier an' dafferdils and wattle blooms once more
Sling sweetness over city streets, an' seem to put to shame
The rotten greed an' butchery that got you on this game—
The same ole sweet September days, an' much the same ole place;
Yet, there's a sort o' *somethin'*, Mick, upon each passin' face—
A sort o' look that's got me beat; a look that you put there,
The day yeh lobbed upon the beach an' charged at Sari Bair . . .

There's bin a lot o' tork, ole mate, uv wot we owe to you,
An' wot yeh've braved an' done fer us, an' wot we mean to do.
We've 'ailed you boys as 'eroes, Mick, an' torked uv just reward
When you 'ave done the job yer at an' slung aside the sword.
I guess it makes yeh think a bit, an' weigh this gaudy praise;
Fer even 'eroes 'ave to eat, an'—there is other days:
The days to come when we don't need no bonzer boys to fight:
When the flamin' picnic's over an' the Leeuwin looms in sight.

Then there's another fight to fight, an' you will find it tough
To sling the Kharki clobber fer the plain civilian stuff.
When orl the cheerin' dies away, an' 'ero-worship flops,

Yeh'll 'ave to face the ole tame life—'ard yakker or 'ard cops.
But, lad, yer land is wantin' yeh, an' wantin' each strong son
To fight the fight that never knows the firin' uv a gun:
The steady fight, when orl you boys will show wot you are worth,
An' punch a cow on Yarra Flats or drive a quill in Perth.

The gilt is on the wattle, Mick, young leaves is on the trees,
An' the bush birds in the gullies swap the ole sweet melerdies;
There's a good, green land awaitin' you when you come 'ome again
To swing a pick at Ballarat or ride Yarrowie Plain.
The streets is gay wiv dafferdils—but, haggard in the sun,
A wounded soljer passes; an' we know ole days is done;
Fer somew'ere down inside us, lad, is somethin' you put there
The day yeh swung a dirty left, fer us, at Sari Bair.

Rosie the Rip they calls 'er in the Lane;
    Fer she wus alwus willin' wiv 'er 'an's,
An' uses 'em to make 'er meanin' plain
    In ways that Spadger's beauties understan's.
But when ole Ginger played to snare 'er 'eart,
Rosie the Rip wus jist the soft, weak tart.

'Igh in 'er winder she wus leanin' out,
    Swappin' remarks wiv fat ole Mother Moon.
The things around I clean fergot about—
    Fergot the fiddle an' its crook Chow toon;
I only seen one woman in the light
Achin' to learn 'er forchin frum the night.

Ole Ginger's Rose! To see 'er sittin' there,
    The moonlight shinin' fair into 'er face,
An' sort o' touchin' gentle on 'er 'air,
    It made me fair fergit the time an' place.
I feels I'm peepin' where I never ought,
An' tries 'arf not to 'ear the words I caught.

One soljer's sweet'eart, that wus wot I seen:
    One out o' thousands grievin' thro' the land.
A tart frum Spadger's or a weepin' queen—
    Wot's there between 'em, when yeh understand?
She 'olds fer Mick, wiv all 'is ugly chiv,
The best a lovin' woman 'as to give.

The best a woman 'as to give—Aw, 'Struth!
    When war, an' grief, an' trouble's on the land
Sometimes a bloke gits glimpses uv the truth

An' sweats 'is soul to try an' understand ...
An' then the World, like some offishus John,
Shoves out a beefy 'and, an' moves 'im on.

So I seen Rose; an' so, on that same night
  I seen a million women grievin' there.
Ole Mother Moon she showed to me a sight
  She sees around the World, most everyw'ere.
Sneakin' beneath the shadder uv the wall
I seen, an' learned, an' understood it all.

An' as I looks at Rosie, dreamin' there,
  'Er 'ead drops on 'er arms ... I seems to wake;
I sees the moonlight streamin' on 'er 'air;
  I 'ears 'er sobbin' like 'er 'eart ud break.
An' me there, pryin' on 'er misery.
"Gawstruth!" I sez, "This ain't no place fer me!"

On my tip-toes I sneaks the way I came—
  (The crook Chow fiddle ain't done yowlin' yet)—
An' tho' I tells it to me bitter shame—
  I'm gittin' soft as 'ell—me eyes wus wet.
An' that stern John, as I go moochin' by
Serloots me wiv a cold, unfeelin' eye.

The fat ole Mother Moon she's got a 'eart.
  An' so I like to think, when she looks down
Wiv 'er soft gaze upon some weepin' tart
  In bonzer gardens or the slums o' town;
She soothes 'em, mother-like, wiv podgy 'ands,
An' makes 'em dream agen uv peaceful lands.

RABBITS

"Ar! Gimme fights wiv foeman I kin see,
   To upper-cut an' wallop on the jor.
Life in a burrer ain't no good to me.
     'Struth! This ain't war!
Gimme a ding-dong go fer 'arf a round,
An' you kin 'ave this crawlin' underground.

"Gimme a ragin', 'owlin', tearin', scrap,
   Wiv room to swing me left, an' feel it land.
This 'idin', sneakin' racket makes a chap
     Feel secon'-'and.
Stuck in me dug-out 'ere, down in a 'ole,
I'm feelin' like I've growed a rabbit's soul."

Ole Ginger's left the 'orspital, it seems;
   'E's back at Anzac, cursin' at the game;
Fer this 'ere ain't the fightin' uv 'is dreams;
     It's too dead tame.
'E's got the oopizootics reely bad,
An' 'idin' in a burrer makes 'im mad.

'E sort o' takes it personal, yeh see.
   'E used to 'awk 'em fer a crust, did Mick.
Now, makin' *'im* play rabbits seems to be
     A narsty trick.
To shove 'im like a bunny down a 'ole
It looks like chuckin' orf, an' sours 'is soul.

"Fair doos," 'e sez, "I joined the bloomin' ranks
   To git away frum rabbits: thinks I'm done
Wiv them Australian pests, an' 'ere's their thanks:
     They makes me one!
An' 'ere I'm squattin', scared to shift about;
Jist waitin' fer me little tail to sprout.

"Ar, strike me up a wattle! but it's tough!
   But 'ere's the dizzy limit, fer a cert—
To live this bunny's life is bad enough,
     But 'ere's reel dirt:
Some tart at 'ome 'as sent, wiv lovin' care,
A coat uv rabbit-skins fer me to wear!

"That's done it! Now I'm nibblin' at the food,
   An' if a dawg shows up I'll start to squeal;
I s'pose I orter melt wiv gratichude:
     'Tain't 'ow I feel.

She might 'a' fixed a note on wiv a pin:
'Please, Mister Rabbit, yeh fergot yer skin!'

"I sees me finish! . . . War? Why, this ain't war!
   It's ferritin'! An' I'm the bloomin' game.
Me skin alone is worth the 'untin' for—
      That tart's to blame!
Before we're done, I've got a silly scare,
Some trappin' Turk will catch me in snare.

"'E'll skin me, wiv the others 'e 'as there,
   An' shove us on a truck, an' bung us 'round
Constantinople at a bob a pair—
      Orl fresh an' sound!
'Eads down, 'eels up, 'e'll 'awk us in a row
Around the 'arems, 'owlin 'Rabbee-oh!'

"But, dead in earnest, it's a job I 'ate.
   We've got to do it, an' it's gittin' done;
But this soul-dopin' game uv sit-an'-wait,
      It ain't no fun.
There's times I wish, if we weren't short uv men,
That I wus back in 'orspital again.

"Ar, 'orspital! There is the place to git.
   If I thort Paradise wus 'arf so snug
I'd shove me 'ead above the parapit
      An' stop a slug;
But one thing blocks me playin' sich a joke;
I want another scrap before I croak.

"I want it bad. I want to git right out
   An' plug some josser in the briskit—'ard.
I want to 'owl an' chuck me arms about,
      An' jab, an' guard.
An' swing, an' upper-cut, an' crool some pitch,
Or git passed out meself—I don't care w'ich.

* * * *

"I'm sittin' in me dug-out day be day—
   It narks us; but Australia's got a name
Fer doin' little jobs like blokes 'oo play
      A clean straight game.
Wiv luck I might see scrappin' 'fore I'm done,
Or go where Craig 'as gone, an' miss the fun.

"But if I dodge, an' keep out uv the rain,
  An' don't toss in me alley 'fore we wins;
An' if I lobs back 'ome an' meets the Jane
    'Oo sent the skins—
These bunnies' overcoats I lives inside—
I'll squeal at 'er, an' run away an' 'ide.

"But, torkin' straight, the Janes 'as done their bit.
  I'd like to 'ug the lot, orl on me pat!
They warms us well, the things they've sewed an' knit:
    An' more than that —
I'd like to tell them dear Australian tarts
The spirit uv it warms Australian 'earts."

THE
GAME

"Ho! the sky's as blue as blazes an' the sun is shinin' bright,
   An' the dicky birds is singin' over'ead,
An' I'm 'ummin', softly 'ummin', w'ile I'm achin' fer a fight,
   An' the chance to fill some blighter full of lead.
An' the big guns they are boomin', an' the shells is screamin' past,
But I'm corperil—lance-corperil—an' found me game at last!"

I ixpects a note frum Ginger, fer the time wus gettin' ripe,
   An I gits one thick wiv merry 'owls uv glee;
Fer they've gone an' made 'im corperil—they've given 'im a stripe,
   An' yeh'd think, to see 'is note, it wus V.C.
Fer 'e chortles like a nipper wiv a bran' noo Noah's Ark
Since forchin she 'as smiled on 'im, an' life's no more a nark.

"Ho! the sky along the 'ill-tops, it is smudged wiv cannon smoke,
   An' the shells along the front is comin' fast,
But the 'eads 'ave 'ad the savvy fer to reckernise a bloke,
   An' permotion's gettin' common-sense at last.
An' they picked me fer me manners, w'ich wus snouted over 'ome,
But I've learned to be a soljer since I crossed the ragin' foam.

"They 'ave picked me 'cos they trust me; an' it's got me where I live,
   An' it's put me on me mettle, square an' all;
I wusn't in the runnin' once when blokes 'ad trust to give,
   But over 'ere I answers to the call;
So some shrewd 'ead 'e marked me well, an' when the time wus ripe
'E took a chance on Ginger Mick, an' I 'ave snared me stripe.

"I've got a push to 'andle now wot makes a soljer proud—
   Yeh ort to see the boys uv my ole squad:
The willin'est, the cheeriest, don'-care-a-damest crowd,
   An' the toughest ever seen outside o' quod.
I reckon that they gimme 'em becos they wus so meek,
But they know me, an' they understan' the lingo that I speak.

"So I'm a little corperil, wiv pretties on me arm,
   But yeh'd never guess it fer to see me now,
Fer me valet 'e's been careless an' me trooso's come to 'arm,
   An' me pants want creasin' badly I'll allow.
But to see me squad in action is a cure for sandy blight,
They are shy on table manners, but they've notions 'ow ter fight.

"There's a little picnic promised that 'as long been overdoo,
   An' we're waitin' fer the order to advance;
An' me bones is fairly achin' fer to see my boys bung thro',
   Fer I know they're dancin' mad to git the chance.

An' there's some'll sure be missin' when we git into the game;
But if they lorst their corperil 'twould be a cryin' shame.

"When it's gettin' near to evenin' an' the guns is slowin' down
   I fergits the playful 'abits uv our foes,
An' finds meself a-thinkin' thorts uv good ole Melbourne town,
   An' dreamin' dilly dreams about ole Rose.
O' course I'll see me girl again, an' give a clean, square deal,
When I come smilin' 'ome again . . . But that ain't 'ow I feel.

"I feel . . . I dunno 'ow I feel. I feel that things is done.
   I seem t've 'it the limit in some way.
Per'aps I'm orf me pannikin wiv sittin' in the sun,
   But I jist wrote to Rose the other day;
An' I wrote 'er sort o' mournful 'cos—I dunno 'ow it seems . . .
Ar, I'm a gay galoot to go an' 'ave these dilly dreams!

"Wot price the bran' noo corperil, wiv sof'nin' uv the 'eart!
   If my pet lambs thort me a turtle dove
I'd 'ave to be reel stern wiv 'em, an' make another start
   To git 'em where I got 'em jist wiv love . . .
But don't fergit, if you or your Doreen sees Rose about,
Jist tell 'er that I'm well an' strong, an' sure uv winnin' out.

"Ho! the sky's as blue as blazes, an' the sun is shinin' still,
   An' the dicky bird is perchin' on the twig,
An' the guns is pop, pop, poppin' frum the trenches on the 'ill,
   An' I'm lookin' bonny in me non-com's rig.
An' when yer writin' me again—don't think I want ter skite—
But don't fergit the 'Corperil'; an' mind yeh spells it right."

"A GALLANT GENTLEMAN"

A month ago the world grew grey fer me;
  A month ago the light went out fer Rose.
To 'er they broke it gentle as might be;
  But fer 'is pal 'twus one uv them swift blows
That stops the 'eart-beat; fer to me it came
Jist, "Killed in Action", an', beneath, *'is* name.

'Ow many times 'ave I sat dreamin' 'ere
  An' seen the boys returnin', gay an' proud.
I've seen the greetin's, 'eard 'is rousin' cheer,
  An' watched ole Mick come stridin' thro' the crowd.
'Ow many times 'ave I sat in this chair
An' seen 'is 'ard chiv grinnin' over there.

'E's laughed, an' told me stories uv the war.
  Changed some 'e looked, but still the same ole Mick,
Keener an' cleaner than 'e wus before;
  'E's took me 'and, an' said 'e's in great nick.
Sich wus the dreamin's uv a fool 'oo tried
To jist crack 'ardy, an' 'old gloom aside.

An' now—well, wot's the odds? I'm only one;
  One out uv many 'oo 'as lost a friend.
Manlike, I'll bounce again, an' find me fun;
  But fer poor Rose it seems the bitter end.
Fer Rose, an' sich as Rose, when one man dies
It seems the world goes black before their eyes.

A parson cove he broke the noos to Rose—
  A friend uv mine, a bloke wiv snowy 'air
An' gentle, soothin' sort o' ways, 'oo goes
  Thro' life jist 'umpin' others' loads uv care.
Instid uv Mick—jist one rough soljer lad—
Yeh'd think 'e'd lost the dearest friend 'e 'ad.

But 'ow kin blows be sof'n'd sich as that?
  Rose took it as 'er sort must take sich things.
An' if the jolt uv it 'as knocked me flat,
  Well, 'oo is there to blame 'er if it brings
Black thorts that comes to women when they frets,
An' makes 'er tork wild tork an' foolish threats?

An' then there comes the letter that wus sent
  To give the strength uv Ginger's passin' out—
A long, straight letter frum a bloke called Trent;
  'Tain't no use tellin' wot it's orl about:

Washing Day

There's things that's in it I kin see quite clear
Ole Ginger Mick ud be ashamed to 'ear.

Things praisin' 'im, that pore ole Mick ud say
  Wus comin' it too 'ot; fer, spare me days!
I well remember that 'e 'ad a way
  Uv curlin' up when 'e wus slung bokays.
An' Trent 'e seems to think that in some way
'E owes Mick somethin' that 'e can't repay.

Well, p'raps 'e does; an' in the note 'e sends
  'E arsts if Mick 'as people 'e kin find.
Fer Trent's an English toff wiv swanky friends,
  An' wants to 'elp wot Ginger's left be'ind.
'E sez strange things in this 'ere note 'e sends:
"He was a gallant gentleman," it ends.

A gallant gentleman! Well, I dunno.
  I 'ardly think that Mick ud like that name.
But this 'ere Trent's a toff, an' ort to know
  The breedin' uv the stock frum which 'e came.
Gallant an' game Mick might 'a' bin; but then—
Lord! Fancy 'im among the gentlemen!

The way 'e died ... Gawd! but it makes me proud
  I ever 'eld 'is 'and, to read that tale.
An' Trent is one uv that 'igh-steppin' crowd
  That don't sling praise around be ev'ry mail.
To 'im it seemed some great 'eroic lurk;
But Mick, I know, jist took it wiv 'is work.

Trent tells 'ow, when they found 'im, near the end,
  'E starts a fag an' grins orl bright an' gay.
An' when they arsts fer messages to send
  To friends, 'is look goes dreamin' far away.
"Look after Rose," 'e sez, "when I move on.
Look after ... Rose ... Mafeesh!" An' 'e wus gone.

"We buried 'im," sez Trent, "down by the beach.
  We put mimosa on the mound uv sand
Above 'im. 'Twus the nearest thing in reach
  To golden wattle uv 'is native land.
But never wus the fairest wattle wreath
More golden than the 'eart uv 'im beneath."

A gallant gentleman ... Well, let it go.
  They sez they've put them words above 'is 'ead,

Out there where lonely graves stretch in a row;
  But Mick 'e'll never mind it now 'e's dead.
An' where 'e's gone, when they weigh praise an' blame,
P'raps gentlemen an' men is much the same.

* * * *

A month ago, fer me the world grew grey;
  A month ago the light went out fer Rose;
Becos one common soljer crossed the way,
  Leavin' a common message as 'e goes.
But ev'ry dyin' soljer's 'ope lies there:
"Look after Rose. Mafeesh!" Gawd! It's a pray'r!

That's wot it is; an' when yeh sort it out,
  Shuttin' yer ears to orl the sounds o' strife—
The shouts, the cheers, the curses—'oo kin doubt
  The claims uv women; mother, sweet'eart, wife?
An' 'oo's to 'ear our soljers' dyin' wish?
An' 'oo's to 'eed? . . . "Look after Rose . . . Mafeesh!"

DOREEN

WASHING DAY

The little gipsy vi'lits, they wus peepin' thro' the green
As she come walkin' in the grass, me little wife, Doreen.
    The sun shone on the sassafras, where thrushes sung a bar;
    The 'ope an' worry uv our lives was yellin' fer 'is Mar.
I watched 'er comin' down the green; the sun wus on 'er 'air—
Jist the woman that I marri'd, when me luck wus 'eadin' fair.

I seen 'er walkin' in the sun that lit our little farm:
She 'ad three clothes-pegs in 'er mouth, an' washin' on 'er arm—
    Three clothes-pegs, fer I counted 'em, an' watched 'er as she come;
    "The stove-wood's low," she mumbles, "an' young Bill 'as cut 'is
        thumb."
Now, it weren't no giddy love-speech, but it seemed to take me
        straight
Back to the time I kissed 'er first beside 'er mother's gate.

Six years uv wedded life we've 'ad, an' still me dreams is sweet . . .
Aw, them bonzer little vi'lits, they wus smilin' round me feet.
    An' wot's a bit uv stove-wood count, wiv paddicks grinnin' green,
    When a bloke gits on to dreamin' uv the old days an' Doreen—
The days I thort I snared a saint; but since I've understood
I 'ave wed a dinkum woman, which is fifty times as good.

I 'ave wed a dinkum woman, an' she's give me eyes to see—
Oh, I ain't been mollycoddled, an' there ain't no fluff on me!
    But days when I wus down an' out she seemed so 'igh above;
    An' a saint is made fer worship, but a woman's made fer love.
An' a bloke is growin' richer as sich things 'e comes to know . . .
(She pegs another sheet an' sez, "The stove-wood's gittin' low.")

A bloke 'e learns a lot uv things in six years wiv a tart;
But thrushes in the sassafras ain't singin' like me 'eart.
    'Tis the thrushes 'oo 'ave tort me in their choonful sort o' way
    That it's best to take things singin' as yeh meet 'em day be day;
Fer I wed a reel, live woman, wiv a woman's 'appy knack
Uv torkin' reason inside out an' logic front to back.

An' I like it. 'Struth, I like it! Fer a wax doll in a 'ome,
She'd give a man the flamin' pip an' longin's fer to roam.
    Aw, I ain't no silk-sock sonkie 'oo ab'ors the rood an' tough.
    Fer, city-born an' gutter-bred, me schoolin' it wus tough.
An' I like the dinkum woman 'oo . . . (She jerks the clothes-prop, so,
An' sez, so sweet an' dangerous, "The stove-wood's gittin' low.")

See, I've studied men in cities, an' I've studied 'em out 'ere;
I've seen 'em 'ard thro' piety an' seen 'em kind thro' beer.

I've seen the meanest doin' deeds to make the angels smile,
An' watched the proudest playin' games that crooks 'ud reckon
    vile.
I 'ave studied 'em in bunches, an' I've read 'em one be one,
An' there isn't much between 'em when the 'ole thing's said an'
    done.

An' I've sort o' studied wimmin—fer I've met a tidy few—
An' there's times, when I wus younger, when I kids meself I knew.
    But 'im 'oo 'opes to count the stars or measure up the sea,
    'E kin 'ave a shot at woman, fer she's fairly flummoxed me ...
("I'll 'ave to 'ave *some* wood," she sez, an' sez it most perlite
An' secret to a pair uv socks; an' jams a peg in, tight.)

Now, a woman, she's a woman. I 'ave fixed that fer a cert.
They're jist as like as rows uv peas from 'at to 'em uv skirt.
    An' then, they're all so different, yeh find, before yeh've done,
    The more yeh know uv all uv 'em the less yeh know uv one.
An' then, the more yeh know uv one ... (She gives 'er 'air a touch:
"The stove-wood's nearly done," she sez. "Not that it matters
    much!")

The little gipsy vi'lits, they wus smilin' round me feet.
An' this dreamin' dilly day-dreams on a Summer day wus sweet.
    I 'eaves me frame frum orf the fence, an' grabs me little axe;
    But, when I'm 'arf way to the shed, she stops me in me tracks.
"Yer lunch is ready. That ole wood kin easy wait a while."
Strike! I'm marri'd to a woman ... But she never seen me smile.

POSSUM

Jist 'ere it gripped me, on a sudden, like a red-'ot knife.
I wus diggin' in the garden, talkin' pleasant to me wife,
   When it got me good an' solid, an' I fetches out a yell,
   An' curses soft down in me neck, an' breathes 'ard fer a spell.
Then, when I tries to straighten up, it stabs me ten times worse.
I thinks per'aps I'm dyin', an' chokes back a reel 'ot curse.

"I've worked too fast," I tells Doreen. "Me backbone's runnin' 'ot.
I'm sick! I've got—Oo, 'oly wars! I dunno *wot* I've got!
   Jist 'ere—*Don't touch!*—Jist round back 'ere, a blazin' little pain.
   Is clawin' up me spinal cord an' slidin' down again."
"You come inside," she sez. "Per'aps it's stoopin' in the sun.
Does it 'urt much?" I sez, "Oh, no; I'm 'avin' lots o' fun."

Then, cooin' to me, woman-like, she pilots me inside.
It stabs me every step I takes; I thort I could 'a' died.
   "There now," she sez. "Men can't stand pain, it's alwus
      understood."
   "Stand pain?" I owls. Then, Jumpin' Jakes! It gits me reely good!
So I gets to bed in sections, fer it give me beans to bend,
An' shuts me eyes, an' groans again, an' jist waits fer the end.

"Now, you lie still," she orders me, "until I think wot's best.
Per'aps 'ot bran, or poultices. You jist lie still, an' rest,"
   Rest? 'Oly Gosh! I clinched me teeth, an' clawed the bloomin'
      bunk;
   Fer a red-'ot poker jabbed me ev'ry time I much as wunk.
I couldn't corf, I couldn't move, I couldn't git me breath.
"Look after Bill," I tells Doreen. "I feels that ... this is ...
      death."

"Death, fiddlesticks," she laughs at me. "You jist turn over now."
I 'owls, "'Ere! Don't you *touch* me, or there'll be a blazin' row!
   I want to die jist as I am." She sez, "Now, Bill, 'ave sense.
   This 'as to go on while it's 'ot." I groans, "I've no defence."
An' so she 'as 'er way wiv me. An', tho' I'm suff'rin' bad,
I couldn't 'elp but noticin' the gentle touch she 'ad.

That ev'nin', when the doctor come, sez 'e, "Ah! 'Urtin' much?
Where is the trouble?" I sez, "Where you ain't allowed to touch!"
   'E mauls an' prods me while I 'owls to beat the bloomin' band.
   Gawbli'me! I'd 'a' cracked 'im if I'd strength to lift me 'and.
"Discribe yer symtims now," sez 'e. I fills meself wiv wind,
An' slung 'im out a catalog while 'e jist stood an' grinned.

"Ar, har!" 'e sez. "Sciatiker! Oh, we'll soon 'ave yeh well."
"Sciatiker?" sez I. "Yer sure yeh don't mean Jumpin' 'Ell?
  It ain't no privit devil wiv a little jagged knife?"
    "Tut, tut," 'e grins. "You'll soon be right. I leaves yeh to yer wife."
I looks at 'er, she smiles at me, an' when I seen that smile:
"Aw, poultices!" I groans. An' she injoys it all the while!

But I'm marri'd to a woman; an', I gives yeh my straight tip,
It makes a man feel glad uv it when sickness gits a grip.
  'Er looks is full uv tenderness, 'er ways is full uv love,
    An' 'er touch is like a blessin' as she gently bends above.
'Er speech is firm, but motherin'; 'er manners strict, but mild:
Yer 'er 'usban', an' 'er patient, an' 'er little orphin child.

When yer marri'd to a woman an' yer feelin' well an' right;
When yer frame is full uv ginger an' yer mouth is full uv skite,
  Then yeh tork about the "missus" in an 'orf'and sort uv way;
    She's 'andy in the 'ouse if she don't 'ave too much to say.
But when Ole Man Sciatiker, 'e does yeh up reel neat,
Then she's yer own reel mate, she is, an' all yer 'ands an' feet.

An' so Doreen, she nurses me while I lie there an' grouch;
Fer I'm snarky when I tumble that it ain't me dyin' couch.
  I barks at 'er, an' snarls at 'er, an' orders 'er about,
    An' nearly wears the feet orf 'er wiv trottin' in an' out.
An' while Ole Man Sciatiker, 'e 'as me in 'is sway
Doreen, she jist gives in to me—an' alwus gits 'er way.

Three solid days I 'as uv it, an' then the pain lets out.
I'm feelin' fit fer graft again, an' wants to git about.
  It's then she lets me see 'er 'and, an' orders, "You stay there
    Until yeh gits yer 'ealth an' strength to sit up in a chair."
"But there's that stove-wood," I begins. Sez she, "Now, don't you
       fret.
I'm very sparin' wiv it, an' there's tons an' tons there yet."

Tell yeh straight; I got to like it. It's a crook thing to confess,
But to 'ave 'er fussin' round me give me chunks uv 'appiness.
  So I gits out in the garden wiv an arm-chair an' a rug,
    An' I comes the floppin' invaleed, an' makes meself reel snug.
I droops me eyes an' 'angs me 'ands, an' looks dead crook an' ill;
An' wriggles ev'ry time she sez, "Wot would yeh like now, Bill?"

An' then, one day, I 'ears the axe down there be'ind the 'ouse;
An' I sees meself a loafer, an' me conscience starts to rouse.
  I 'eaves me frame out uv the chair, an' wanders down the yard.

She's beltin' at a knotty log, an' beltin' good an' 'ard.
I grabs the axe. "Give up," I sez. "I ain't no shattered wreck.
This 'ere's my job." An' then, Gawstruth! I gits it in the neck!

"Am I yer wife?" she asks me straight. "Why can't yeh trust me,
    Bill?
Am I not fit to see to things when you are weak an' ill?"
  I tries to say I'm possumin', an' reely well an' strong;
  But ev'ry time I starts to tork she's got me in the wrong.
"Yeh can't deceive me, Bill," she sez. "Yer 'ealth is fur frum good.
Yeh jist can't trust yer wife to chop a little bit uv wood!

"Yeh got to come out in the cold," she sez, "wivout yer wraps.
An' now I'll 'ave yeh on me 'ands fer days wiv a relapse!"
  "I been pretendin'," I ixplains. She sez, "Am I yer wife?
  Yet sooner than yeh'd trust to me yeh go an' risk yer life."
Well, I'm marri'd to a woman, an—it might seem sort uv meek—
I goes back into bed again . . . an' *'ates* it . . . fer a week!

ROSE OF SPADGERS

THE
FALTERING
KNIGHT

It knocks me can in, this 'ere game uv life,
  A bloke gets born, grows up, looks round fer fun,
Dreams dilly dreams, then wakes to find a wife
  An' fambly round 'im—all 'is young days done.
An', gazin' back, sees in 'is youth a man
Scarce reckernised. It fair knocks in me can!

Ther's me. I never seemed to mark no change
  As I mooched on through life frum year to year;
An' yet, at times it seems to me dead strange
  That me, uv old, is me, 'oo's sittin' 'ere.
Per'aps it ain't. 'E was a crook young coot,
While I'm a sturdy farmer, growin' froot.

But, all the same, 'e wouldn't back an' fill,
  An' argue with 'imself, an' 'esitate,
Once 'e 'ad seen the way. 'E'd find the will
  To go an' do the thing 'e 'ad to, straight.
That's 'ow I was; an' now—Ar, strike a light!
Life gits so mixed I can't git nothin' right . . .

All marrid blokes will un'erstand me well.
  I ain't addressin' no remarks to those
'Oo've learnt but 'arf uv life. The things I tell
  Is fer the ears uv fellermen that *knows*:
Them symperthetic 'usbands 'oo 'ave 'eard
The fog-'orn soundin' in the wifely word.

Fer when stern jooty grips a 'usband's 'eart
  (That's me) an' eggs 'im on to start a scene
That's like to tear two 'appy lives apart,
  In spite uv all 'er carin' (That's Doreen)
Why, there you 'ave a story that would make
A bonzer movie—with a bit uv fake.

But 'ere's the plot. When my pal, Ginger Mick,
  Chucked in 'is alley in this war we won,
'E left things tangled; fer 'e went too quick
  Fer makin' last requests uv anyone.
'E jist sez to the world, when last 'e spoke,
"Look after Rose!" . . . 'E was a trustful bloke.

Rose lives in Spadgers Lane. She lived, them days,
  Fer Mick's returnin'. When 'e never came,
If she lost 'old, an' took to careless ways,
  Well, I ain't sayin' she was much to blame.

An' I don't worry, till I 'ear she's took,
Or thinks uv takin' on to ways that's crook.

Although I'm vegetatin' on a farm,
  I gets a city whisper now an' then.
An' when I 'ear she's like to come to 'arm
  Amongst a push uv naughty spieler men,
I gets the wind up. This is all I see:
Mick was my cobber; so it's up to me.

That's all I see, quite clear, with my two eyes.
  But marrid blokes will understand once more,
When I remarks that marrid blokes is wise
  'Oo 'ave the sense to take a squint through four.
Four eyes is needed in reviewin' plans—
Their vision's broader than a single man's.

But when them four eyes sees two ways at once—
  Gets crossed—Ar, well, ther's things in marrid life
For which a hint's enough fer any dunce.
  Ther's certin things between a man an' wife
That can't be quite—But take this fer a fack:
Don't start things uv a mornin'. It ain't tack.

That was me first bad break. I should 'ave seen
  The supper things washed up, an' 'elped a bit,
An' then 'ave broke it gently to Doreen,
  Promiscus, like I jist 'ad thought uv it.
But I done worse. I blurts wot I'd to say
Upon the mornin' uv a *washin'* day!

I owns me ta'tic's crook. But, all the same,
  Ther' weren't no need fer certin things she said.
Wantin' to do good acts don't call fer blame,
  Even on tackless 'usban's, eight years wed.
A bloke 'oo jist suggests a 'armless plan
Don't need remindin' 'e's a *marrid* man.

'Struth! Don't I know it? Can I well ferget
  While I still 'ave two 'ealthy ears to 'ark?
Not that she torks an' mags a lot; but yet
  Ther's somethin' in 'er choice uv a remark
That gets there, worse than yappin' all day long,
An' makes me pure intentions look dead wrong.

It seems it ain't right fer a marrid bloke
  To rescue maids. I starts to answer back;

But got took up before I 'ardly spoke,
   An' innercent designs is painted black.
I calls attention to the knights uv old;
But tin knights an' romance jist leaves 'er cold.

I read 'er meanin' plain in 'er cool eye.
   Aw, strike! I ain't *admirin'* Rose! ... Wot? ... Me!
But when 'er look sez "Rats!" where's the reply
   A man can give, an' keep 'is dignity?
It can't be done. When they git on that lay,
Wise coves adjourns the meet, an' fades away.

That's wot I done. I gits out uv the 'ouse
   All dignified. An', jist to show 'er 'ow
Reel unconcerned I am, I starts to rouse
   Me neighbour, Wally Free, about 'is cow
Wot's got in to me cabbages, an' et
Close on a row uv 'em. I'll shoot 'er yet!

(A batchelor 'e is, this Wally Free—
   A soljer bloke that come this way last year
An' took the little farm nex' door to me.)
   When I gets mad, 'e grins frum ear to ear,
An' sez, "Cool orf," 'e sez. "It's plain your wool
'As been pulled 'ard this mornin'." 'E's a fool!

If 'e don't mend that fence ... Ar, wot's the good?
   I lets 'im go, an' sneaks be'ind the shed,
An' sits there broodin' on a pile uv wood ...
   Ther's certin things she might 'ave left unsaid.
Ther' wasn't nothin' fer to make 'er go
An' dig up chance remarks uv years ago.

Me problem's this: Either I 'urts Doreen,
   By doin' things with which she don't agree,
Or lets Rose slide, an' treats me cobber mean—
   Ole Ginger Mick, 'oo 'ad no friend but me.
I ain't a ringtail; but, by gum, it's tough.
I loves me wife too much to treat 'er rough.

If I was single ... 'Struth! 'Oo wants to be?
   Fool batchelors can larf their silly larf,
An' kid theirselves they got a pull on me.
   I'm out uv sorts, that's all; an' more than 'arf
Inclined to give some coot a crack, right now
Fer pref'rince, some insultin' single cow!

A HOLY
WAR

"Young friend!" . . . I tries to duck, but miss the bus.
    'E sees me first, an' 'as me by the 'and.
"Young friend!" 'e sez, an' starts to make a fuss
    At meetin' me. "Why, this," 'e sez, "is grand!
    Events is workin' better than I planned.
It's Providence that I should meet you thus.
    You're jist the man," 'e sez, "to make a stand,
      An' strive for us.

"Young friend," 'e sez, "allow me to explain . . ."
    But wot 'e 'as to say too well I knows.
I got the stren'th uv it in Spadgers Lane
    Not 'arf an hour before'and, when I goes
    To see if I could pick up news uv Rose,
After that dentist let me off the chain.
    ("Painless," 'e's labelled. So 'e is, I s'pose.
      I 'ad the pain.)

"Young friend," 'e sez. I let 'im 'ave 'is say;
    Though I'm already wise to all 'e said—
The queer old parson, with 'is gentle way—
    ('E tied Doreen an' me when we was wed)
    I likes 'im, from 'is ole soft, snowy 'ead
Down to 'is boots. 'E ain't the sort to pray
      When folks needs bread.

Yeh'd think that 'e was simple as a child;
    An' so 'e is, some ways; but, by and by,
While 'e is talkin' churchy-like an' mild,
    Yeh catch a tiny twinkle in 'is eye
    Which gives the office that 'e's pretty fly
To cunnin' lurks. 'E ain't to be beguiled
    With fairy tales. An' when I've seen 'em try
      'E's only smiled.

But, all the same, I didn't want to meet
    'Is 'oly nibs jist then; fer well I knoo,
When I fell up against 'im in the street,
    'E 'ad a little job fer me to do.
    Fer I 'ad gethered up a tip or two
In Spadgers, where 'is rev'rince 'as 'is beat,
    Tryin' to make that Gorfergotten crew
      'Olesome an' sweet.

"Young friend," 'e sez, "I am beset by foes.

The Church," 'e sez, "is in a quandary."
An' then 'e takes an' spills out all 'is woes,
   An' 'ints that this 'ere job is up to me.
   "Yer aid—per'aps yer strong right arm," sez 'e,
"Is needed if we are to rescue Rose
   From wot base schemes an' wot iniquity
     Gawd only knows."

This is the sorry tale. Rose, sick, an' low
   In funds an' frien's, an' far too proud to beg,
Is gittin' sorely tempted fer to go
   Into the spielin' trade by one Spike Wegg.
   I knoo this Spike uv old; a reel bad egg,
'Oo's easy livin' is to git in tow
   Some country mug, an' pull 'is little leg
     Fer all 'is dough.

A crooked crook is Spike amongst the crooks,
   A rat, 'oo'd come the double on 'is friends;
Flash in 'is ways, but innercint in looks
   Which 'e works well fer 'is un'oly ends.
   "It's 'ard to know," sez Snowy, "why Fate sends
Sich men among us, or why Justice brooks
   Their evil ways, which they but seldom mends—
     Except in books.

"Young friend," 'e sez, "You're known in Spadgers Lane.
   You know their ways. We must seek out this man.
With 'er, pray'r an' persuasion 'ave been vain.
   I've pleaded, but she's bound to 'is vile plan.
   I'd 'ave you treat 'im gently, if you can;
But if you can't, well—I need not explain."
   ('E twinkles 'ere) "I'm growin' partisan;
     I must refrain."

"Do you mean stoush?" I sez. "Fer if yeh do
   I warn yeh that a scrap might put me queer."
"Young friend," sez 'e, "I leave the means to you.
   Far be it from the Church to interfere
   With noble works." But I sez, "Now, look 'ere,
I got a wife at 'ome; you know 'er, too.
   Ther's certin things I never could make clear
     If once she knoo.

"I got a wife," I sez, "an' loves 'er well,
   Like I loves peace an' quite. An' if I goes

Down into Spadgers, raisin' merry 'ell,
  Breakin' the peace an' things account uv Rose,
  Where that might land me goodness only knows.
'Ow women sees these things no man can tell.
  I've done with stoush," I sez. "'Ard knocks an' blows
    'Ave took a spell.

"I've done with stoush," I sez. But in some place
  Deep in me 'eart a voice begun to sing;
A lurin' little voice, with motives base . . .
  It's ten long years since I was in a ring,
  Ten years since I gave that left 'ook a swing.
Ten weary years since I pushed in a face;
  An' 'ere's a chance to 'ave a little fling
    With no disgrace.

"Stoush? Stoush, young friend?" 'e sez. "Where 'ave I 'eard
  That term? I gather it refers to strife.
But there," 'e sez, "why quarrel with a word?
  As you 'ave said, indeed, I know yer wife;
  An' should she 'ear you went where vice is rife
To battle fer the right—But it's absurd
  To look fer gallantry in modrin life.
    It's a rare bird.

"Young friend," 'e sez. An' quicker than a wink
  'Is twinklin' eyes grew sudden very grave.
"Young friend," 'e sez, "I know jist wot yeh think
  Uv 'ow us parsons blather an' be'ave.
  But I 'ave 'ere a woman's soul to save—
A lonely woman, tremblin' on the brink
  Uv black perdition, blacker than the grave.
    An' she must sink.

"Yes, she must sink," 'e sez. "For I 'ave done
  All that a man uv my poor parts can do.
An' I 'ave failed! There was not anyone
  That I could turn to, till I met with you.
  But now *that* 'ope 'as gone—an' 'er 'ope too."
"'Old on," I sez. "Just let me think for one
  Brief 'alf-a-mo. I'd love a crack or two
    At this flash gun."

"Righto," I sez (an' turns me back on doubt)
  "I'm with yeh, parson. I go down to-night
To Spadgers, an' jist looks this Spike Wegg out."

"Young friend," 'e sez, "be sure you've chosen right.
    Remember, I do not desire a fight.
But if—" "Now don't you fret," I sez, "about
    No vi'lince. If I'm forced, it will be quite
        A friendly clout."

"Young friend," 'e sez, "if you go, I go too.
    Maybe, by counsel, I may yet injuce
This evil man—" "It ain't no game for you,"
    I argues with 'im. But it ain't no use.
"I go!" 'e sez, an' won't take no ixcuse.
So that's all fixed. An' us crusaders two
    Goes down to-night to Spadgers, to cut loose
        Till all is blue.

'Ow can Doreen make trouble or git sore?
    (Already I can 'ear 'er scold an' sob)
But this ain't stoushin'. It's a 'oly war!
    The blessin' uv the Church is on the job.
    I'm a church-worker, with full leave to lob
A sacrid left on Spike Wegg's wicked jor.
    Jist let me! Once! An' after, s'elp me bob,
        Never no more!

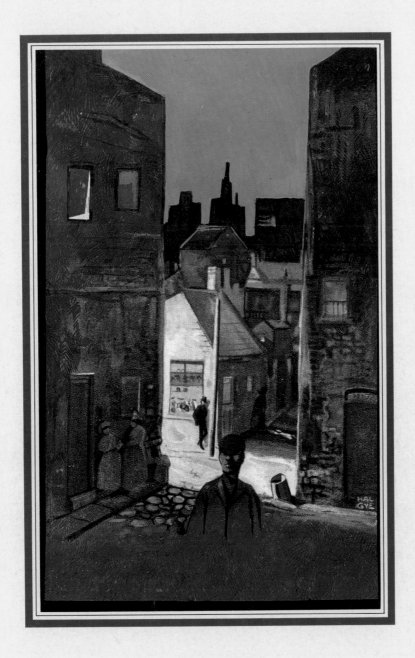

Cover illustration for
Rose of Spadgers

THE CRUSADERS

"Peter the 'Ermit was a 'oly bloke,"
  The parson sez, "wot chivvied coves to war."
  "Too right," I chips. "I've 'eard that yarn before."
"Brave knights sprung straight to arms where'er 'e spoke."
"Sure thing," sez I. "It muster been no joke
  Tinnin' yer frame in them dead days uv yore
  Before yeh starts to tap a foeman's gore."

"Peter the 'Ermit was a man inspired,"
  The parson sez. We're moochin' up the Lane,
  Snoopin' around for news we might obtain
Uv this Spike Wegg, the man 'oo I am 'ired
To snatch by 'ook or crook, jist as required
  By circs, frum out the sev'ril sins wot stain
  'Is wicked soul. I 'ope me meanin's plain.

"Peter the 'Ermit," sez the parson, "saw
  No 'arm in vi'lince when the cause was just.
  While 'e deplored, no doubt, the fightin' lust,
'E preached—" "'Old on," I sez. "'Ere comes the Law:
'Ere's Brannigan, the cop. Pos'pone the jaw
  Till we confer. I got idears 'e must
  Keep track uv Spike; if 'e toils fer 'is crust."

"Spike Wegg?" growls Brannigan. "I know that bloke;
  An' 'e's the one sweet soul I long to see.
  That shrinkin' vi'lit 'ates publicity
Jist now," sez Brannigan. "Spike Wegg's in smoke.
Oh, jist concerns a cove 'e tried to croak.
  'E's snug in some joint round about, maybe.
  If you should meet, remember 'im to me."

The cop passed on. "Peter the 'Ermit was
  A ri'chus man," the parson sez, "wot knoo—"
  "'Old 'ard!" I begs. "Jist for a hour or two
I wouldn't go an' nurse sich thorts, becoz
Too much soul-ferritin' might put the moz
  On this 'ere expedition. I'll 'elp you
  To search our conscience when the job is through.

"I know yer doubts," I sez, "an' 'ow you 'ate
  The thorts uv stoush, an' 'old 'ard blows in dread.
  But Pete the 'Ermit's been a long time dead.
'E'll keep. But we are in the 'ands uv Fate,
An' 'oly spruikers uv a ancient date

Don't 'elp. I quite agrees with all you've said
But—" "Say no more," 'e answers. "Lead ahead."

"But, all the same," 'e sez, "I want no fight."
    "Right 'ere, be'ind this 'oardin'," I replies,
    "A two-up school's in session. If we spies
About a bit, there is a chance we might
Git news—" Jist then the spotter comes to light.
    I word 'im gentle, with some 'asty lies:
    I'm seekin' Spike. See? Can 'e put me wise?

"Spike Wegg?" (At first 'e only twigs meself)
    "'E's gone—" ('E spots the parson standin' by)
    A cold, 'ard glimmer comes in 'is fish eye:
"'Ere! Wot's the game?" 'e yelps. "Are you a shelf?"
"'Ave sense!" I larfs. "I got a bit uv pelf,
    An' thort I'd like to take a little fly—"
    "Buzz orf!" 'e orders. So we done a guy.

"Blank number one," I sez. The parson sighed.
    "Joshuer fought, an' never seemed to shrink—"
    "Now, look," I tells 'im. "Honest. Don't you think
Them Bible blokes 'oo've 'ad their day an' died
Is best fergot until we're 'ome an' dried?
    Now, up the street 'ere, is a little sink
    Uv sin that does a traffic in strong drink."

"Sly grog?" 'e arsts. But I sez, "'Ush! This place
    Is kep' by Mother Weems, 'oo's sof', blue eye
    An' snow-white 'air would make yeh 'shamed an' shy
To brand 'er name with any sich disgrace.
'Er kind, sweet smile, 'er innercint ole face.
    Beams like a blessin'. Still, we'll 'ave a try
    To word the dear ole dame, an' pump 'er dry.

'Is nibs stands in the shadders while I knock.
    Mother unlocks the door, an' smiles, an' peers
    Into me face. She wears 'er three score years
Reel sweet, in lacy cap an' neat black frock.
Then: "Bill," she cries. "You've give me quite a shock!
    Why, dearie, I ain't seen you for long years.
    Come in." 'Er kind ole eyes seem close to tears.

"Dearie, come in," she chirps. But I pretend
    I'm on reel urgent biz; I got to 'aste

"Jist for ole times," she pleads. "One little taste."
"I can't," I sez. "I'm lookin' for a friend,
Spike Wegg, for 'oo I've certin news no end
   Important; an' I got no time to waste."
   "Wot? Spike?" she sez. "I 'ear 'e's bein' chased.

"'E's bein' chased," she sez, "by D's, I've 'eard."
   "Too true," I owns. "'E's got no time to lose."
   "Well, maybe, if you was to try Ah Foo's—
The privit room—" Then, as 'is rev'rince stirred,
She seen 'is choker. "'Oo the 'ell's this bird?
   Is this a frame?" she shrieks . . . Without adoos,
   We slap the pavemint with four 'asty shoes.

But, as along the sloppy lane we race,
   'Er 'ot words tumble after in a flood:
   "You pimps! You dirty swine! I'll 'ave yer blood!"
"'Eavings!" the parson gasps. "With that sweet face!"
"'Er words," I answer, "do seem outer place."
   "Vile words, that I 'ave scarce 'arf understud."
   Sez Snowy, shoshin' in a pool uv mud.

We reach Ah Foo's. "Now, 'ere," I sez, "is where
   You stop outside. Twice you 'ave put me queer
   It's a lone 'and I mean to play in 'ere.
You 'ang around an' breathe the 'olesome air."
"Young friend," 'e sez, "I go with you in there.
   I've led you into this. Why should I fear
   The danger? 'Tis me jooty to be near."

Snowy's a game un! I lob in the shop,
   The parson paddin' after on the floor.
   Ah Foo looks up. "Not there!" 'e squeaks. "Wha' for?"
But we sail past the Chow without a stop,
Straight for the little crib up near the top
   That I knoo well in sinful days uv yore . . .
   I turn the knob; an' sling aside the door.

Beside a table, fearin' 'arm from none,
   Spike an' another bloke is teet-ah-teet.
   Quick on the knock, Spike Wegg jumps to 'is feet
An' jerks a 'and be'ind 'im for 'is gun.
I rush 'im, grab a chair up as I run,
   An' swing it with a aim that ain't too neat.
   Spike ducks aside; an', with a bump, we meet.

93

An' then we mix it. Strife an' merry 'ell
   Breaks loose a treat, an' things git movin' fast.
   An', as a Chinese jar goes crashin' past,
'Igh o'er the din I 'ears the parson's yell:
   "Hit! Hit 'im 'ard young friend. Chastise 'im well!
   "Hit 'im!" ... The 'oly war is in full blast;
   An' Pete the 'Ermit's come to light at last.

"'AVE A 'EART!"

"'Ere! 'Ave a 'eart!" 'e sez. "Why, love a duck!
   A 'uman bein' ain't a choppin' block!
There ain't no call fer you to go an' chuck
   A man about when 'e 'as took the knock.
Gaw! Do yeh want to bust 'im all apart!
     'Ere! 'Ave a 'eart!

"Aw, 'ave a 'eart!" 'e weeps. "A fight's a fight;
   But, strike me bandy, this is bloody war!
It's murder! An' you got no blasted right
   To arst a 'uman man to come fer more.
'E 'ad no chance with you right frum the start.
     Aw, 'ave a 'eart!

"Yeh've pulped 'is dile," 'e whines; "yeh've pinched 'is gun;
   Yeh've bunged 'is eye 'an bashed in 'arf 'is teeth.
'Struth! Ain't yeh satisfied with wot yeh've done?
   Or are you out to fit 'im fer a wreath?
The man's 'arf dead a'ready! Wot's yer dart?
     Say, 'ave a 'eart!"

I never did 'ear sich a bloke to squeal
   About a trifle. This 'ere pal uv Spike's
Don't seem to 'ave the stummick fer a deal
   Uv solid stoush: rough work don't soot 'is likes.
'E ain't done much but blather frum the start,
     "'Ere 'ave a 'eart!"

A rat-face coot 'e is, with rat-like nerves
   That's got all jangled with ixceedin' fright,
While I am 'andin' Spike wot 'e deserves.
   But twice 'e tried to trip me in the fight,
The little skunk, now sobbin' like a tart,
     "Aw, 'ave a 'eart!"

This 'ere's the pretty pitcher in Ah Foo's
   Back privit room: Spite Wegg, well on the floor,
Is bleedin' pretty, with a bonzer bruise
   Paintin' one eye, an' 'arf 'is clobber tore.
While me, the conq'rin' 'ero, stan's above
     'Owlin' me love.

The rat-face mutt is dancin' up an' down;
   Ah Foo is singin' jazz in raw Chinee;
The parson's starin' at me with a frown,
   As if 'e thort sich things could never be;

An' I'm some bloke 'e's but 'arf rekernised
    'E's 'ipnertised."

Foo's furniture is scattered any'ow,
    Artisic like, in bits about the floor.
An' 'arf a dozen blokes, drawn by the row,
    Nosey but nervis, 'overs near the door.
I ain't no pitcher orf no chocklit box.
    I've took some knocks.

I ain't no pitcher. But—O Glory!—*But*
    Ther's dicky-birds awarblin' in me soul!
To think that I ain't lost that upper-cut!
    An' my left-'ook's still with me, good an' whole.
I feared me punch was dead; but I was wrong.
    Me 'eart's all song!

Then, as Spike makes a move, I raised me mits
    Fearin' a foul; an' Rat-face does 'is block.
'E loosens up a string uv epi-tits
    That seem to jolt the parson with a shock.
Filthy an' free they was, make no mistakes.
    Then Snowy wakes.

All through the fight 'e 'ad seemed kind uv dazed,
    Ubsorbin' it like some saint in a dream.
But now 'e straightened up, 'is ole eyes blazed
    An', as the filth flowed in a red-'ot stream,
'Is voice blew in like cool winds frum the south:
    "Shut that foul mouth!"

"Shut your vile mouth, or, by the Lord!—" 'Is 'and
    Went up, an' there was anger on 'is face.
But Rat-face ducked. 'E weren't the man to stand
    Agin that figger uv avengin' grace.
Ducked, or 'e might uv stopped one 'oly smite
    Frum Snowy's right.

"Young friend," 'E turns to me. An' then I 'ear
    A yell: "The cops! The cops is in the Lane!
"Parson," I sez, "we are de tropp, I fear.
    Mid 'appier scenes I'll vencher to ixplain.
'Ang to me 'and, an' wave no fond farewell;
    But run like 'ell!"

Some say wrong livin' reaps no good reward.
    Well, I dunno. If I 'ad not cut loose

In Spadgers, in them days long, long deplored,
  'Ow could I knowed the run uv Foo's caboose?
That back-way entrance, used fer Chiner's friends'
    Un'oly ends.

Out by a green door; down a flight uv stair;
  Along a passige; up another flight;
Through 'arf a dozen rooms, broodcastin' scares
  To twenty yellow men, pea-green with fright;
Me an' the parson, through that 'eathen land,
    Trips 'and in 'and.

Out uv dark corners, voices 'ere an' there
  Break sudden with a jabberin' sing-song,
Like magpies flutin' on the mornin' air.
  We pays no 'eed to them, but plug along,
  Twistin' an' turnin' through them secret ways,
    Like in a maze.

I bust a bolted door. The parson gasps:
  The air inside is 'eavy with the drug.
A fat Chow goggles at the broken hasps;
  Another dreams un'eedin' on a rug.
Out by the other door—past piles uv fruit—
    'Ow we did scoot!

Red lanterns—lacquer-work—brass pots—strange smells—
  Silk curtains—slippers—baskets—ginger jars—
A squealin' Chinee fiddle—tinklin' bells—
  Queer works uv art—filth—fowls—ducks—iron bars
To winders—All pass by us in a stream,
    Like 'twuz a dream.

Down to a cellar; up agen, an' out—
  Bananers—brandy jars—we rush pell-mell,
Turnin' to left, to right, then round about
  (The parson, after, said it seemed like 'ell)
Through one last orful pong, then up a stair
    Into clean air.

We're in a little yard; no thing to stop
  Our flight to freedom but a fence. "Now, jump!"
I grabs 'is rev'rince, 'eaves 'im to the top,
  An' bungs me own frame over with a bump.
"Dam!" sez the parson—or it sounded so.
    But I dunno.

Seems that 'is coat got 'itched up on a nail.
  'E jerks it free an' gently comes to earth.
"Peter the 'ermit's 'ome!" I sez. "All 'ail!"
  An' makes punk noises indicatin' mirth.
The parson, 'e walks on, as still as death.
    Seems out o' breath.

I walk beside 'im; but 'e sez no word.
  To put it straight, I'm feelin' pretty mean—
Feelin' a bit ashamed uv wot's occurred—
  But still, I never planned to 'ave no scene
With Spike. I didn't start the flamin' row,
    Not any'ow.

I tells 'im so. But still 'e never spoke.
  I arsts 'im 'ow else could the thing be done.
I tells 'im straight I'd let no flamin' bloke
  Take pot shots at me with no flamin' gun.
'E stops, an' pats me shoulder with 'is 'and:
    "I understand.

"Young friend." 'Is face is orful stern an' grave.
  "The brawl was not your seekin', we'll suppose.
But does it 'elp this girl we wish to save?
  'Ow can sich mad brutality serve Rose?
May be, in anger, you fergot, young friend,
    Our Christian end?"

"Not on yer life!" I tells 'im. "Spike's in soak,
  Whether the cops 'ave got 'im now or not.
An' that removes one interferin' bloke
  Wot 'ad a mind to queer our 'oly plot.
Tomorrer we'll find Rose, an' work good works
    With gentler lurks."

"Gentler?" 'e sez. "I 'ope so." Still 'e's grave.
  "The ways uv 'Eaven's strange," 'e sez, "an' yours
Is stranger still. Yet all may work to save
  One strugglin' soul, if 'Eaven's grace endures."
'E's dreadful solemn. "I must own I feel
    Grieved a great deal.

"Your face," 'e sez, "is very badly cut—"
  "Now, look," I chips. "'Old on. Let's git this right.
'Oo was it tried to stoush that rat-face mutt?
  'Oo was it barracked for me in the fight?

'Oo was it used that word uv evul sense
   Up on that fence?"

"Young friend!" . . . Indignant? 'Struth! I see 'im try
  To keep reel stern. But soon I rekernise
The little twinkle stealin' in 'is eye,
  That won't keep out, no matter 'ow 'e tries.
An' then—'is twitchin' lips smile wide apart:
    "Aw, 'ave a 'eart!"

THE KNIGHT'S RETURN

The conq'rin' 'ero! Me? Yes, I don't think.
  This mornin' when I catch the train fer 'ome,
It's far more like a walloped pup I slink
  To kennel, with resolves no more to roam.
Crusades is orf. I'm fer the simple life,
  'Ome with me trustin' wife
    All safe frum strife.

I've read uv knights returnin' full uv gyp,
  Back to the bewchus lady in the tower.
They never seemed to git dumestic pip
  In them brave days when knight'ood was in flower.
But times is changed; an' 'usbands 'as to 'eed;
  Fer knight'ood's run to seed;
    It 'as indeed.

Snowy, the parson, came to say farewell
  "Young friend," 'e sez, "You've did a Christian ack—
A noble deed that you'll be glad to tell
  An' boast uv to yer wife when you git back."
"Too true," I sez, reel chirpy. "She'll be proud,
  I'll blab it to the crowd—
    If I'm allowed."

"Good-bye! Good Luck!" 'e sez. "I'll see to Rose,
  Make yer mind easy. Ierdine yer face.
Bless yeh! Good luck, young friend!" An' orf we goes—
  Me an' me conscience arguin' the case.
An', as we pick up speed an' race along,
  The rails make up a song:
    "Yer in all wrong!"

"Yer in all wrong! Yer in all wrong! Yeh blob!
  Why did yeh want to go an' 'unt fer Spike?
Yer in all wrong! Becoz yeh liked the job.
  That's wot. An' don't pretend yeh didn't like.
Yer in all wrong! Wot will yeh tell Doreen?
  Yeh'll 'ate to 'ave a scene.
    Don't yeh feel mean?"

Gawstruth, I do! It ain't so much the fack
  That I 'ave soiled me soul be breakin' trust;
But 'ere's me lip swole up an' one eye black
  An' all me map in gen'ril bunged an' bust.

'Ow can a 'omin' 'usband 'ave the neck
   To 'arf ixplain that wreck
     With self-respeck?

An' then ther's Rose. Wot 'ave I got to say
   About that invite? 'Struth! Doreen an' Rose!
Arstin' strange dames (comparative) to stay
   Ain't done since knights 'ad buttons to their clo'es.
Wot's after, if I do pull orf the coop?
   I feel me spirits droop.
     I'm in the soup!

Two stations on, a w'iskered coot gits in
   I seem to sort uv rekernise, some'ow.
But all at once I place 'im, an' I grin.
   But 'e don't jerry; 'e's stone sober now.
It's 'im I scragged in Spadgers—number one—
   The late suspected gun.
     It's Danny Dunn.

"Sold that watch yet, ole cobber?" I remarks.
   'E grabs 'is bag, an' views me battered dile,
With sudden fears uv spielers an' their larks.
   But I ixplain, an' 'e digs up a smile.
"Ah, yes," 'e drawls. "We met two nights ago
   But I was—well, you know—
     Well—jist so-so."

'E pipes me dile again, then stammers out,
   "I'm sorry, sonny. Stone the crows! It's sad
To see yer face so orful cut about.
   I never thort I walloped you so bad.
I'm sorry, lad, that we should come to blows.
   Black eye? An' wot a nose!
     Oh, stone the crows!"

I ease 'is guilty mind about me phiz,
   An' we're good cobbers in a 'arf a tick.
Then 'e wades in an' tells me 'oo 'e is—
   ('E ain't a bad ole coot when 'e ain't shick)—
"I ain't dead broke," 'e sez. "That night, yeh know,
   I was cleaned out uv dough,
     An'—well—so-so."

Lookin' fer land 'e is; an' 'as 'is eye
  Upon a little farm jist close to me.
If 'e decides to take it by-an'-by,
  "Why, stone the crows! I'll look yous up," sez 'e.
"I need some friends: I ain't got wife nor chick;
  An' yous will like me quick—
    When I ain't shick."

I leaves 'im tork. Me own affairs won't let
  Me pay much 'eed to all 'e 'as to say.
But, while 'e's spoutin', sudden like I get
  A bright idear that brings one 'opeful ray.
One thing I 'eard pertickler while 'e spoke;
  'E is a single bloke.
    I lets that soak.

But later on I wished 'e'd sling 'is mag.
  The nearer 'ome I get the worse I feel;
The worse I feel, the more I chew the rag;
  The more I chew the rag, this crooked deal
I've served Doreen looks black an' blacker yet.
  I worry till I get
    All one cold sweat.

I walk 'ome frum the station, thinkin' 'ard.
  Wot can I tell me wife? Gawstruth! I been
Eight long years wed, an' never 'ad to guard
  Me tongue before. Wot can I tell Doreen?
An' there she's waitin' 'arf ways down our hill ...
  She takes one look ... "Why! Bill!"
    I stands stock still.

"Oh, yes, me face," I larfs. "O' course. Me face.
  I clean fergot. I—well—to tell the truth,
I—Don't look scared—I—Oh, it's no disgrace.
  That dentist. Yes, yes! Pullin' out me tooth.
Reel butcher. Nearly frachered both me jors.
  Yes, dear, let's go indoors."
    (Wow! 'Oly wars!)

Poor Bill! Poor Dear! 'E must 'ave been a brute."
  She kisses me fair on me busted lip;
An' all me fears is stilled be that serloot.
  Ar, wot a fool I was to 'ave the pip.

The game is mine before I 'ardly tried.
  Dead easy, 'ow I lied!
    I'm 'ome an' dried.

Yet . . . I dunno. Me triump' don't last long.
  'Twuz low down, some way, 'ow I took 'er in—
Like pinchin' frum a kid. I feel dead wrong.
  The parson calls it "conshusniss uv sin."
I might be; but it's got me worried now:
    An' conshuns is a cow,
      That I'll allow.

Take it frum me. To 'ave a lovin' wife
  Fussin' an' pettin' you, jist through a lie—
Like 'er this ev'nin'—crools all married life.
  If you can't look 'er fair bang in the eye
An' feel you've earned that trust frum first to last.
  You're 'eadin' downward fast . . .
    But Rose—Oh, blast!

A
WOMAN'S
WAY

Women is strange. You take my tip; I'm wise.
  I know enough to know I'll never know
The 'uman female mind, or wot su'prise
  They 'as in store to bring yer boastin' low.
They keep yeh guessin' wot they're up to nex',
An' then, odds on, it's wot yeh least expecks.

Take me. I know me wife can twist me round
  'Er little finger. I don't mind that none.
Wot worries me is that I've never found
  Which way I'm gittin' twisted, till it's done.
Women is strange. An' yet, I've got to own
I'd make a orful 'ash uv it, alone.

There's this affair uv Rose. I tells yeh straight,
  Suspicious don't describe me state uv mind.
The calm way that Doreen 'as fixed the date
  An' all, looks like there's somethin' else be'ind.
Somethin'—not spite or meanness; don't think that.
Me wife purrs sometimes, but she ain't a cat.

But somethin'. I've got far too wise a nob
  To be took in by 'er airs uv repose.
I know I said I'd chuck the 'ole darn job
  An' leave 'er an' the parson deal with Rose.
But now me mind's uneasy, that's a fack.
I've got to manage things with speshul tack.

That's 'ow I feel—uneasy—when I drive
  Down to the train. I'm thinkin' as I goes,
There ain't two women, that I know, alive
  More dif'rint than them two—Doreen an' Rose.
'Ow they will mix together I dunno.
It all depends on 'ow I run the show.

Rose looks dead pale. She ain't got much to say
  ('Er few poor bits uv luggage make no load)
She smiles when we shake 'ands, an' sez Goodday
  Shy like an' strange; an' as we take the road
Back to the farm, I see 'er look around
Big-eyed, like it's some queer new land she's found.

I springs a joke or two. I'm none too bright
  Meself; but it's a slap-up sort uv day.
Spring's workin' overtime; to left an' right
  Blackwood an' wattle trees is bloomin' gay,

Botchin' the bonzer green with golden dust;
An' magpies in 'em singin' fit to bust.

I sneak a glance at Rose. I can't look long.
  'Er lips is trem'lin'; tears is in 'er eye.
Then, glad with life, a thrush beefs out a song
  'Longside the road as we go drivin' by.
"Oh, Gawd A'mighty! 'Ark!" I 'ear 'er say,
"An' Spadgers Lane not fifty mile away!"

Not fifty mile away: the frowsy Lane,
  Where only dirt an' dreariness 'as sway,
Where every second tale's a tale uv pain,
  An' devil's doin's blots the night an' day.
But 'ere is thrushes tootin' songs uv praise.
An' golden blossoms lightin' up our ways.

I speaks a piece to boost this bonzer spot;
  Tellin' 'er 'ow the neighbour'ood 'as grown,
An' 'ow Dave Brown, jist up the road, 'as got
  Ten ton uv spuds per acre, usin' bone.
She don't seem to be list'nin'. She jist stares,
Like someone dreamin' dreams, or thinkin' pray'rs.

Me yap's a dud. No matter 'ow I try,
  Me conversation ain't the dinkum brand.
I'm 'opin' that she don't bust out an' cry:
  It makes me nervis. But I understand.
Over an' over I can 'ear 'er say,
"An' Spadgers less than fifty mile away!"

We're 'ome at last. Doreen is at the gate.
  I hitch the reins, an' quite the eager pup;
Then 'elp Rose down, an' stand aside an' wait
  To see 'ow them two size each other up.
But quick—like that—two arms 'as greeted warm
The sobbin' girl ... Doreen's run true to form.

"'Ome on the bit!" I thinks. But as I turn,
  'Ere's Wally Free 'as got to poke 'is dile
Above the fence, where 'e's been cuttin' fern.
  The missus spots 'im, an' I seen 'er smile.
An' then she calls to 'im: "Oh, Mister Free,
Come in," she sez, "an' 'ave a cup uv tea."

There's tack! A woman dunno wot it means.
    What does that blighter want with cups uv tea?
A privit, fambly meet—an' 'ere Doreen's
    Muckin' it all by draggin' in this Free.
She might 'ave knowed that Rose ain't feelin' prime,
An' don't want no strange comp'ny at the time.

Free an' 'is thievin' cow! But, all the same,
    'Is yap did seem to cheer Rose up a lot.
An' after, when 'e'd bunged 'is lanky frame
    Back to 'is job, Doreen sez, "Ain't you got
No work at all to do outside to-day?
Us two must 'ave a tork; so run away."

I went ... I went becoz, if I 'ad stayed,
    Me few remarks might 'ave been pretty 'ot.
Gawbli'me! 'Oo *is* 'ead uv this parade?
    Did I plan out the scheme, or did I not?
I've worked fer this, I've worried night an' day;
An' now it's fixed, I'm tole to "run away."

Women is strange. I s'pose I oughter be
    Contented; though I never un'erstands.
But when I score, it 'urts me dignerty
    To 'ave the credit grabbed out uv me 'ands.
I shouldn't look fer credit, p'raps; an' then,
Women is strange. But bli'me! So is men!

LISTENER'S LUCK

"My sort," she sez, "don't meet no fairy prince." . . .
   I can't 'elp 'earin' part uv wot was said
   While I am sortin' taters in the shed.
They've 'ad these secret confabs ever since
   Rose came. 'Er an' Doreen's been 'eart to 'eart,
   'Oldin' pow-wows in which I got no part.

Not that I want to. This 'ere women's craze
   Fer torkin' over things is jist 'ot air;
   An' never reely gits 'em anywhere.
It don't concern me if they yap fer days.
   My bloomin' troubles! But, as I jist said,
   I can't 'elp 'earin' as they pass the shed.

"My sort," sez Rose, "don't meet no fairy prince."
   'Er voice seems sort uv lonely like an' sad.
   "Ah well," she sez, "there's jobs still to be 'ad
Down in the fact'ries. I ain't one to wince
   Frum all the knocks I've 'ad—an' will 'ave. Still,
   Sometimes I git fed-ip against me will.

"Some women 'ave the luck," she sez; "like you.
   Their lives seem made fer love an' joy an' sport,
   But I'm jist one uv the unlucky sort.
I've give up dreamin' dreams: they don't come true.
   There ain't no love or joy or sport fer me.
   Life's made me 'ard; an' 'ard I got to be."

"Oh, rubbidge!" sez Doreen. "You've got the blues,
   We all 'ave bad luck some times, but it mends.
   An' you're still young, my dear; you 'ave your friends.
Why should you think that you must alwiz lose?
   The sun's still shinin'; birds still sing, an' court;
   An' men still marry." Rose sez, "Not my sort.

"Ah, wot's the use?" she sez. "You 'ave been good—
   Too good—an' it's ungrateful I should grieve;
   But when it comes the time that I must leave
All this an'—Oh, I should 'ave understood.
   I was a fool to come. I should 'ave know
   'Ow it would be. I should 'ave stayed alone."

An' then—Aw, well, I thort I knoo me wife,
   'Ow she can be so gentle an' so kind,
   An' all the tenderness that's in 'er mind;
As I've 'ad cause to know through married life.

But never 'ave I 'eard 'er wisdom speak
Sich words before. It left me wond'rin'—meek.

Yes, meek I felt—an' proud, all in the one:
Proud fer to know 'ow fine my wife can be;
Meek fer to think she cares fer sich as me.
"'Ope lasts," I 'ear 'er say, "till life is done.
An' life can bring us joy, I know it can.
I know; fer I've been lucky in my man."

There's a wife for yeh! Would n't any bloke
Feel great to 'ear 'is wife say things like that?
I know I've earned it; but it knocked me flat.
"Been lucky in 'er man." That's 'ow she spoke.
"The dear ole simple block'ead," sez Doreen.
"'E's reel good 'earted, though 'e's orful green."

There's a wife for yeh! Green! Think in the 'ead!
To think she'd go an' tork be'ind me back,
Gossip, an' paint me character that black!
I'm glad I can't 'ear more uv wot was said.
They wander off, down by the creek somewhere.
Green! Well, I said that women talk 'ot air.

I thinks uv Danny Dunn, an' wot I've planned.
Doreen don't know wot I got up me sleeve;
An' Rose don't know that she won't 'ave to leave,
Not once I come to light an' take a 'and.
Block'ead won't be the name they'll call me then.
Women can tork; but action needs us men.

Yet, I dunno. Some ways it ain't so fine.
Spite uv 'is money, Danny ain't much catch.
It seems a pity Rose can't make a match
That's reel romantic, like Doreen's an' mine;
But then again, although 'e's old an' plain,
Danny's a kinder fate than Spadgers Lane.

Bit later on I see Rose standin' by
That bridge frum where Mick waved 'is last farewell
When 'e went smilin' to the war, an' fell.
'Ow diff'rint if 'e 'ad n't come to die,
I thinks. Life's orful sad, some ways.
Though it's 'ard to be sad on these Spring days.

Doreen 'as left, fer reasons uv 'er own;
    An' Rose is gazin' down into the stream,
    Lost, like it seems, in some un'appy dream.
She looks perthetic standin' there alone.
    Wis'ful she looks. But when I've turned away
    I git a shock to 'ear 'er larfin' gay.

It's that coot Wally Free; 'e's with 'er now.
    Funny 'ow 'is fool chatter makes 'er smile,
    An' shove 'er troubles under fer a while.
(Pity 'e don't pay more 'eed to 'is cow
    Instid uv loafin' there. 'E's got no sense.
    I'm sick uv tellin' 'im to mend that fence.)

'Er sort don't meet no fairy prince ... Ar, well.
    Fairy gawdfathers, p'raps, wot once was knights,
    Might take a turn at puttin' things to rights.
Green? Block'ead, am I? You can't alwiz tell.
    Wait till I wave me magic mit at Rose,
    An' turn 'er into "Mrs. Stone-the-crows."

THE
DANCE

"Heirlums," 'e sez. "I've 'ad the trousiz pressed.
    Me father married in 'em, that 'e did.
See this 'ere fancy vest?
        See this 'ere lid?
Me gran'dad brought that frum 'is native land
In forty-two—an' then 'twas second-'and."

Clobber? Oh, 'el! Pants uv wild shepherd's plaid,
    A coat that might 'ave knocked the cliners flat
When father was a lad,
        A tall, pot 'at
That caught the mange back in the diggin's days,
A fancy vest that called fer loud 'oorays.

But loud 'oorays don't 'arf ixpress my rage
    When Danny comes up'olstered fer the jig.
I've seen it on the stage,
        That comic rig;
But never at a country dance before
'Ave I seen sich crook duds as Danny wore.

"You want to crool my scheme," I sez, "with rags
    Like that? This ain't no fancy dress affair.
Wot sort uv tile an' bags
        Is them to wear?
But 'e don't tumble; 'e's as pleased as pie.
"By gum," 'e sez, "this ort to catch 'er eye."

"You posin' fer a comic film, or wot?"
    I arsts 'im—"with noorotic togs like those!
Jazz clobber! Ain't you got
        No decent clo'es?"
But 'e's too tickled with 'imself to 'eed.
"This orter catch 'er eye," 'e sez, "this tweed."

It caught 'er eye, all right, an' many more.
    They starts to come before the daylight fades;
An', fer a hour before
        The crowd parades,
Ole Danny 'eld the centre uv the stage,
While I stood orf an' chewed me silent rage.

That's 'ow it alwiz is: I try to show
    'Ow I can use me bean in deep-laid lurks;
An' then some fool must go
        An' bust the works.

'Ere, I 'ave planned a coop in slap-up-style,
An' Danny spikes me guns with gran'pa's tile.

Rose never seemed so free frum ugly dreams,
    Not since she came, as that night at the dance;
But my matchmakin' schemes
        Makes no advance;
Fer every time I gits a chance to score,
Doreen butts in, an' crools me pitch once more.

Reel thortless, women is. She ort to seen
    I 'ad intents—in spite uv Danny's clo'es—
An' that 'e was reel keen.
        Cocernin' Rose.
Not 'er. She larfs, an' chatters with the push,
As if rich 'usbands grew on every bush.

Once, f'rinstance, I gits busy when I seen
    Rose sittin' out; an' brings Dan on the run.
"Why, mercy!" sez Doreen.
        "'Ere's Mister Dunn
Perlite enough to arst *me* fer a dance.
'E knows us marrid ones don't git much chance."

An' there she grabs 'im, fair out uv me 'ands!
    An' lets young Wally Free git off with Rose;
While like a fool I stands,
        Kickin' me toes
An' cursin' all the fool things women do.
I'd think 'twas done apurpis, less I knoo.

That's 'ow it was all night. I schemed a treat,
    Workin' shrood points, an' sweatin' blood, almost;
But every time I'm beat
        Right on the post.
All me matchmakin's bust—the task uv days—
Through Danny's duds an' my wife's tackless ways.

Nice chaperong she is! While Free an' Rose
    Dance 'arf the night Doreen jist sits an' beams.
When I seen that, up goes
        My 'opes an' schemes.
But all that Danny sez is, "Stone the crows!
Yeh'd think I'd took 'er eye, with them good clo'es."

When we git 'ome that night I shows me spleen
    By 'intin' Rose will be left on the shelf.

An' then I see Doreen
   Smile to 'erself.
"I would n't be su'prised," she sez, "to see
Rose marrid, some fine day, to Wally Free."

To Wally Free! Yeh could 'ave knocked me flat
  With 'arf a brick. I seen it in a flash.
A grinnin' coot like that!
   Without no cash!
Besides, a man 'oo'd keep a thievin' cow
Like 'is, won't make no 'usband any'ow.

I'm sick uv everything. It ain't no joke.
  I've tried to do good works; an' now I've found
When you git 'elpin' folk
   They jist turn round
An' bite the 'and that feeds 'em, so to speak.
An' yet they sez the strong should 'elp the weak.

Wot rot! . . . I wisht I 'ad some reel ixcuse
  To push some face in, jist to ease me mind.
Spike Wegg, 'e 'ad 'is use—
   'Im an' 'is kind.
If I could give me ole left-'ook one swing,
I might feel kinder like to everything.

S P I K E
W E G G

Me photer's in the papers! 'Oly wars!
  A 'ero, I've been called in big, black type.
  I 'ad idears the time was close on ripe.
    Fer some applorse
To come my way, on top uv all me bumps.
Now it's come sudden, an' it's come in lumps.

I've given interviews, an' 'ad me dile
  Bang on the front page torkin' to a 'tec'.
  Limelight? I'm swimmin' in it to the neck!
    Me sunny smile
Beams on the crowd. Misun'erstandin's past;
An' I 'ave come into me own, at last.

But all the spot-light ain't alone fer me;
  'Arf, I am glad to say, is made to shine
  Upon that firm an' trusted friend uv mine,
    Ole Wally Free—
A man, I've alwiz said, 'oo'd make 'is mark . . .
But, case you 'ave n't 'eard the story, 'ark:

Spike Wegg—Yes, 'im. I thort, the same as you,
  That 'e was dished an' done fer in the Lane.
  I don't ixpeck to cross 'is tracks again;
    An' never knoo
That 'e 'ad swore to git me one uv those
Fine days, an' make 'is alley good with Rose.

'Spike 'ad been aimin' 'igh in 'is profesh.
  Bank robberies, an' sich, was 'is noo lurk;
  An' one big job 'ad set the cops to work
    To plan a fresh
Campaign agin this crook. They want 'im more
Than ever they 'ave wanted 'im before.

They yearn fer 'im, reel passionit, they do.
  Press an' perlice both 'ankers fer 'im sore.
  "Where is Spike Wegg?" the daily 'eadlines roar.
    But no one knoo.
Or them that did 'ad fancies to be dumb.
The oysters uv the underworld was mum.

It was the big sensation uv the day.
  Near 'arf the Force was nosin' fer the bloke
  Wot done the deed; but Spike was well in smoke,
    An' like to stay.

Shots 'ad been fired; an' one poor coot was plugged.
An' now the crowd arsts, "Why ain't no one jugged?"

That's 'ow the land lies when, one day, I go
  Down to the orchid paddick, where I see
  A strange cove playin' spy be'ind a tree.
    I seem to know
The shape uv that there sneakin', slinkin' frame,
An' walk across to git on to 'is game.

Oh, yes; it's 'im; an' a reel vicious Spike.
  Venom is in the eye that looks in mine—
  A cold, 'ard, snaky eye. "Well, Bill, yeh swine.
    'Ow would yeh like
To make cold meat?" This is the pleasant way
'E greets me on a nice, bright, warm, Spring day.

Though it is warm, I feel a sudden cold
  Creep up me spine. I 'speck to 'ear a gun
  Tork any minute; so I make a run
    To git a hold,
An' keep in close to use that upper-cut.
But Spike is fly this time, an' works 'is nut.

'E side-steps pretty. Then we git to grips.
  I plant a short-arm jolt; an', as I land,
  I see a flash uv somethin' in 'is 'and.
    Nex' thing, 'e rips
A knife beneath me guard an' gives a dig—
Sticks me fair in the bellers, like a pig.

It was red-'ot! I grunt, an' break away
  To 'old 'im orf. I'm battlin' fer me life—
  All-in, a cert; fer 'e's still got the knife.
    An', by the way
'E looks, I know it's either 'im or me
'As an appointment at the cemet'ry.

I've often wondered 'ow a feller feels
  When 'e is due to wave the world good-bye.
  They say 'is past life flicks before 'is eye
    Like movie reels.
My past life never troubled me a heap.
All that I want to do is go to sleep.

I'm gittin' weak; I'm coughin', chokey like;
  Me legs is wobbly, an' I'm orful ill.

But I 'ave got some fight left in me still.
   I look at Spike;
An' there I see the dirty look wot shows
'E's got me where 'e wants me—an' 'e knows.

'E's smilin'. Not a pretty smile, I own.
   But, sudden, there's a fear springs in 'is eye;
   An', frum be'ind me, some thing flashes by.
     I 'ear Spike groan;
I 'ear the squishy thud uv flesh on flesh;
An' gits idears there's somethin' doin' fresh.

I think that's where I fell. Nex' thing I see
   Is Spike Wegg down, an' fair on top uv 'im
   Some one that's breathin' ard an' fightin' grim.
     It's Wally Free!
It's good old Wally! 'E 'as got Spike pinned,
Both 'ands, an' kneelin' 'eavy on 'is wind.

So fur so good. But I ain't outed yet.
   On 'ands an' knees I crawls to reach 'em, slow.
   (Spike's got the knife, an' Wally dare n't let go)
     Then, as I get
Close up, I 'ear Rose screamin', then me wife.
I'm faint. I twist Spike's arm—an' grab the knife.

That's all. At least, as far as I'm concerned,
   I took no further interest in the show.
   The things wot 'appened subsekint I know
     Frum wot I learned
When I come-to, tucked in me little bed,
Me chest on fire, an' cold packs on me 'ead.

I 'ear they tied Spike up with 'arness straps
   An' bits uv 'ay-band, till the John 'Ops come;
   An' watched 'im workin' out a mental sum—
     Free an' some chaps—
Uv 'ow much time 'e'd git fer this last plot
An' other jobs. The answer was, a lot.

Then that nex' day! an' after, fer a week!
   Yeh'd think I owned the winner uv a Cup.
   Pressmen, perlice, the parson, all rush up;
     An' I've to speak
Me piece, to be took down in black an' white,
In case I chuck a seven overnight.

The papers done us proud. Near every day
  Some uv 'em printed photers uv me map
  (Looked at some ways, I ain't too crook a chap)
    But, anyway
I've 'ad enough. I wish they'd let me be.
I'm sick uv all this cheap publicity.

But I'm reel glad ole Wally's won a name.
  'E saved my life; I'm wise to that, all right.
  Besides, I alwiz said that 'e was white
    Since 'e first came
To live 'ere, but 'e never got 'is due.
Now 'im an' Rose—Ah, well; I fixed that too.

But sich is fame. Less than a month ago.
  The whole thing started with a naggin' tooth.
  Now I am famis; an', to tell the truth—
    Well, I dunno—
I'd 'ardly like to bet yeh that I don't
Git arst to act in pitchers—but I won't.

NARCISSUS

A man's a mug. I've worked the 'ole thing out
   To-day, down in the orchard where I sat
   Runnin' the wheels red-'ot beneath me 'at,
An' wras'lin' fervud with a sudden doubt—
   A doubt wot's plugged me fair bang on the point
   An' jolted all me glad dreams out uv joint.

It's been a pearlin' day. The birds above
   Up in the trees sung fit to break their 'earts.
It seemed, some'ow, the 'ole world's makin' love,
   Ixceptin' me. An' then an' there I starts
To think things out an' git me bearin's straight,
Becoz—Well, I ain't been meself uv late.

I've flopped. It was the parson put me wise,
   Before 'e left. I 'ad been full uv skite.
   I was the 'ero uv the piece all right.
Me chest was out, me 'ead was twice the size
   It used to be. I felt I was king-pin.
   Did n't the papers 'ave me photer in?

I was that puffed with pride I never stopped
   To search me soul fer signs uv wear an' tear.
I loved meself so much I never dropped
   To any blot or blemish anywhere.
The Lord 'Igh Muck-a-muck, wot done the trick,
An' dug the Murray with 'is little pick.

When I think back on it I go all 'ot.
   I was that blind I never even seen,
   Nor looked to see no changes in Doreen.
I was content to 'ave 'er on the spot
   Dodgin' about the 'ouse in 'er calm way,
   To chirp, "Yes, Bill," to everything I say.

The parson punchered me. 'E's alwiz 'ad
   A trick uv callin' me by fancy names.
In town 'e christened me "Sir Gally'ad,"
   'Oo was, it seems, a knight wot rescued dames,
But never spoke out uv 'is turn to none,
Becoz 'is 'eart was pure. 'E took the bun.

But now "Narcissy" is the moniker
   'E wishes on me; an' I arst fer light.
   "Narcissy?" I remarks. "Don't sound perlite.
'Oo was this bird? There looks to be a slur

Or somethin' sly about that cissy touch."
"A bloke," 'e sez, "'oo liked 'imself too much."

I looks quick fer that twinkle in 'is eye
    Wot tells me if 'e's kiddin' me or not.
But it ain't there. "Fair dinkum," I reply,
    "You don't mean—You ain't 'intin' that I've got—"
"I mean," 'e sez, "you should give thanks through life
That you 'ave been so lucky in your wife."

'E don't 'arp on the toon; but turns away.
    "Your daffydils," 'e sez, "makes quite a show."
    An' latter, when it came 'is time to go,
'E shakes me 'and reel 'arty, twinklin' gay . . .
    But, "lucky in me wife?" Where did I 'ear
    Somethin' like that before? It sounds dead queer.

I turns to 'er, after we've waved good-byes,
    To try an' figure wot the parson meant.
An' sudden, I see somethin' in 'er eyes
    I never noticed there before 'e went:
That troubled, mother look I've seen so plain.
The times she's said, "Poor Bill! 'Ow is the pain?"

I seeks the orchard, with a sickly grin,
    To sort meself out straight an' git a grip.
    Them 'ints the parson drops give me the pip.
I don't quite see where daffydils comes in;
    But, "lucky in me wife!" Why, spare me days,
    Yeh'd think I beat 'er, by the things 'e says!

I tries to kid meself: to back me skite,
    An' 'old that wad uv self-content I 'ad.
It ain't no use. I know the parson's right:
    Clean through the piece I 'ave been actin' bad.
I've been so full uv Me, I've treated 'er
Like she was—well, a bit uv furnicher.

Yet, "furnicher" don't seem to put it good.
    Nothin' so wooden don't describe Doreen.
    All through the game, some'ow, she's alwiz been—
Well, somewhere 'andy, 'elpin' where she could,
    An' manidgin', an' . . . Bli'me! Now I see!
    Wot she *did* manidge was the block'ead—me! . . .

Well, I'm the goat. I s'pose I should 'ave seen
  I was n't 'ead an' tail uv all the show.
A bit uv putty in 'er 'ands I been!
  An' so bull-'eaded that I did n't know.
Only fer 'er things might 'ave—Spare me days!
I never will git used to women's ways.

Only fer 'er Rose might ... But wot's the use?
  Shakespeare 'as said it right: the world's a stage;
  An' all us 'uman ducks an' dames ingage
In actin' parts. Mostly the men cut loose,
  An' fights, an' throws their weight about a lot.
  But, listen. It's the women weave the plot.

The women ... Well, it's been a bonnie day.
  Blue-bonnets, dodgin' in an' out the ferns,
Looks like blue chips uv sky come down to play.
  An' down the valley, where the creek track turns,
I see Rose, arm-in-arm with Wally Free.
The 'ole world's makin' love, ixceptin' me.

Huh! Women! ... Yes; a man's a mug, all right ...
  I sees the sof' clouds sailin' in the sky,
  An' bits uv thistledown go driftin' by.
"Jist like men's lives," I think. An' then I sight,
  Fair in me cabbages, ole Wally's cow.
  That fence—But them plants ain't worth savin', now.

Women ... I wonder 'oo Narcissy was ...
  Green trees agin blue 'ills don't look 'arf bad ...
I s'pose 'e got the cissy part becoz
  'Is ways was womanish. Well, serve 'im glad ...
That cow uv Wally's ort to milk a treat
With plenty good young cabbage plants to eat.

Women *is* often 'elpful—in a sense ...
  Lord, it's a lazy day! Before it fails,
  I better git a 'ammer an' some nails
An' dodge acrost an' mend that bit uv fence.
  It's up to me to try an' put things right,
  An'—well, I'll 'elp Doreen wash up tonight.

119

DIGGER SMITH

Cover illustration for *Digger Smith*

BEFORE THE WAR

"Before the war," she sighs. "Before the war."
    Then blinks 'er eyes, an' tries to work a smile.
"Ole scenes," she sez, "don't look the same no more.
    Ole ways," she sez, "seems to 'ave changed their style.
    The pleasures that we 'ad don't seem worth while—
Them simple joys that passed an hour away—
    An' troubles, that we used to so revile,
'Ow small they look," she sez. "'Ow small to-day.

"This war!" sighs ole Mar Flood. An' when I seen
    The ole girl sittin' in our parlour there,
Tellin' 'er troubles to my wife, Doreen,
    As though the talkin' eased 'er load uv care,
    I thinks uv mothers, 'ere an' everywhere,
Similin' a bit while they are grievin' sore
    For grown-up babies, fightin' Over There;
An' then I 'ears 'em sigh, "Before the war."

My wife 'as took the social 'abit bad.
    I ain't averse—one more new word I've learned—
Averse to tea, when tea is to be 'ad;
    An' when it comes I reckon that it's earned.
    It's jist a drink, as fur as I'm concerned,
Good for a bloke that's toilin' on the land;
    But when a caller comes, 'ere I am turned
Into a social butterfly, off-'and.

Then drinkin' tea becomes an 'oly rite.
    So's I won't bring the fam'ly to disgrace
I gits a bit uv coachin' overnight
    On ridin' winners in this bun-fed race.
    I 'ave to change me shirt, an' wash me face,
An' look reel neat, from me waist up at least,
    An' sling remarks in at the proper place,
An' not makes noises drinkin', like a beast.

"'Ave some more cake. Another slice, now do.
    An' won't yeh 'ave a second cup uv tea?
'Ow is the children?" Ar, it makes me blue!
    This boodoor 'abit ain't no good to me.
    I likes to take me tucker plain an' free:
Tea an' a chunk out on the job for choice,
    So I can stoke with no one there to see.
Besides, I 'aven't got no comp'ny voice.

Uv course, I've 'ad it all out with the wife.
　　I argues that there's work that must be done,
An' tells 'er that I 'ates this tony life.
　　She sez there's jooties that we must not shun.
　　You bet that ends it; so I joins the fun,
An' puts 'em all at ease with silly grins—
　　Slings bits uv repartee like "'Ave a bun,"
An' passes bread an' butter, for me sins.

Since I've been marri'd, say, I've chucked some things,
　　An, learned a whole lot more to fill the space.
I've slung all slang; crook words 'ave taken wings,
　　An' I 'ave learned to entertain with grace.
　　But when ole Missus Flood comes round our place
I don't object to 'er, for all 'er sighs;
　　Becos I likes 'er ways, I likes 'er face,
An', most uv all, she 'as them mother's eyes.

"Before the war," she sighs, the poor ole girl.
　　'Er talk it gets me thinkin' in between,
While I'm assistin' at this social whirl . . .
　　She comes across for comfort to Doreen,
　　To talk about the things that might 'ave been
If Syd 'ad not been killed at Suvla Bay,
　　Or Jim not done a bunk at seventeen,
An' not been 'eard uv since 'e went away.

They 'ave a little farm right next to us—
　　'Er an' 'er 'usband—where they live alone.
Spite uv 'er cares, she ain't the sort to fuss
　　Or serve up sudden tears an' sob an' moan,
　　An' since I've known 'er some'ow I 'ave grown
To see in 'er, an' all the grief she's bore,
　　A million brave ole mothers 'oo 'ave known
Deep sorrer since them days before the war.

"Before the war," she sez. "Yeh mind our Syd?
　　Poor lad . . . But then, yeh never met young Jim—
'Im 'oo was charged with things 'e never did.
　　Ah, both uv you'd 'ave been reel chums with 'im.
　　'Igh-spirited 'e was, a perfect limb.
It's six long years now since 'e went away—
　　Ay, drove away." 'Er poor ole eyes git dim.
"That was," she sighs, "that was me blackest day.

"Me blackest day! Wot am I sayin' now?
　There was the day the parson come to tell
The news about our Syd . . . . An', yet, some'ow . . .
　My little Jim!" She pauses for a spell . . .
　"Your 'olly'ocks is doin' reely well,"
She sez, an' battles 'ard to brighten up.
　"An' them there pinks uv yours, 'ow sweet they smell.
An'—Thanks! I think I *will* 'ave one more cup."

As fur as I can get the strength uv it,
　Them Floods 'ave 'ad a reel tough row to hoe.
First off, young Jim, 'oo plays it 'igh a bit,
　Narks the ole man a treat, an' slings the show.
　Then come the war, an' Syd 'e 'as to go.
'E run 'is final up at Suvla Bay—
　One uv the Aussies I was proud to know.
An' Jim's cracked 'ardy since 'e went away.

'Er Jim! These mothers! Lord, they're all the same.
　I wonders if Doreen will be that kind.
Syd was the son 'oo played the reel man's game;
　But Jim 'oo sloped an' left no word be'ind,
　His is the picter shinin' in 'er mind.
'Igh-spirited! I've 'eard that tale before.
　I sometimes think she'd take it rather kind
To 'ear that 'is 'igh spirits run to war.

"Before the war," she sez. "Ah, times was good.
　The little farm out there, an' jist us four
Workin' to make a decent liveli'ood.
　Our Syd an' Jim! . . . Poor Jim! It grieves me sore;
　For Dad won't 'ave 'im mentioned 'ome no more.
'E's 'urt, I know, cos 'e thinks Jim 'urt me.
　As if 'e could, the bonny boy I bore . . .
But I must off 'ome now, an' git Dad's tea."

I seen 'er to the gate. (Take if frum me,
　I'm some perlite.) She sez, "Yeh mustn't mind
Me talkin' so uv Jim, but when I see
　Your face it brings 'im back; 'e's jist your kind.
　Not quite so 'an'some, p'r'aps, nor so refined.
I've got some toys uv 'is," she sez. "But there—
　This is ole woman's talk, an' you be'ind
With all yer work, an' little time to spare."

She gives me 'and a squeeze an' turns away,
   Sobbin', I thort; but when she looks be'ind,
Smilin', an' wavin', like she felt reel gay,
   I wonders 'ow the women works that blind,
   An' jist waves back; then goes inside to find
A lookin'-glass, an' takes a reel good look ...
   "'Not quite so 'an'some, p'r'aps, nor so refined!'
Gawd 'elp yeh, Jim," I thinks. "Yeh must be crook."

DIGGER SMITH

'E calls me Digger; that's 'ow 'e begins.
'E sez 'e's only 'arf a man; an grins.
  Judged be 'is nerve, I'd say 'e was worth two
    Uv me an' you.
Then 'e digs 'arf a fag out uv 'is vest,
Borrers me matches, an' I gives 'im best.

The first I 'eard about it Poole told me.
"There is a bloke called Smith at Flood's," sez 'e;
  Come there this mornin', sez 'e's come to stay,
    An' won't go 'way.
Sez 'e was sent there be a pal named Flood;
An' talks uv contracts sealed with Flanders mud.

"No matter wot they say, 'e only grins,"
Sez Poole. "'E's rather wobbly on 'is pins.
  Seems like a soldier bloke. An' Peter Begg
    'E sez one leg
Works be machinery, but I dunno;
I only know 'e's there an' 'e won't go.

"'E grins," sez Poole, "at ev'rything they say.
Dad Flood 'as nearly 'ad a fit to-day.
  'E's cursed, an' ordered 'im clean off the place;
    But this cove's face
Jist goes on grinnin', an' 'e sez, quite carm,
'E's come to do a bit around the farm."

The tale don't sound too good to me at all.
"If 'e's a crook," I sez, "'e wants a fall.
  Maybe 'e's dilly. I'll go down an' see.
    'E'll grin at me
When I 'ave done, if 'e needs dealin' with."
So I goes down to interview this Smith.

'E 'ad a fork out in the tater patch.
Sez 'e, "Why, 'ello, Digger. Got a match?"
  "Digger?" I sez. "Well, you ain't digger 'ere.
    You better clear.
You ought to know that you can't dig them spuds.
They don't belong to you; they're ole Dad Flood's."

"Can't I?" 'e grins. "I'll do the best I can,
Considerin' I'm only 'arf a man.
  Give us a light. I can't get none from Flood,
    An' mine is dud."

I parts; an' 'e stands grinnin' at me still;
An' then 'e sez, "'Ave yeh fergot me, Bill?"

I looks, an' seen a tough bloke, short an' thin.
Then, Lord! I recomembers that ole grin.
  "It's little Smith!" I 'owls, "uv Collin'wood.
    Lad, this is good!
Last time I seen yeh, you an' Ginger Mick
Was 'owling rags, out on yer final kick."

"Yer on to it," 'e sez. "Nex' day we sailed.
Now 'arf uv me's back 'ome, an' 'arf they nailed
  An' Mick ... Ar, well, Fritz took me down a peg."
    'E waves 'is leg.
"It ain't too bad," 'e sez, with 'is ole smile;
"But when I starts to dig it cramps me style.

"But I ain't grouchin'. It was worth the fun.
We 'ad some picnic stoushin' Brother 'Un—
  The only fight I've 'ad that some John 'Op
    Don't come an' stop.
They pulled me leg a treat, but, all the same,
There's nothin' over 'ere to beat the game.

"An' now," 'e sez, "I'm 'ere to do a job
I promised, if it was me luck to lob
  Back 'ome before me mate," 'e sez, an' then,
    'E grins again.
"As clear as mud," I sez. "But I can't work
Me brains to 'old yer pace. Say, wot's the lurk?"

So then 'e puts me wise. It seems that 'im
An' this 'ere Flood—I tips it must be Jim—
  Was cobbers up in France, an' things occurred.
    (I got 'is word
Things did occur up there.) But, anyway,
Seems Flood done somethin' good for 'im one day.

Then Smith 'e promised if 'e came back 'ome
Before 'is cobber o'er the flamin' foam,
  'E'd see the ole folks 'ere, an' 'e agreed,
    If there was need,
'E'd stay an' do a bit around the farm
So long as 'e 'ad one sound, dinkum arm.

"So, 'ere I am," 'e sez, an' grins again.
"A promise is a promise 'mong us men."
   Sez I, "You come along up to the 'ouse,
    Ole Dad won't rouse
When once 'e's got yer strength, an' as for Mar,
She'll kiss yeh when she finds out 'oo yeh are."

So we goes up, an' finds 'em both fair dazed
About this little Smith; they think 'e's crazed.
   I tells the tale in words they understand;
    Then it was grand
To see Dad grab Smith's 'and an' pump it good,
An' Mar, she kissed 'im, like I said she would.

Mar sez 'e must be starved, an' right away
The kettle's on, she's busy with a tray;
   An', when I left, this Digger Smith 'e looked
    Like 'e was booked
For keeps, with tea an' bread an' beef inside.
"Our little Willie's 'ome," 'e grins, "an' dried!"

WEST

"I've seen so much uv dirt an' grime
  I'm mad to 'ave things clean.
I've seen so much uv death," 'e said—
"So many cobbers lyin' dead—
  You won't know wot I mean;
But, lad, I've 'ad so much uv strife
I want things straightened in my life.

"I've seen so much uv 'ate," 'e said—
  "Mad 'ate an' silly rage—
I'm yearnin' for clear thoughts," said 'e.
"Kindness an' love seem good to me.
  I want a new, white page
To start all over, clean an' good,
An' live me life as reel men should."

We're sittin' talkin' by the fence,
  The sun's jist goin' down,
Paintin' the sky all gold an' pink.
Said 'e, "When it's like that, I think—"
  An' then 'e stops to frown.
Said 'e, "I think, when its jist so,
Uv . . . God or somethin': I dunno.

"I ain't seen much uv God," said 'e;
  "Not 'ere nor Over There;
But, partly wot the padre said,
  It gits me when I stare
Out West when it's like that is now.
There must be somethin' else—some'ow.

"I've thought a lot," said Digger Smith—
  "Out There I thought a lot.
I thought uv death, an' all the rest,
An' uv me mates, good mates gone West;
  An' it ain't much I've got;
But things get movin' in me 'ead
When I look over there," 'e said.

"I've seen so much uv death," said 'e,
  "Me mind is in a whirl.
I've 'ad so many thoughts uv late." . . .
Said I, "Now, tell me, tell me straight,
  Own up; ain't there a girl?"
Said 'e, "I've done the best I can.
Wot does she want with 'arf a man?"

It weren't no use. 'E wouldn't talk
  Uv nothin' but the sky.
Said 'e. "Now, dinkum, talkin' square,
When you git gazin' over there
  Don't you 'arf want to cry?
I wouldn't be su'prised to see
An angel comin' out," said 'e.

The gold was creepin' up, the sun
  Was 'arf be'ind the range:
It don't seem strange a man should cry
To see that glory in the sky—
  To me it don't seem strange.
"Digger!" said 'e. "Look at it now!
There *must* be somethin' else—some'ow."

OVER THE FENCE

'Tain't my idea uv argument to call a man a fool,
An' I ain't lookin' round for bricks to 'eave at ole man Poole;
    But when 'e gets disputin' 'e's inclined to lose 'is 'ead.
    It ain't so much 'is choice uv word as 'ow the words is said.

'E's sich a coot for takin' sides, as I sez to Doreen.
Sez she, "'Ow can 'e, by 'imself?"—wotever that may mean.
    My wife sez little things sometimes that nearly git me riled.
    I knoo she meant more than she said be that soft way she smiled.

Today, when I was 'arrowin', Poole comes down to the fence
To get the loan uv my long spade; an' uses that pretence
    To 'ave a bit uv friendly talk, an' one word leads to more,
    As is the way with ole man Poole, as I've remarked before.

The spade reminds 'im 'ow 'e done some diggin' in 'is day,
An' diggin' brings the talk to earth, an' earth leads on to clay,
    Then clay quite natural reminds a thinkin' bloke uv bricks,
    An' mortar brings up mud, an' then, uv course, it's politics.

Now, Poole sticks be 'is Party, an' I don't deny 'is right;
But when 'e starts abusin' mine 'e's lookin' for a fight.
    So I delivers good 'ome truths about 'is crowd; then Poole
    Wags 'is ole beard across the fence an' tells me I'm a fool.

Now, that's the dizzy limit; so I lays aside the reins,
An' starts to prove 'e's storin' mud where most blokes keeps their
        brains.
    'E decorates 'is answers, an' we're goin' it ding-dong,
    When this returned Bloke, Digger Smith, comes saunterin' along.

Poole's gripped the fence as though 'e means to tear the rail in two,
An' eyes my waggin' finger like 'e wants to 'ave a chew.
    Then Digger Smith 'e-grins at Poole, an' then 'e looks at me,
    An' sez, quite soft an' friendly-like, "Winnin' the war?" sez 'e.

Now, Poole deserves it, an' I'm pleased the lad give 'im that jolt.
'E goes fair mad in argument when once 'e gets a holt.
    "Yeh make me sad," sez Digger Smith; "the both uv you," sez 'e.
    "The both uv us! Gawstruth!" sez I. "You ain't includin' me?"

"Well, it takes two to make a row," sez little Digger Smith.
"A bloke can't argue 'less 'e 'as a bloke to argue with
    I've come 'ome from a dinkum scrap to find this land uv light.
    Is chasin' its own tail around an' callin' it a fight.

"We've seen a thing or two, us blokes 'oo've fought on many fronts;
An' we've 'ad time to think a bit between the fightin' stunts.

We've seen big things, an' thought big things, an' all the silly fuss,
That used to get us rattled once, seems very small to us.

"P'r'aps we 'ave 'ad some skite knocked out, an p'r'aps we see more
     clear;
But seems to us there's plenty cleanin'-up to do round 'ere.
     We've learnt a little thing or two, an' we 'ave unlearnt 'eaps,
     An' silly partisans, with us, is counted out for keeps.

This takin' sides jist for the sake uv takin' sides—Aw, 'Struth!
I used to do them things one time, back in me foolish youth.
     Out There, when I remembered things, I've kicked meself reel good.
     In football days I barracked once red 'ot for Collin'wood.

"I didn't want to see a game, nor see no justice done.
It never mattered wot occurred as long as my side won;
     The other side was narks an' cows an' rotters to a man,
     But mine was all reel bonzer chaps. I was a partisan.

"It might sound like swelled-'ead," sez Smith. "But show me, if yeh
     can." . . . .
"'Old 'ard," sez Poole. "Jist tell me this: wot is a partisan?"
     Then Digger Smith starts to ixplain; Poole interrupts straight out;
     An' I wades in to give my views, an' 'as to nearly shout.

We battles on for one good hour. My team sleeps where it stands;
An' Poole 'as tossed the spade away to talk with both 'is 'ands;
     An' Smith 'as dropped the maul 'e 'ad. Then I looks round to see
     Doreen quite close. She smiles at us. "Winnin' the war?" sez she.

A DIGGER'S TALE

"'My oath!" the Duchess sez. 'You'd not ixpect
    Sich things as that. Yeh don't mean kangaroos?
Go hon!' she sez, or words to that effect—
    (It's 'ard to imitate the speech they use)—
I tells 'er, 'Straight; I drives 'em four-in-'and
        'Ome in my land.'

"You 'ear a lot," sez little Digger Smith,
    "About 'ow English swells is so stand-off.
Don't yeh believe it; it's a silly myth.
    I've been reel cobbers with the British toff
While I'm on leave; for Blighty liked our crowd,
        An' done us proud.

"Us Aussies was the goods in London town
    When I was there. If they jist twigged yer 'at
The Dooks would ask yeh could yeh keep one down.
    An' Earls would 'ang out 'Welcome' on the mat
An' sling yeh invites to their stately 'alls
        For fancy balls.

"This Duchess—I ain't quite sure uv 'er rank;
    She might uv been a Peeress. I dunno.
I meets 'er 'usband first. 'E owns a bank,
    I 'eard, an' 'arf a dozen mints or so.
A dinkum toff. 'E sez, 'Come 'ome with me
        An' 'ave some tea.'

"That's 'ow I met this Duchess Wot's-er-name—
    Or Countess—never mind 'er moniker;
I ain't no 'and at this 'ere title game—
    An' right away, I was reel pals with 'er.
'Now, tell me all about yer 'ome,' sez she,
        An' smiles at me.

"That knocks me out. I know it ain't no good
    Paintin' word-picters uv the things I done
Out 'ome 'ere, barrackin' for Collin'wood,
    Or puntin' on the flat at Flemington.
I know this Baroness uv Wot-yeh-call
        Wants somethin' tall.

"I thinks reel 'ard; an' then I lets it go.
    I tells 'er, out at Richmond, on me Run—
A little place uv ten square mile or so—
    I'm breedin' boomerangs; which is reel fun,

When I ain't troubled by the wild Jonops
    That eats me crops.

"I talks about the wondrous Boshter Bird
    That builds 'er nest up in the Cobber Tree,
An' 'atches out 'er young on May the third,
    Stric' to the minute, jist at 'arf pas' three.
'Er eyes get big. She sez, 'Can it be true?'
    'Er eyes was blue.

"An' then I speaks uv sport, an' tells 'er 'ow
    In 'untin' our wild Wowsers we imploy
Large packs uv Barrackers, an' 'ow their row
    Wakes echoes in the forests uv Fitzroy,
Where lurks the deadly Shicker Snake 'oo's breath
    Is certain death.

"I'm goin' on to talk uv kangaroos,
    An' 'ow I used to drive 'em four-in-'and.
'Wot?' sez the Marchioness. 'Them things in Zoos
    That 'ops about? I've seen 'em in the Strand
In *double 'arness*; but I ain't seen four.
    Tell me some more.'

"I baulks a bit at that; an' she sez, 'Well,
    There ain't no cause at all for you to feel
Modest about the things you 'ave to tell;
    An' wot yeh say sounds wonderfully reel.
Your talk'—an' 'ere I seen 'er eyelids flick—
    'Makes me 'omesick.

"'I reckerlect,' she sez—'Now, let me see—
    In Gippsland, long ago, when I was young,
I 'ad a little pet Corroboree'
    (I sits up in me chair like I was stung);
'On its 'ind legs,' she sez, 'it used to stand.
    Fed from me 'and.'

"Uv course, I threw me alley in right there.
    This Princess was a dinkum Aussie girl.
I can't do nothin' else but sit an' stare,
    Thinkin' so rapid that me 'air roots curl.
But 'er? She sez, 'I ain't 'eard talk so good
    Since my child'ood.

"'I wish,' sez she, 'I could be back again
  Beneath the wattle an' that great blue sky.
It's like a breath uv 'ome to meet you men.
  You've done reel well,' she sez. 'Don't you be shy.
When yer in Blighty once again,' sez she,
    'Come an' see me.'

"I don't see 'er no more; 'cos I stopped one.
  But, 'fore I sails, I gits a billy doo
Which sez, 'Give my love to the dear ole Sun,
  An' take an exile's blessin' 'ome with you.
An' if you 'ave some boomerangs to spare,
    Save me a pair.

"'I'd like to see 'em play about,' she wrote,
  'Out on me lawn, an' stroke their pretty fur.
God bless yeh, boy.' An' then she ends 'er note,
  'Yer dinkum cobber,' an' 'er moniker.
A sport? You bet! She's marri'd to an Earl—
    An Aussie girl."

HALF
A MAN

"I wash me 'ands uv 'im," I tells 'em, straight.
　"You women can do wot yeh dash well like
I leave this 'arf a man to 'is own fate;
　I've done me bit, an' now I'm gone on strike.
Do wot yeh please; but don't arsk 'elp from me;
'E's give me nerves; so now I'll let 'im be."

Doreen an' ole Mar Flood 'as got a scheme.
　They've been conspirin' for a week or more
About this Digger Smith, an' now they dream
　They've got 'is fucher waitin' in cool store
To 'and 'im out, an' fix 'im up for life.
But they've got Buckley's, as I tells me wife.

I've seen 'em whisperin' up in our room.
　Now they wants me to join in the debate;
But, "Nix," I tells 'em. "I ain't in the boom,
　An' Digger Smith ain't risin' to me bait;
'E's fur too fly a fish for me to catch,
An' two designin' women ain't 'is match."

I puts me foot down firm, an' tells 'em, No!
　Their silly plan's a thing I wouldn't touch.
An' then me wife, for 'arf an hour or so,
　Talks to me confident, of nothin' much;
Then, 'fore I know it, I am all red 'ot
Into the scheme, an' leader uv the plot.

'Twas Mar Flood starts it. She got 'old uv 'im—
　You know the way they 'ave with poor, weak men—
She drops a tear or two concernin' Jim;
　Tells 'im wot women 'ave to bear; an' then
She got 'im talkin', like a woman can.
'E never would 'ave squeaked to any man.

She leads 'im on—it's crook the way they scheme—
　To talk about this girl 'e's left be'ind.
Not that she's pryin'! Why, she wouldn't dream!—
　But speakin' uv it might jist ease 'is mind.
Then, 'fore 'e knows, 'e's told, to 'is su'prise,
Name an' address—an' colour uv 'er eyes!

An' then she's off 'ere, plottin' with Doreen—
　Bustin' a confidence, I tells 'em, flat.

But all me roustin' leaves 'em both serene:
  Women don't see a little thing like that.
An' I ain't cooled off yet before they've got
Me workin' for 'em in this crooked plot.

Nex' day Mar Flood she takes 'er Sund'y dress
  An' 'er best little bonnet up to town.
'Er game's to see the girl at this address
  An' sprag 'er in regard to comin' down
To take Smith be su'prise. My part's to fix
A meetin' so there won't be any mix.

I tips, some'ow, that girl won't 'esitate.
  She don't. She comes right back with Mar nex' day,
All uv a fluster. When I seen 'er state
  I thinks I'd best see Digger straight away;
'Cos, if I don't, 'e's bound to 'ear the row,
With 'er: "Where is 'e? Can't I see 'im now?"

I finds 'im in the paddick down at Flood's
  I 'ums an' 'ars a bit about the crops.
'E don't say nothin': goes on baggin' spuds.
  "'Ow would yeh like?" I sez to 'im, an' stops.
"'Ow would it be?" ... 'E stands an' looks at me:
"Now, wot the 'Ell's got into you?" sez 'e.

That don't restore me confidence a bit—
  The drarmer isn't goin' as I tipped.
I corfs, an' makes another shot at it,
  While 'e looks at me like 'e thinks I'm dipped.
"Well—jist suppose?" I sez; an' then I turn
An' see 'er standin' there among the fern.

She don't want no prelimin'ries, this tart;
  She's broke away before they rung the bell;
She's beat the gun, an' got a flyin' start.
  Smith makes a funny noise, an' I sez, "'Ell!"
An' gives 'em imitations uv the chase.
But, as I went, I caught sight uv 'er face.

That's all I want to know. An', as I ran,
  I 'ears 'er cry, "My man! Man an' a 'arf!
Don't fool me with yer talk uv 'arf a man!" ...
  An' then I 'ears ole Digger start to larf.

Frontispiece from *Digger Smith*

It was a funny larf, so 'elp me bob:
Fair in the middle uv it come a sob . . .

I don't see Digger till the other night.
   "Well, 'Arf-a-man," I sez. "'Ow goes it now?"
"Yes, 'arf a man," sez 'e. "Yeh got it right;
   I can't change that, alone, not any'ow.
But she is mendin' things." 'E starts to larf.
"Some day," 'e sez, "she'll be the better 'arf."

JIM

"Now, be the Hokey Fly!" sez Peter Begg.
"Suppose 'e comes 'ome with a wooden leg.
  Suppose 'e isn't fit to darnce at all,
  Then, ain't we 'asty fixin' up this ball?
A little tournament at Bridge is my
Idear," sez Peter. "Be the Hokey Fly!"

Ole Peter Begg is gettin' on in years.
'E owns a reel good farm; an' all 'e fears
  Is that some girl will land 'im, by an' by,
  An' share it with 'im—be the Hokey Fly.
That's 'is pet swear-word, an' I dunno wot
'E's meanin', but 'e uses it a lot.

"Darncin'!" growls Begg. We're fixin' up the 'all
With bits uv green stuff for a little ball
  To welcome Jim, 'oo's comin' 'ome nex' day.
  We're 'angin' flags around to make things gay,
An' shiftin' chairs, an' candle-greasin' floors,
As is our way when blokes come 'ome from wars.

"A little game uv Bridge," sez Peter Begg,
"Would be more decent like, an' p'r'aps a keg
  Uv somethin' if the 'ero's feelin' dry.
  But this 'ere darncin'! Be the Hokey Fly,
These selfish women never thinks at all
About the guest; they only wants the ball.

"Now, cards," sez Begg, "amuses ev'ry one.
An' then our soldier guest could 'ave 'is fun
  If 'ed lost *both* 'is legs. It makes me sick—
  'Ere! Don't yeh spread that candle-grease too thick.
Yeh're wastin' it; an' us men 'as to buy
Enough for nonsense, be the Hokey Fly!"

Begg, 'e ain't never keen on wastin' much.
"Peter," I sez, "it's you that needs a crutch.
  Why don't yeh get a wife, an' settle down?"
  'E looks reel fierce, an' answers, with a frown,
"Do you think I am goin' to be rooked
For 'arf me tucker, jist to get it cooked?"

I lets it go at that; an' does me job;
An' when a little later on I lob
  Along the 'omeward track, down by Flood's gate
  I meet ole Digger Smith, an' stops to state

Me views about the weather an' the war . . .
'E tells me Jim gets 'ere nex' day, at four.

An', as we talk, I sees along the road
A strange bloke 'umpin' some queer sort uv load.
　　I points 'im out to Smith an' sez, "'Oo's that?
　　Looks like a soldier, don't 'e, be 'is 'at?"
"Stranger," sez Digger, "be the cut uv 'im."
But, trust a mother's eyes . . . *"It's Jim! My Jim!"*

"My Jim!" I 'ears; an', scootin' up the track
Come Missus Flood, with Flo close at 'er back.
　　It was a race, for lover an' for son;
　　They finished neck an' neck; but mother won,
For it was 'er that got the first good 'ug.
(I'm so took back I stands there like a mug).

Then come Flo's turn; an' Jim an' Digger they
Shake 'ands without no fancy, gran'-stand play.
　　Yeh'd think they parted yesterd'y, them two,
　　For all the wild 'eroics that they do.
"Yeh done it, lad," sez Jim. "I knoo yeh would."
"You bet," sez Smith; "but I'm all to the good."

Then, uv a sudden, all their tongues is loosed.
They finds me there an' I am intrajuiced;
　　An' Jim tells 'ow it was 'e come to land
　　So soon, while Mar an' Flo each 'olds a 'and.
But, jist as sudden, they all stop an' stare
Down to the 'ouse, at Dad Flood standin' there.

'E's got 'is 'and up shadin' off the sun.
Then 'e starts up to them; but Dad don't run:
　　'E isn't 'owlin' for 'is lost boy's kiss;
　　'E's got 'is own sweet way in things like this.
'E wanders up, an' stands an' looks at Jim;
An', spare me days, that look was extra grim!

I seen the mother pluckin' at 'er dress;
I seen the girl's white face an' 'er distress.
　　An' Digger Smith, 'e looks reel queer to me:
　　Grinnin' inside 'imself 'e seemed to be.
At last Dad sez—oh, 'e's a tough ole gun!—
"Well, are yeh sorry now for wot yeh done?"

Jim gives a start; but answers with a grin,
"Well, Dad, I 'ave been learnin' discipline.

An' tho' I ain't quite sure wot did occur
Way back"—'e's grinnin' worse—"I'm sorry, sir."
(It beats me, that, about these soldier blokes:
They're always grinnin', like all things was jokes.)

P'r'aps Dad is gettin' dull in 'is ole age;
But 'e don't seem to see Jim's cammyflage.
  P'r'aps 'e don't want to; for, in 'is ole eye,
  I seen a twinkle as 'e give reply.
"Nex' week," 'e sez, "we will begin to cart
The taters. Yeh can make another start."

But then 'e grabs Jim's 'and. I seen the joy
In mother's eyes. "Now, welcome 'ome, me boy."
  Sez Dad; an' then 'e adds, "Yeh've made me proud;"
  That's all. An' 'e don't say it none too loud.
Dad don't express 'is feelin's in a shout;
It cost 'im somethin' to git that much out.

                    * * * *

We 'ad the darnce. An', spite uv all Begg's fears,
Jim darnced like 'e could keep it up for years;
  Mostly with Flo. We don't let up till three;
  An' then ole Peter Begg, Doreen an' me
We walk together 'ome, an' on the way,
Doreen 'as quite a lot uv things to say.

"Did you see Flo?" sez she. "Don't she look grand?
That Jim's the luckiest in all the land—
  An' little Smith—that girl uv 'is, I'm sure,
  She'll bring 'im 'appiness that will endure."
She 'ugs my arm, then sez, "'Usband or wife,
If it's the right one, is the wealth uv life."

I sneaks a look at Begg, an' answers, "Yes,
Yeh're right, ole girl; that's the reel 'appiness.
  An' if ole, lonely growlers was to know
  The worth uv 'appy marridge 'ere below,
They'd swap their bank-books for a wife," sez I.
Sez Peter Begg, *"Well! Be the—Hokey—Fly!"*

THE GLUGS OF GOSH

THE
GLUG
QUEST

Follow the river and cross the ford,
  Follow again to the wobbly bridge,
Turn to the left at the notice-board,
  Climbing the cow-track over the ridge;
Tip-toe soft by the little red house,
  Hold your breath if they touch the latch,
Creep to the slip-rails, still as a mouse
  Then . . . run like mad for the bracken patch.

Worm your way where the fern-fronds tall
  Fashion a lace-work over your head,
Hemming you in with a high, green wall;
  Then, when the thrush calls once, stop dead.
Ask of the old grey wallaby there—
  Him prick-eared by a woollybutt tree—
How to encounter a Glug, and where
  The country of Gosh, famed Gosh, may be.

  But if he is scornful, if he is dumb,
  Hush! There's another way left. Then come.

On a white, still night, where the dead tree bends
  Over the track, like a waiting ghost
Travel the winding road that wends
  Down to the shore on an Eastern coast.
Follow it down where the wake of the moon
  Kisses the ripples of silver sand;
Follow it on where the night seas croon
  A traveller's tale to the listening land.

Step not jauntily, not too grave,
  Till the lip of the languorous sea you greet;
Wait till the wash of the thirteenth wave
  Tumbles a jellyfish out at your feet.
Not too hopefully, not forlorn,
  Whisper a word of your earnest quest;
Shed not a tear if he turns in scorn
  And sneers in your face like a fish possessed.

  Hist! Hope on! There is yet a way.
  Brooding jellyfish won't be gay.

Wait till the clock in the tower booms three,
  And the big bank opposite gnashes its doors,
Then glide with a gait that is carefully free
  By the great brick building of seventeen floors;

Haste by the draper who smirks at his door,
  Straining to lure you with sinister force,
Turn up the lane by the second-hand store,
  And halt by the light bay carrier's horse.

By the carrier's horse with the long, sad face
  And the wisdom of years in his mournful eye;
Bow to him thrice with a courtier's grace,
  Proffer your query, and pause for reply.
Eagerly ask for a hint of the Glug,
  Pause for reply with your hat in your hand;
If he responds with a snort and a shrug
  Strive to interpret and understand.

  Rare will a carrier's horse condescend.
  Yet there's another way. On to the end!

Catch the four-thirty; your ticket in hand,
  Punched by the porter who broods in his box;
Journey afar to the sad, soggy land,
  Wearing your shot-silk lavender socks;
Wait at the creek by the moss-grown log
  Till the blood of a slain day reddens the West.
Hark for the croak of a gentleman frog,
  Of a corpulent frog with a white satin vest.

Go as he guides you, over the marsh,
  Treading with care on the slithery stones,
Heedless of night winds moaning and harsh
  That seize you and freeze you and search for your bones.
On to the edge of a still, dark pool,
  Banishing thoughts of your warm wool rug;
Gaze in the depths of it, placid and cool,
  And long in your heart for one glimpse of a Glug.

  "Krock!" Was he mocking you? "Krock! Kor-r-rock!"
  Well, you bought a return, and it's past ten o'clock.

Choose you a night when the intimate stars
  Carelessly prattle of cosmic affairs.
Flat on your back, with your nose pointing Mars,
  Search for the star who fled South from the Bears.
Gaze for an hour at that little blue star,
  Giving him, cheerfully, wink for his wink;
Shrink to the size of the being you are;
  Sneeze if you have to, but softly; then think.

Throw wide the portals and let your thoughts run
    Over the earth like a galloping herd.
Bounds to profundity let there be none,
    Let there be nothing too madly absurd.
Ponder on pebbles or stock exchange shares,
    On the mission of man or the life of a bug,
On planets or billiards, policemen or bears,
    Alert all the time for the sight of a Glug.

Meditate deeply on softgoods or sex,
    On carraway seeds or the causes of bills,
Biology, art, or mysterious wrecks,
    Or the tattered white fleeces of clouds on blue hills.
Muse upon ologies, freckles and fog,
    Why hermits live lonely and grapes in a bunch,
On the ways of a child or the mind of a dog,
    Or the oyster you bolted last Friday at lunch.

Heard you no sound like a shuddering sigh?
Or the great shout of laughter that swept down the sky?
Saw you no sign on the wide Milky Way?
Then there's naught left to you now but to pray.

Sit you at eve when the Shepherd in Blue
    Calls from the West to his clustering sheep,
Then pray for the moods that old mariners woo,
    For the thoughts of young mothers who watch their babes sleep.
Pray for the heart of an innocent child,
    For the tolerant scorn of a weary old man,
For the petulant grief of a prophet reviled,
    For the wisdom you lost when your whiskers began.

Pray for the pleasures that he who was you
    Found in the mud of a shower-fed pool,
For the fears that he felt and the joys that he knew
    When a little green lizard crept into the school.
Pray as they pray who are maddened by wine:
    For distraction from self and a spirit at rest.
Now, deep in the heart of you search for a sign—
    If there be naught of it, vain is your quest.

Lay down the book, for to follow the tale
Were to trade in false blame, as all mortals who fail.
And may the gods salve you on life's dreary round;
For 'tis whispered: "Who finds not, 'tis he shall be found!"

**JOI,
THE GLUG**

The Glugs abide in a far, far land
That is partly pebbles and stones and sand,
  But mainly earth of a chocolate hue,
  When it isn't purple or slightly blue.
And the Glugs live there with their aunts and wives,
In draught-proof tenements all their lives.
  And they climb the trees when the weather is wet,
  To see how high they can really get.
    Pray, don't forget,
  This is chiefly done when the weather is wet.

And every shadow that flits and hides,
And every stream that glistens and glides
  And laughs its way from a highland height,
  All know the Glugs quite well by sight,
And they say, "Our test is the best by far;
For a Glug is a Glug; so there you are!
  And they climb the trees when it drizzles or hails
  To get electricity into their nails;
    And the Glug that fails
  Is a luckless Glug, if it drizzles or hails."

Now, the Glugs abide in the land of Gosh;
And they work all day for the sake of Splosh.
  For Splosh, the First, is the nation's pride,
  And King of the Glugs on his uncle's side.
And they sleep at night, for the sake of rest,
For their doctors say this suits them best.
  And they climb the trees, as a general rule,
  For exercise, when the weather is cool.
    They're taught at school
  To climb the trees when the weather is cool.

And the whispering grass on the gay green hills,
And every cricket that skirls and shrills,
  And every moonbeam, gleaming white,
  All know the Glugs quite well by sight.
And they say, "It is safe, is the test we bring;
For a Glug is an awfully Gluglike thing.
  And they climb the trees when there's sign of a fog,
  To scan the land for a feasible dog;
    They love to jog
  Thro' dells in quest of a feasible dog."

The Glugs eat meals three times a day
Because their fathers ate that way;
   Their grandpas said the scheme was good
   To help the Glugs digest their food.
And 'tis wholesome food the Glugs have got
For it says so plain on the tin and pot.
   And they climb the trees when the weather is dry
   To get a glimpse of the pale green sky.
     We don't know why,
   But they like to gaze on a pale green sky.

And every cloud that sails aloft,
And every breeze that blows so soft,
   And every star that shines at night,
   All know the Glugs quite well by sight.
For they say, "Our test, it is safe and true;
What one Glug does, the other Glugs do;
   And they climb the trees when the weather is hot
   For a bird's-eye view of the garden plot.
     Of course, it's rot,
   But they love that view of the garden plot."

At half-past two on a Wednesday morn
A most peculiar Glug was born;
   And, later on, when he grew a man,
   He scoffed and sneered at the Chosen Plan.
"It's wrong!" said this Glug, whose name was Joi.
"Bah!" said the Glugs. "He's a crazy boy!"
   And they climbed the trees, as the West wind stirred,
   To hark to the note of the Guffer Bird.
     It seems absurd,
   But they're foolishly fond of the Guffer Bird.

And every reed that rustles and sways
By the gurgling river that plashes and plays,
   And the beasts of the dread, neurotic night
   All know the Glugs quite well by sight.
And, "Why," say they; "It is easily done;
For a dexter Glug's like a sinister one!"
   And they climb the trees. Oh, they climb the trees!
   And they bark their knuckles and chafe their knees;
   And 'tis one of the world's great mysteries
     That things like these
   Get into serious histories.

THE
STONES
OF GOSH

Now, here is a tale of the Glugs of Gosh,
And a wonderful tale I ween,
   Of the Glugs of Gosh and their great King Splosh
   And Tush, his virtuous Queen.
And here is a tale of the crafty Ogs,
   In the neighbouring land of Podge;
Of their sayings and doings and plottings and brewings,
   And something about Sir Stodge.
     Wise to profundity,
     Stout to rotundity,
   That was the Knight, Sir Stodge.

Oh, the King was rich, and the Queen was fair,
And they made a very respectable pair.
   And whenever a Glug in that peaceful land,
   Did anything no one could understand,
The Knight, Sir Stodge, he looked in a book,
And charged that Glug with the crime called Crook;
   And the great Judge Fudge, who wore for a hat
   The sacred skin of a tortoiseshell cat,
He fined that Glug for his action rash,
And frequently asked a deposit in cash.
   Then every Glug, he went home to his rest
   With his head in a bag and his toes to the West;
     For they knew it was best,
   Since their grandpas slept with their toes to the West.

But all of the tale that is so far told
   Has nothing whatever to do
With the Ogs of Podge, and their crafty dodge,
   And the trade in pickles and glue.
To trade with the Glugs came the Ogs to Gosh,
   And they said in seductive tones,
   "We'll sell you pianers and pickles and spanners
For seventeen shiploads of stones:
     Smooth 'uns or nobbly 'uns,
     Firm 'uns or wobbly 'uns,
   All that we ask is stones."

And the King said, "What?" and the Queen said, "Why,
That is awfully cheap to the things I buy!
   For that grocer of ours in the light brown hat
   Asks two and eleven for pickles like that!"

But a Glug stood up with a wart on his nose,
And cried, "Your Majesties! Ogs is foes!"
   But the Glugs cried, "Peace! Will you hold your jaw!
   How did our grandpas fashion the law?"

Said the Knight, Sir Stodge, as he opened his Book,
"When the goods were cheap then the goods they took."
   So they fined the Glug with the wart on his nose
   For wearing a wart with his everyday clothes.
And the goods were bought thro' a Glug named Ghones,
And the Ogs went home with their loads of stones,
     Which they landed with glee in the land of Podge.
     Do you notice the dodge?
   Nor yet did the Glugs, nor the Knight, Sir Stodge.

In the following Summer the Ogs came back
   With a cargo of eight-day clocks,
And hand-painted screens, and sewing machines,
   And mangles, and scissors, and socks.
And they said, "For these excellent things we bring
   We are ready to take more stones;
     And in bricks or road-metal
     For goods you will settle
   Indented by your Mister Ghones."
     Cried the Glugs praisingly,
     "Why, how amazingly
   Smart of industrious Ghones!"

And the King said, "Hum," and the Queen said, "Oo!
That curtain! What a bee—ootiful blue!"
   But a Glug stood up with some very large ears,
   And said, "There is more in this thing than appears!
And we ought to be taxing these goods of the Ogs,
Or our industries soon will be gone to the dogs."
   And the King said, "Bosh! You're un-Gluggish and rude!"
   And the Queen said, "What an absurd attitude!"
Then the Glugs cried, "Down with political quacks!
How did our grandpas look at a tax?"
   So the Knight, Sir Stodge, he opened his Book,
   "No tax," said he, "wherever I look."
Then they fined the Glug with the prominent ears
For being old-fashioned by several years;
     And the Ogs went home with the stones, full-steam.
     Do you notice the scheme?
   Nor yet did the Glugs in their dreamiest dream.

Then every month to the land of Gosh
  The Ogs, they continued to come,
With buttons and hooks, and medical books,
  And rotary engines, and rum,
Large cases with labels, occasional tables,
  Hair tonic, and fiddles and 'phones;
And the Glugs, while concealing their joy in the dealing,
  Paid promptly in nothing but stones.
    Why, it was screamingly
    Laughable, seemingly—
  Asking for nothing but stones!

And the King said, "Haw!" and the Queen said, "Oh!
Our drawing-room now is a heavenly show
  Of large overmantels, and whatnots, and chairs,
  And a statue of Splosh at the head of the stairs!"
But a Glug stood up with a cast in his eye,
And he said, "Far too many such baubles we buy;
  With all the Gosh factories closing their doors,
  And importers' warehouses lining our shores."
  But the Glugs cried, "Down with such meddlesome fools!
What did our grandpas state in their rules?"
  And the Knight, Sir Stodge, he opened his Book:
  "To Cheapness," he said, "was the road they took."
Then every Glug who was not too fat
Turned seventeen handsprings, and jumped on his hat.
  They fined the Glug with the cast in his eye
  For looking both ways—which he did not deny—
And for having no visible precedent, which
Is a crime in the poor and a fault in the rich.

So the Glugs continued, with greed and glee,
To buy cheap clothing, and pills, and tea;
  Till every Glug in the land of Gosh
  Owned three clean shirts and a fourth in the wash.
But they all grew idle, and fond of ease,
And easy to swindle, and hard to please;
  And the voice of Joi was a lonely voice,
  When he railed at Gosh for its foolish choice.
But the great King grinned, and the good Queen gushed,
As the goods of the Ogs were madly rushed.
  And the Knight, Sir Stodge, with a wave of his hand,
  Declared it a happy and prosperous land.

OGS

I chanced one day, in the middle of May,
  There came to the great King Splosh
A policeman, who said, while scratching his head,
  "There isn't a stone in Gosh
To throw at a dog; for the crafty Og,
  Last Saturday week, at one,
Took our last blue-metal, in order to settle
  A bill for a toy pop-gun."
    Said the King, jokingly,
    "Why, how provokingly
  Weird; but we have the gun."

And the King said, "Well, we are stony broke."
But the Queen could not see it was much of a joke.
  And she said, "If the metal is all used up,
  Pray what of the costume I want for the Cup?
It all seems so dreadfully simple to me.
The stones? Why, import them from over the sea."
  But a Glug stood up with a mole on his chin,
  And said, with a most diabolical grin,
"Your Majesties, down in the country of Podge,
A spy has discovered a very 'cute dodge.
  And the Ogs are determined to wage a war
  On Gosh, next Friday, at half-past four."
Then the Glugs all cried, in a terrible fright,
"How did our grandfathers manage a fight?"

Then the Knight, Sir Stodge, he opened his Book,
And he read, "Some very large stones they took,
  And flung at the foe, with exceeding force;
  Which as very effective, tho' rude, of course."
And lo, with sorrowful wails and moans,
The Glugs cried, "Where, Oh, where are the stones?"
  And some rushed North, and a few ran West;
  Seeking the substitutes seeming best.
And they gathered the pillows and cushions and rugs
From the homes of the rich and middle-class Glugs.
  And a hasty message they managed to send
  Craving the loan of some bricks from a friend.

On the Friday, exactly at half-past four,
  Came the Ogs with triumphant glee.
And the first of their stones hit poor Mister Ghones,
  The captain of industry.
Then a pebble of Podge took the Knight, Sir Stodge,

In the curve of his convex vest.
He gurgled "Un-Gluggish!" His heart growing sluggish,
He solemnly sank to rest.
   'Tis inconceivable,
   Scarcely believable,
Yet, he was sent to rest.

And the King said, "Ouch!" and the Queen said, "Oo!
My bee-ootiful drawing-room! What shall I do?"
   But the warlike Ogs, they hurled great rocks
   Thro' the works of the wonderful eight-day clocks
They had sold to the Glugs but a month before—
Which was very absurd; but, of course, 'twas war.
   And the Glugs cried, "What would our grandfathers do
   If they hadn't the stones that they one time threw?"
But the Knight, Sir Stodge, and his mystic Book
Oblivious slept in a grave-yard nook.

Then a Glug stood out with a pot in his hand,
As the King was bewailing the fate of his land,
   And he said, "If these Ogs you desire to retard,
   Then hit them quite frequent with *anything* hard."
So the Glugs seized anvils, and editors' chairs,
And smote the Ogs with them unawares;
   And bottles of pickles, and clocks they threw,
   And books of poems, and gherkins, and glue,
Which they'd bought with the stones—as, of course, you know—
From the Ogs but a couple of months ago.
   Which was simply inane, when you reason it o'er;
   And uneconomic, but then, it was war.

When they'd fought for a night and the most of a day,
The Ogs threw the last of their metal away.
   Then they went back to Podge, well content with their fun,
   And, with much satisfaction, declared they had won.
And the King of the Glugs gazed around on his land,
And saw nothing but stones strewn on every hand:
   Great stones in the palace, and stones in the street,
   And stones on the house-tops and under the feet.
And he said, with a desperate look on his face,
"There is nothing so ghastly as stones out of place.
   And, no doubt, this Og scheme was a very smart dodge.
   But whom does it profit—my people, or Podge?"

153

**EMILY
ANN**

Government muddled, departments dazed,
Fear and confusion wherever he gazed;
  Order insulted, authority spurned,
  Dread and distraction wherever he turned—
Oh, the great King Splosh was a sad, sore king,
With never a statesman to straighten the thing.

Glugs all importunate urging their claims,
With selfish intent and ulterior aims,
  Glugs with petitions for this and for that,
  Standing ten deep on the royal door-mat,
Raging when nobody answered their ring—
Oh, the Great King Splosh was a careworn king.

And he looked to the right, and he glanced to the left,
And he glared at the roof like a monarch bereft
  Of his wisdom and wits and his wealth all in one;
  And, at least once a minute, asked, "What's to be done?"
But the Swanks stood around him and answered, with groans,
"Your Majesty, Gosh is half buried in stones!"

"How now?" cried the King. "Is there not in my land
One Glug who can cope with this dreadful demand:
  A rich man, a poor man, a beggar man, thief—
  I reck not his rank so he lessen my grief—
A soldier, a sailor, a—?" Raising his head,
With relief in his eye, "Now, I mind me!" he said:

"I mind me a Tinker, and what once befel,
When I think, on the whole, he was treated not well.
  But he shall be honoured, and he shall be famed
  If he read me this riddle. But how is he named?
Some commonplace title, like—Simon?—No—Sym!
Go, send out my riders, and scour Gosh for him."

They rode for a day to the sea in the South,
Calling the name of him, hand to the mouth.
  They rode for a day to the hills in the East,
  But signs of a tinker saw never the least.
Then they rode to the North thro' a whole day long,
And paused in the even to hark to a song.

"Kettles and pans! Kettles and pans!
Oh, who can show tresses like Emily Ann's?
  Brown in the shadow and gold at the tips.
  Bright as the smile on her beckoning lips.

Great King Splosh
and Tush his Virtuous Queen

Bring out your kettle! O kettle or pan!
So I buy me a ribband for Emily Ann."

With his feet in the grass, and his back to a tree,
Merry as only a tinker can be,
   Busily tinkering, mending a pan,
   Singing as only a merry man can . . .
"Sym!" cried the riders. "'Tis thus you are styled?"
And he paused in his singing, and nodded and smiled.

Said he: "Last eve, when the sun was low,
Down thro' the bracken I watched her go—
   Down thro' the bracken, with simple grace—
   And the glory of eve shone full on her face;
And there on the sky-line it lingered a span,
So loth to be leaving my Emily Ann."

With hands to their faces the riders smiled.
"Sym," they said—"be it so you're styled—
   Behold, great Splosh, our sorrowing King,
   Has sent us hither, that we may bring
To the palace in Gosh a Glug so named,
That he may be honoured and justly famed."

"Yet," said Sym, as he tinkered his can,
"What should you know of her, Emily Ann?
   Early as cock-crow yester morn
   I watched young sunbeams, newly born,
As out of the East they frolicked and ran,
Eager to greet her, my Emily Ann."

"King Splosh," said the riders, "is bowed with grief;
And the glory of Gosh is a yellowing leaf.
   Up with you, Tinker! There's work ahead,
   With a King forsaken, and Swanks in dread,
To whom may we turn for the salving of man?"
And Sym, he answered them, "Emily Ann."

Said he: "Whenever I watch her pass,
With her skirts so high o'er the dew-wet grass,
   I envy every blade the bruise
   It earns in the cause of her twinkling shoes.
Oh, the dew-wet grass, where this morn she ran,
Was doubly jewelled for Emily Ann."

"But haste!" they cried. "By the palace gates
A sorrowing king for a tinker waits.

And what shall we answer our Lord the King
If never a tinker hence we bring,
To tinker a kingdom so sore amiss?"
But Sym, he said to them, "Answer him this:

'Every eve, when the clock chimes eight,
I kiss her fair, by her mother's gate:
    Twice, all reverent, on the brow—
    Once for a pray'r, and once for a vow;
Twice on her eyes that they may shine,
Then, full on the mouth because she's mine.'"

"Calf!" sneered the riders. "O Tinker, heed!
Mount and away with us, we must speed.
    All Gosh is agog for the coming of Sym.
    Garlands and greatness are waiting for him:
Garlands of roses, and garments of red,
And a chaplet for crowning a conqueror's head.

"Listen," quoth Sym, as he stirred his fire.
"Once in my life have I known desire.
    Then, Oh, but the touch of her kindled a flame
    That burns as a sun by the candle of fame.
And a blessing and boon for a poor tinker man
Looks out from the eyes of my Emily Ann."

Then they said to him, "Fool! Do you cast aside
Promise of honour, and place, and pride,
    Gold for the asking, and power o'er men—
    Working your will with the stroke of a pen?
Vexed were the King if you ride not with us."
But Sym, he said to them, "Answer him thus:

'Ease and honour and leave to live—
These are the gifts that a king may give ... '
    'Twas over the meadow I saw her first;
    And my lips grew parched like a man athirst.
Oh, my treasure was ne'er in the gift of man;
For the gods have given me Emily Ann."

"Listen," said they, "O you crazy Sym.
Roses perish, and eyes grow dim.
    Lustre fades from the fairest hair.
    Who weds a woman links arms with care.
But women there are in the city of Gosh—
Ay, even the daughters of good King Splosh ..."

"Care," said Sym, "is a weed that springs
Even to-day in the garden of kings.
   And I, who have lived 'neath the tent of the skies,
   Know of the flowers, and which to prize . . .
Give you good even! For now I must jog."
And he whistled him once to his little red dog.

Into the meadow and over the stile,
Off went the tinker man, singing the while;
   Down by the bracken patch, over the hill,
   With the little red dog at the heel of him still.
And back, as he soberly sauntered along,
There came to the riders the tail of his song:

"Kettles and pans! Kettles and pans!
Strong is my arm if the cause it be man's.
   But a fig for the cause of a cunning old king;
   For Emily Ann will be mine in the Spring.
Then naught shall I labour for Splosh or his plans;
Tho' I'll mend him a kettle. Ho, kettles and pans!"

THE LITTLE RED DOG

The Glugs still live in the land of Gosh,
Under the rule of the great King Splosh;
   And they climb the trees in the Summer and Spring,
   Because it is reckoned the regular thing.
Down in the Valley they live their lives,
Taking the air with their aunts and wives.
   And they climb the trees in the Winter and Fall,
   And count it improper to climb not at all.

And they name their trees with a thousand names,
Calling them after their Arts and Aims;
   And some, they climb for the fun of the thing,
   But most go up at the call of the King.
Some scale a tree that they fear to name,
For it bears great blossoms of scarlet shame.
   But they eat of the fruit of the nameless tree,
   Because they are Glugs, and their choice is free.

But every eve, when the sun goes West,
Over the mountain they call The Blest,
   Whose summit looks down on the city of Gosh,
   Far from the reach of the great King Splosh,
The Glugs gaze up at the heights above,
And feel vague promptings to wondrous love.
   And they whisper a tale of a tinker man,
   Who lives in the mount with his Emily Ann.

A great mother mountain, and kindly is she,
Who nurses young rivers and sends them to sea.
   And, nestled high up on her sheltering lap,
   Is a little red house with a little straw cap
That bears a blue feather of smoke, curling high,
And a bunch of red roses cocked over one eye.
   And the eyes of it glisten and shine in the sun,
   As they look down on Gosh with a twinkle of fun.

There's a gay little garden, a tidy white gate,
And a narrow brown pathway that will not run straight;
   For it turns and it twists and it wanders about
   To the left and the right, as in humorous doubt.
'Tis a humorous path, and a joke from its birth
Till it ends at the door with a wriggle of mirth.
   And here in the mount lives the queer tinker man
   With his little red dog and his Emily Ann.

And, once in a while, when the weather is clear,
When the work is all over, and even is near,
   They walk in the garden and gaze down below
   On the Valley of Gosh, where the young rivers go;
Where the houses of Gosh seem so paltry and vain,
Like a handful of pebbles strewn over the plain;
   Where tiny black forms crawl about in the vale,
   And stare at the mountain they fear them to scale.

And Sym sits him down by his little wife's knee,
With his feet in the grass and his back to a tree;
   And he looks on the Valley and dreams of old years,
   As he strokes his red dog with the funny prick ears.
And he says, "Still they climb in their whimsical way,
While we stand on earth, yet are higher than they.
   Oh, who trusts to a tree is a fool of man!
   For the wise seek the mountains, my Emily Ann."

So lives the queer tinker, nor deems it a wrong,
When the spirit so moves him, to burst into song.
   'Tis a comical song about kettles and pans,
   And the graces and charms that are Emily Ann's.
'Tis a mad, freakish song, but he sings it with zest,
And his little wife vows it of all songs the best.
   And he sings quite a lot, as the Summer days pass,
   With his back to a tree and his feet in the grass.

And the little red dog, who is wise as dogs go,
He will hark to that song for a minute or so,
   With his head on one side, and a serious air.
   Then he makes no remark; but he wanders elsewhere.
And he trots down the garden to gaze now and then
At the curious pranks of a certain blue wren:
   Not a commonplace wren, but a bird marked for fame
   Thro' a grievance in life and a definite aim.

Now, they never fly far and they never fly high,
And they probably couldn't, suppose they should try.
   So the common blue wren is content with his lot:
   He will eat when there's food, and he fasts when there's not.
He flirts and he flutters, his wife by his side,
With his share of content and forgiveable pride.
   And he keeps to the earth, 'mid the bushes and shrubs,
   And he dines very well upon corpulent grubs.

But the little blue wren with a grievance in life,
He was rude to his neighbours and short with his wife.
  For, up in the apple-tree over his nest,
  There dwelt a fat spider who gave him no rest:
A spider so fat, so abnormally stout
That he seemed hardly fitted to waddle about.
  But his eyes were so sharp, and his legs were so spry,
  That he could not be caught; and 'twas folly to try.

Said the wren, as his loud lamentations he hurled
At the little red dog, "It's a rotten old world!
  But my heart would be glad, and my life would be blest
  If I had that fat spider well under my vest.
Then I'd call back my youth, and be seeking to live,
And to tase of the pleasures the world has to give.
  But the world is all wrong, and my mind's in a fog!"
  "Aw, don't be a Glug!" said the little red dog.

Then, up from the grass, where he sat by his tree,
The voice of the Tinker rose fearless and free.

The little dog listened, his head on one side;
Then sought him a spot where a bored dog could hide.

"Kettles and pans! Ho, kettles and pans!
The stars are the gods' but the earth, it is man's!
  Yet down in the shadow dull mortals there are
  Who climb in the tree-tops to snatch at a star;
Seeking content and a surcease of care,
Finding but emptiness everywhere.
  Then make for the mountain, importunate man!
  With a kettle to mend ... and your Emily Ann."

As he cocked a sad eye o'er a sheltering log,
"Oh, a Glug *is* a Glug!" sighed the little red dog.

JIM OF THE HILLS

A MORNING SONG

The thrush is in the wattle tree, an', "O, you pretty dear!"
He's callin' to his little wife for all the bush to hear.
  He's wantin' all the bush to know about his charmin' hen;
  He sings it over fifty times, an' then begins again.
For it's Mornin'! Mornin'! The world is wet with dew,
With tiny drops a-twinkle where the sun comes shinin' thro'.

The thrush is in the wattle tree, red robin's underneath,
The little blue-cap's dodgin' in an' out amongst the heath;
  An' they're singin', boy, they're singin' like they'd bust 'emselves
    to bits;
  While, up above, old Laughin' Jack is havin' forty fits.
For it's Mornin'! Mornin'! The leaves are all ashine:
There's treasure all about the place; an' all of it is mine.

Oh, it's good to be a wealthy man, it's grand to be a king
With mornin' on the forest-land an' joy in everything.
  It's fine to be a healthy man with healthy work to do
  In the singin' land, the clean land, washed again with dew.
When sunlight slants across the trees, an' birds begin to sing,
Then kings may snore in palaces, but I'm awake—and king.

But the king must cook his breakfast, an' the king must sweep the
    floor;
Then out with axe on shoulder to this kingdom at the door,
  His old dog sportin' on ahead, his troubles all behind,
  An' joy mixed in the blood of him because the world is kind.
For it's Mornin'! Mornin'! Time to out an' strive!
Oh, there's not a thing I'm askin' else but just to be alive!

My friends are in the underbrush, my friends are in the trees,
An' merrily they welcome me with mornin' melodies.
  Above, below, from bush an' bough each calls his tuneful part;
  An' best of all, one trusty friend is callin' in my heart.
For it's Mornin'! Mornin'! When night's black troubles end.
An' never man was friendless yet who stayed his own good friend.

Grey thrush is in the wattle, an' it's, "O, you pretty dear!"
He's callin' to his little wife, an' don't care who should hear
  In the great bush, the fresh bush, washed again with dew;
  An' my axe is on my shoulder, an' there's work ahead to do.
Oh, it's Mornin'! Singin' Mornin'! in the land I count the best,
An' with the heart an' mind of me I'm singin' with the rest.

A FREAK
OF SPRING

At any other time of year
It might have passed, but Spring is queer.
    He says somethin'—I dunno—
    Somethin' nasty. I says, "Ho!"
"Ho, yourself!" he says, an' glares.
I says nothin'—only stares.
    "Coot!" says he . . . Then up she goes!
    An' I land him on the nose.

It was Spring, Spring, Spring! Just to hear the thrushes sing
Would make a fellow laugh, or love, or fight like anything.
    Which mood called I wasn't carin'; I was feelin' fine an' darin';
So I fetches him a beauty with a lovely left-arm swing.
    Ben Murray staggered back a bit an' howled a wicked word
    Which gave me feelin's of great joy . . . An' that's how it occurred.

"On the sawdust!" yells old Pike,
Gloatin' an' bloodthirsty-like.
    "On the sawdust with yeh both!"
    Truth to tell, I'm nothin' loth.
I peel off my coat an' vest.
Murray, with his rage suppressed,
    Comes up eager, pale with spite.
    "Glory!" shouts old Pike. "A fight!"

It was Spring, glad Spring, an' the swallows on the wing
Made a man feel kind an' peaceful with their cherry twittering.
    As I watched their graceful wheelin' with a pleasant sort of feelin'
Old man Pike pulled out his ticker, an' the mill-hands made a ring.
    There was gold upon the wattle an' the blackwood was in bud,
    An' I felt the call for action fairly sizzin' in my blood.

Murray comes on like a bull;
Both his eyes with spleen are full.
    Let him have it—left an' right . . .
    Pike is bustin' with delight . . .
Right eye once and left eye twice—
Then he grabs me like a vise . . .
    Down into the dust we go—
    Bull-dog grip and short-arm blow.

It was Spring! Mad Spring! Just to feel him clutch an' cling
Told me plain that life was splendid an' my strength a precious thing.
    On the sawdust heap we scrambled, while the fellows yell an'
        gambled
On the fight; an' Ben loosed curse-words in a never-endin' string.

Oh, I glimpsed the soft sky shinin' an' I smelled the fresh-cut wood;
An' as we rolled I pummelled him, an' knew the world was good.

"'Tain't a dog-fight!" shouts Bob Blair.
"Stand up straight an' fight it fair."
  I get end-up with a grin.
  "Time!" yells Pike, an' bangs a tin.
"Corners, boys. A minute's spell."
"Good lad, Jim! You're doin' well,"
  Says the little Dusty, Dick . . .
  Murray's eye is closin' quick.

It was Spring, sweet Spring, an' a man must have his fling:
Healthy men must be respondin' to the moods the seasons bring.
  That sweet air, with scrub scents laden, all my body was invadin',
Till each breath I drew within me made me feel I was a king.
  'Twas the season to be doin'—fondlin' maids, or fightin' men—
An' I felt my spirit yearnin' for another crack at Ben.

Pike bangs on his tin again.
"Time!" he roars. "Get to it, men!"
  I come eager, fit to dance;
  Ben spars cautious for a chance.
With a laugh I flick him light;
Then—like lightnin' comes his right
  Full an' fair upon the jaw—
  Lord, the purple stars I saw!

It was Spring, wild Spring! When I felt the sudden sting
Of a clout all unexpected, I was just a maddened thing—
  Just a savage male thing ragin'; battle all my wits engagin'.
Instant I was up an' at him, an' I punched him round the ring.
  I forgot the scents an' season; I lost count of time an' place;
An' my only aim an' object was to batter Murray's face.

Pike is dancin' wild with joy;
Dusty Dick howls, "At him, boy!"
  I am at him, fast an' hard.
  Then, as Murray drops his guard,
I get in one, strong an' straight,
Full of enmity an' weight.
  Down he goes; the fellows shout.
  "One!" starts Pike, then . . . "Ten—an' out!"

It was Spring, gay Spring. Still were swallows on the wing,
An', on a sudden, once again I heard the thrushes sing.
  There was gold upon the wattle, an' my recent wish to throttle
Murray, as he lay there groanin', was a far-forgotten thing.
  In the soft blue sky were sailin' little clouds as fine as fluff.
"Wantin' more?" I asked him gently; but Ben Murray said, "Enough."

"Well done, Jim," says old Bob Blair.
"'Tis the brave deserves the fair."
  An' he laughs an' winks at Pike
  In a way that I don't like.
"Widders," grins young Dusty Dick,
"Likes a bloke whose hands is quick.
  Now poor Ben can take the sack."
But I frowns, an' turns my back.

It was Spring, the fickle Spring; an' a most amazin' thing
Came upon me sudden-like an' set me marvelling.
  For no longer was I lookin' for a wife to do my cookin',
But for somethin' sweet an' tender of the kind that kiss an' cling.
  Oh, for such a one I'd battle, an' I'd win by hook or crook;
  But it did seem sort of foolish to go fightin' for a cook.

Standin' on the sawdust heap
I feel mean an' rather cheap,
  Widows? Let the widow go!
  What we fought for I don't know.
Murray offers me his hand:
"Jim, you've won; so, understand,
  I don't mean to block your road . . ."
  But I answer, "That be blowed!"

"Why, it's Spring, man, Spring!" (An' I gave his fist a wring)
"If you reckoned me your rival, give up thinkin' such a thing.
  I just fought for fun an' frolic, so don't you get melancholic;
An', if you have notions yonder, why, buck up an' buy the ring!
    Put some beefsteak on your eye, lad, an' learn how to keep your
        guard."
    Then I put my coat an' vest on, an' walked homeward . . . thinkin'
        hard.

THE
VISION

Of things that roam about the bush I ain't got many fears,
For I knows their ways an' habits, an' I've chummed with them for
     years.
  For man or beast or gully ghost I've pluck enough to spare;
  But I draws the line at visions with the sunlight in their hair.

I was feelin' fine this mornin' when I started out to work;
An' I caught myself high-steppin' with a boastful sort of jerk;
  With my head a trifle higher an' my eye a little stern.
  I thought the world was mine for keeps; but I'd a lot to learn.

I was workin' at the rip saw; for the boss had called me in
From the peaceful bush an' quiet to the sawmill's fuss an' din;
  An' there he put me tailin' out—a game I never like;
  But, "Likin' isn't gettin' in the bush," says Daddy Pike.

I was workin' at the rip saw, cursin' at my achin' back,
When I saw the blessed vision comin' down the log-yard track;
  There were others in the party, but the one that got my stare
  Was her with two brown, laughin' eyes an' sunlight in her hair.

"More visitors!" growled old man Pike. "Another city push.
I'll bet a quid they ask us why we 'spoil the lovely bush'."
  I hardly heard him saying it, for like a fool I stand,
  My eyes full of the vision an' a batten in my hand.

"You gone to sleep?" the sawyer said. "What's got you mesmerized?"
I start to work like fury, but my thoughts can't be disguised.
  "Oh, Jim's gone dippy with the Spring," replies old Pike an' grins.
  I turn to answer dignified; but trip, an' bark my shins.

Next thing I know the boss is there, an' talkin' fine an' good,
Explainin' to the visitors how trees are made of wood.
  They murmur things like "Marvellous!" an' "What a monster tree!"
  An' then the one with sunlit hair comes right bang up to me.

"I saw you fall," she sort of sung: you couldn't say she talked,
For her voice had springtime in it, like the way she looked an'
     walked.
  "I saw you fall," she sung at me. "I hope you were not hurt?"
  An' suddenly I was aware I wore my oldest shirt.

"It never hurt me half as much as your two smilin' eyes."
That's how I could have answered her—an' watched old Pike's
     surprise—
  "It never harmed me half as much as standin' here like this

With tattered shirt an' grimy hands" ... But I just says, "No,
   Miss."

"Oh, no," I says. "We're pretty hard, an' have to take them
   cracks."
(But, just to see her sudden smile, made me as soft as wax.)
   "You're strong," she smiles. I answers, "Oh, I'm pretty strong, all
   right."
   An' close behind I heard old Pike observin', "Hear 'im skite!"

That finished me. I lost what little nerve I had, an' grew
Dead certain that I looked a fool, an' that she thought so, too.
   She talked some more; but I can't tell what other things she said—
   I went all cold, except my ears, an' they were burnin' red.

I only know her eyes were soft, her voice was kind an' low.
I never spoke another word exceptin' "Yes" an' "No".
   I never felt a bigger chump in all my livin' days,
   Well knowin' I was gettin' worse at every work she says.

An' when the knock-off whistle blew, Ben Murray he came by,
An' says he'd like a private talk; but, "Pickle it," says I.
   "'Twill have to keep till later on." He answers, "As you like."
   Soon after that I saw him talkin' earnest with old Pike.

If I'd been right, I might have known there's somethin' in the air
By the way the blokes were actin'; but a fat lot did I care.
   Swell visions an' the deadly pip was what was wrong with me.
   I slung a word to my old dog, an' we trudged home to tea.

An' after, in the same old way, we sits beside the fire,
To have a talk, my dog an' me, on fools an' vain desire.
   I tell him I'm a silly chump to think the things I do;
   An', with a waggle of his tail, he says he thinks so too.

I tell him I suppose she's rich, or so she seems to be;
Most likely some reel city swell—an' he don't disagree.
   I says to him the chances are I'll not see her no more.
   Then he gives me a funny look, an' curls up on the floor.

But I was slow to take the tip, an' went on talkin' rot
About injustice in the world, an' boiled up good an' hot.
   I spouts of wrongs of workin' men an' how our rulers fail.
   His eyes are shut, but he just seconds motions with his tail.

All beauty's only for the rich, all times, an' every way.
The toilers just take what is left, as I've heard Murray say

When he's been talkin' to the boys about the workers' rights,
An' spoutin' of equality, down at the huts, of nights.

I turned the social system inside-out for my old dog,
Tho' he don't seem much entertained, but lies there like a log.
    I spoke of common people's wrongs—especially of mine;
    But when I came to mention love I thought I heard him whine.

But I went on, an' said straight out that, tho' I seemed above
Such nonsense once, I'd changed a bit, an' I believed in love.
    I said love was a splendid thing! ... Then, true as I am born,
    He rose, an' yawned, an' shut me up with one crook glance of
        scorn.

It's bad enough to be a bloke without one reel close friend;
But when your dog gives you the bird it's pretty near the end.
    Ashamed, I sneaked away to bunk; an' fell to dreamin' there
    Of a little brown-eyed vision with the sunlight in her hair.

THE
WOOER

I nearly fell fair in my tracks.
I'm trudgin' homeward with my axe
   When I come on her suddenly.
   "I wonder if I'm lost?" says she.
"It's risky on such roads as this."
I lifts my hat an' says, "Yes, miss."
   I knew 'twas rude for me to stare,
   But, oh, that sunlight in her hair!

"I wonder if I'm lost?" says she,
An' gives a smile that staggers me.
   "An' yet, it wouldn't matter much
   Supposing that I was, with such
A glorious green world about,
With bits of blue sky peepin' out.
   Do *you* think there will be a fog?"
   "No, miss," says I, an' pats my dog.

"Oh, what a dear old dog!" says she.
"Most dogs are pretty fond of me."
   She calls him to her, an' he goes.
   (He didn't find it hard, I s'pose;
I know I wouldn't, if she called.)
"It's wondrous how the tracks are walled
   With these great trees that touch the sky
   On either side." "Yes, miss," says I.

She fondles my old dog a bit;
I wait to make a bolt for it.
   (There ain't no call to stand an' talk
   With one who'd be too proud to walk
A half-a-yard with such as me.)
"The wind seems workin' up," says she.
   "Yes, miss," I says, an' lifts me hat.
   An' she just lets it go at that.

She lets me reach the dribblin' ford—
That day to me it fairly roared.
   (At least, that's how the thing appears;
   But blood was poundin' in my ears.)
She waits till I have fairly crossed:
"I thought I told you I was lost?"
   She cries. "An' you go walkin' off,
   Quite scornful, like some proud bush toff!"

She got me thinkin' hard with that.
"Yes, miss," I says, an' lifts my hat.
　　But she just waits there on the track,
　　An' lets me walk the whole way back.
"An' are you reely lost?" says I.
"Yes, sir," says she, an' drops her eye . . .
　　I wait, an' wait for what seems days;
　　But not another word she says.

I pats my dog, an' lifts my hat;
But she don't seem to notice that.
　　I looks up trees an' stares at logs,
　　An' long for twenty hats an' dogs.
"The weather's kept reel good to-day,"
I blurts at last. Says she, "Hurray!"
　　"Hurray!" she says, an' then, "Encore!"
　　An' gets me wonderin' what for.

"Is this the right road to 'The Height'?"
I tell her it's the road, all right,
　　But that the way she's walkin' ain't.
　　At that she looked liked she would faint.
"Then I *was* lost if I had gone
Along this road an' walked right on—
　　An unfrequented bush track, too!
　　How fortunate that I met you!"

"Yes, miss," I says. "Yes—what?" says she.
Says I, "Most fortunate . . . for me."
　　I don't know where I found the pluck
　　To blurt that out an' chance my luck.
"You'll walk," she says, "a short way back,
So you can put me on the track?"
　　"I'll take you *all* the way," says I,
　　An' looks her fair bang in the eye.

Later, I let myself right out,
An' talked; an' told her all about
　　The things I've done, an' what I do,
　　An' nearly all I'm hopin' to.
Told why I chose the game I'm at
Because my folks were poor, an' that.
　　She seemed reel pleased to hear me talk,
　　An' sort of steadied up the walk.

Title page from
Jim of the Hills

An' when I'd spoke my little bit,
She just takes up the thread of it;
   An' later on, near knocks me down
   By tellin' me, she *works*—in town.
Works? Her? I thought, the way she dressed,
She was quite rich; but she confessed
   That makin' dresses was her game,
   An' she was dead sick of the same.

When Good-bye came, I lifts my hat;
But she holds out her hand at that.
   I looked at mine, all stained with sap,
   An' told her I'm a reel rough chap.
"A worker's hand," says she, reel fine,
"An' marked with toil; but so is mine.
   We're just two toilers; let us shake,
   An' be good friends—for labour's sake."

At home I looks around the place,
An' sees the dirt's a fair disgrace;
   So takes an' tidies up a bit,
   An' has a shave; an' then I sit
Beside my fire to have a think.
But my old dog won't sleep a wink;
   He fools, an' whines, an' nudges me,
   Then all at once I thinks of tea.

I beg his pardon with a smile,
An', talkin' to him all the while,
   I get it ready, tellin' him
   About that girl; but, "Shut up, Jim!"
He says to me as plain as plain.
"First have some food, an' then explain."
   (I don't know how she came to tell,
   But I found out her name is Nell.)

We gets our bits to eat at last
(An', just for spite, he et his fast) . . .
   I think that Nell's a reel nice name . . .
   "All right, old dog, I ain't to blame
If you" . . . Just as I go to sup
My tea I stop dead, with my cup
   Half up, an' . . . By the Holy Frost!
   I wonder was Nell reely lost?

RED ROBIN

Hi, it's a funny world! This mornin', when I woke
I saw red robin on the fence, an' heard the words he spoke.
  Red robin, he's a perky chap, an' this was his refrain:
  "Dear, it's a pity that poor Jenny is so plain."

To talk like that about his wife! It had me scandalized.
I'd heard him singin' so before, but never recognized
  The meaning of his chatter, or that he could be so vain:
  "Dear, it's a pity that poor Jenny is so plain."

I don't know how, I don't know why, but this reminded me
I was promised to the widow for this Sunday night to tea.
  I'd promised her for weeks an' weeks, until she pinned me down.
  I recollects this is the day, an' gets up with a frown.

I was thinkin' of the widow while I gets me clobber on—
Like a feller will start thinkin' of the times that's past an' gone.
  An', while my thoughts is runnin' so, that bird chips in again:
  "Dear, it's a pity that poor Jenny is to plain."   .

Now, the widow's name is Jenny, an' it strikes me sort of queer
That my thoughts should be upon her when that robin's song I
            hear.
  She ain't so homely neither; but she never could compare
  With a certain bonzer vision with the sunlight in her hair.

When I wander down that evenin', she come smilin' to the gate,
An' her look is calculatin', as she scolds because I'm late.
  She takes my hat an' sits me down an' heaves a little sigh
  But I get a queer sensation from that glimmer in her eye.

She starts to talk about the mill, an' then about the strike,
An' then she digs Ben Murray up an' treats him nasty-like;
  She treats him crool an' cattish, as them soft, sweet women can,
  But I ups an' tells her plainly that I think Ben is a man.

First round to me. But she comes back, an' says Ben is a cad
Who's made a laughin'-stock of her, an' treated her reel bad.
  I twig she's out for sympathy; so counters that, an' says
  That Ben's a broken-hearted man about the mill these days.

The second round to me on points; an' I was havin' hopes.
(I might have known that widows were familiar with the ropes.)
  "But he'd *never* make a husband!" says the widow, with a sigh.
  An' again I gets a warnin' from that glimmer in her eye.

I says I ain't no judge of that; an' treats it with a laugh.
But she keeps the talk on husbands for a minute an' a half.

I can't do much but spar a bit, an' keep her out of range;
So the third round is the widow's; an' the fight takes on a change.

I'm longin' for a breather, for I've done my nerve a lot,
When suddenly she starts on "Love", an' makes the pace reel hot.
    In half a jiff she has me on the ropes, an' breathin' hard,
    With not a fight inside me—I can only duck an' guard.

She uppercuts me with a sigh, an' jabs me with a glance.
(When a widow is the fighter, has a single bloke a chance?)
    Her short-arm blows are amorous, most lovin' is her lunge;
    Until it's just a touch an' go I don't throw up the sponge.

I use my head-piece here a bit to wriggle from the fix;
For the widow is a winner 'less I fluke a win by tricks.
    An' I gets a reel mean notion (that I don't seek to excuse),
    When I interrupts her rudely with, "But have you heard the
        news?"

Now, to a woman, that's a lead dead certain of a score,
An' a question that the keenest is unable to ignore.
    An' good old Curiosity comes in to second me,
    As I saw her struggle hopeless, an' "What news is that?" says she.

An' here I spins a lovely yarn, a gloomy, hard-luck tale
Of how I've done my money in, an' I'm about to fail,
    How my house an' land is mortgaged, how I've muddled my
        affairs
    Through foolin' round the racin' bets an' rotten minin' shares.

I saw the fight was easy mine the minute I begun;
An', after half a dozen words, the time-keep counted "one".
    An' when I finish that sad tale there ain't the slightest doubt
    I am the winner of the contest, an' the widow's down an' out.

But not for long. Although she's lost, the widow is dead game:
"I'm sorry, Mister Jim," says she, "for both your loss an' shame.
    All things is changed between us now, of course; the past is dead.
    An' what you were about to say you please will leave unsaid."

* * * *

I was thinkin' in the evenin' over how I had escaped,
An' how the widow took it all—the way she stared an' gaped.
    She looked her plainest at that time; but that don't matter now;
    For, plain, or fair, I know of one who's fairer, anyhow.

I tells meself that beauty ain't a thing to count with man,
An' I would never choose a wife on that unthinkin' plan.
  No robin was awake, I swear; but still I heard that strain:
  "Dear, it's a pity that poor Jenny is so plain."

FLAMES

It's human nature for a bashful bloke
     To bottle up, an' hesitate, an' doubt
Till grinnin' Fate plays him some low-down joke;
     Then, in excitement, he goes blurtin' out
The tale his sane mind never would impart,
So all the nearly-by world knows it by heart.

Good luck for me, the near-by world that day,
     When I ran sobbin' thro' the scorchin' fern,
Held few to hear the foolish things I say:
     No one was there my secret thought to learn,
As I went shoutin' down the mountain spur,
Only the scared birds, an' the trees, an' Her.

In fancy, many men have been thro' Hell,
     Tortured by fear, when hope has almost died;
But few have gone thro' that, an' fire as well
     To come on Heaven at the other side
With just one angel in it, safe an' well—
A cool, calm angel by the name of Nell.

The day the fire came sweepin' down the hill,
     Lickin' the forest up like some mad beast,
We had our work cut out to save the mill;
     An', when the wind swung round into the East,
An' blew the roarin' flames along the spur,
Straight for "The Height", I gets quick fear for Her.

Flat out I was with fightin' all day long—
     (We saved the mill-shed, but the huts were done)—
When some bloke, weak with sprintin', comes along—
     (Comic, it seemed to me, the way he run)—
Shoutin' that someone's missin' from "The Height",
An' all the forest at the back's alight.

I don't know what he thought, an' never cared,
     When I grabs at his coat, an' starts to yell.
I only know that I was dreadful scared . . .
     In half a minute more, I guessed 'twas Nell.
He tells me when an' where they thought she went,
An' of the useless searchers they had sent.

I never waits for more; but turned an' ran
     Straight for the spur, along the scorchin' track.
Behind me, as I went, I hear some man—
     I think it's Pike—bawlin', "You fool! Come back!"

What plan was in my mind I cannot tell;
I only know I want to find my Nell.

Next thing I mind, I've left the track, an' turned
  Into the blackened scrub—my eyes feel bad—
Above my head the messmate trees still burned.
  An' Lord, them awful fancies that I had!
I seen her lyin' there—her face—her hair . . .
Why, even now, them thoughts give me a scare.

I stumble on. Against a red-hot butt
  I burn my hand, but never even swear;
But keep on sayin', "Make the splitter's hut,
  The splitter's hut! Get to the clearin' there.
She's at the splitter's hut; an' if she ain't . . ."
My heart turns over, an' I feel dead faint.

An', as I plug along, I hear some fool
  Repeatin' words till they sound like a spell.
"I'm goin' mad," I thinks. "Keep cool! Keep cool!"
  But still that voice goes on: "My Nell! My Nell!"
I whips round quick to see who he can be,
This yappin' fool—then realize it's me.

I don't know how I reached the splitter's hut,
  I only saw the ragin' fire—an' Nell.
My clothes were torn, my face an' hands were cut,
  An' half a dozen times, at least, I fell.
I burst into the clearin' . . . an' I look . . .
She's sittin' on a log there—*with a book!*

I seem to cross that clearin' in a stride,
  Still sobbin' like a kid: "My Nell! My Nell!"
I was clean mad. But, as I reach her side,
  I sort of wake, an' give that song a spell.
But, by her eyes, for all she seemed so cool,
I know she must have heard, an' feel a fool.

"Why, Mister Jim! You do look hot," says she.
  (But still her eyes say oceans more than that.)
"Did you come all the way up here for me?"
  Coolness? I tell you straight, it knocked me flat.
By rights, she should fall sobbin' in my arms;
But no; there weren't no shrieks an' no alarms.

I pulls meself together with a jerk.
  "Oh, just a stroll," I says. "Don't mention it.
The mill's half burnt, an' I am out of work;
  They missed you, so I looked around a bit."
"Now, that *was* good of you," says she, reel bright.
"Wasn't the bush-fire just a splendid sight?"

She looks me up an' down. "Why, Mister Jim,"
  She says to me, "you do look hot, indeed.
If you go strollin' that way for a whim
  Whatever would you do in case of need?"
That's what she said. But with her eyes she sent
More than her thanks; an' I was quite content.

I seen her home; or, rather, she seen me,
  For I was weak, an' fumbled in my stride.
But, when we reached "The Height", I seen that she
  Was just on breakin'; an' she went inside . . .
I stumbles home. "Well, Jim, lad, anyway,"
I tells myself, "you've had a fine, full day."

GREY THRUSH

Grey thrush was in the wattle tree, an', "Oh, you pretty dear!"
He says in his allurin' way; an' I remarks, "Hear, hear!
    That does me nicely for a start; but what do I say next?"
    But then the Jacks take up the song, an' I get very vexed.

The thrush was in the wattle tree, an' I was underneath.
I'd put a clean white collar on, I'd picked a bunch of heath;
    For I was cleaned an' clobbered up to meet my Nell that day.
    But now my awful trouble comes: What is a man to say?

I mean to tell her all I've thought since first I saw her there,
On the bark-heap by the mill-shed, with the sunlight in her hair.
    I mean to tell her all I've done an' what I'll do with life;
    An', when I've said all that an' more, I'll ask her for my wife.

I mean to tell her she's too good, by far, for such as me,
An' how with lonely forest life she never may agree.
    I mean to tell her lots of things, an' be reel straight an' fine;
    And, after she's considered that, I'll ask her to be mine.

I don't suppose I've got much hope—a simple country yob.
I'd like to have a word with Blair—He's wise, is good old Bob;
    He's got such common sense an' that, he'd tip me what to say.
    But I'm not nervous, not a bit; I'll do it my own way ...

I seen her by the sassafras, the sun was on her hair;
An' I don't know what come to me to see her standin' there.
    I never even lifts my hat, I never says "Good day"
    To her that should be treated in a reel respectful way.

I only know the girl I want is standin' smilin' there
Right underneath the sassafras. I never thought I'd dare,
    But I holds out my arms to her, an' says, as I come near—
    Not one word of that speech of mine—but, "Oh, you pretty
        dear!"

It was enough. Lord save a man! It's simple if he knew
There's one way with a woman if she loves you good an' true.
    Next moment she is in my arms; an' me? I don't know where.
    If Heaven can compare with it I won't fret much up there.

"Why, Mister Jim," she says to me. "You're very bold," says she.
"Yes, miss," I says. Then she looks up—an' that's the end of me ...
    "O man!" she cries. "O modest man, if you go on like this—"
    But I interrupt a lady, an' I do it with a kiss.

"Jim, do you know what heroes are?" says she, when I'd "behaved".
"Why, yes," says I. "They're blokes that save fair maids that won't
      be saved."
   "You're mine," says she, an' smiles at me, "an' will be all my
      life—
   That is, if it occurs to you to ask me for your wife."

* * * *

Grey thrush is in the wattle tree when I get home that day—
Back to my silent, lonely house—an' still he sings away.
   There is no other voice about, no step upon the floor;
   An' none to come an' welcome me as I get to the door.

Yet in the happy heart of me I play at make-believe:
I hear one singin' in the room where once I used to grieve;
   I hear a light step on the path, an', as I reach the gate,
   A happy voice, that makes me glad, tells me I'm awful late.

Now what's a man to think of that, an' what's a man to say,
Who's been out workin' in the bush, tree-fallin', all the day?
   An' how's a man to greet his wife, if she should meet him here?
   But Grey Thrush in the wattle tree says, "Oh, you pretty dear!"

ROUNDABOUT

THE
BAKER

I'd like to be a baker, and come when morning breaks,
  Calling out "Beeay-ko!" (that's the sound he makes)—
Riding in a rattle-cart that jogs and jolts and shakes.
Selling all the sweetest things a baker ever bakes;
Currant-buns and brandy-snaps, pastry all in flakes;
  But I wouldn't be a baker if . . .
    I couldn't eat the cakes.
      Would you?

THE ANT EXPLORER

Once a little sugar ant made up his mind to roam—
To fare away far away, far away from home.
He had eaten all his breakfast, and he had his ma's consent
To see what he should chance to see and here's the way he went—
Up and down a fern frond, round and round a stone,
Down a gloomy gully where he loathed to be alone,
Up a mighty mountain range, seven inches high,
Through the fearful forest grass that nearly hid the sky,
Out along a bracken bridge, bending in the moss,
Till he reached a dreadful desert that was feet and feet across.
'Twas a dry, deserted desert, and a trackless land to tread;
He wished that he was home again and tucked-up tight in bed.
His little legs were wobbly, his strength was nearly spent,
And so he turned around again and here's the way he went—
Back away from desert lands feet and feet across,
Back along the bracken bridge bending in the moss,
Through the fearful forest grass shutting out the sky,
Up a mighty mountain range seven inches high,
Down a gloomy gully, where he loathed to be alone,
Up and down a fern frond and round and round a stone.
A dreary ant, a weary ant, resolved no more to roam,
He staggered up the garden path and popped back home.

THE TRAM-MAN

I'd like to be a Tram-man, and ride about all day,
Calling out, "Fares, please!" in quite a 'ficious way,
With pockets full of pennies which I'd make the people pay.
But in the hottest days I'd take my tram down to the Bay;
And when I saw the nice cool sea I'd shout "Hip, hip, hooray!"
   But I wouldn't be a tram-man if . . .
     I couldn't stop and play.
       Would you?

THE
SWAGMAN

Oh, he was old and he was spare;
His bushy whiskers and his hair
Were all fussed up and very grey;
He said he'd come a long, long way
And had a long, long way to go.
Each boot was broken at the toe,
And he'd a swag upon his back.
His billy-can, as black as black.
Was just the thing for making tea
At picnics, so it seemed to me.

'Twas hard to earn a bit of bread,
He told me. Then he shook his head,
And all the little corks that hung
Around his hat-brim danced and swung
And bobbed about his face; and when
I laughed he made them dance again.
He said they were for keeping flies—
"The pesky varmints"—from his eyes.
He called me "Codger" ... "Now you see
The best days of your life," said he.
"But days will come to bend your back,
And, when they come, keep off the track.
Keep off, young codger, if you can."
He seemed a funny sort of man.

He told me that he wanted work,
But jobs were scarce this side of Bourke,
And he supposed he'd have to go
Another fifty mile or so.
"Nigh all my life the track I've walked,"
He said. I liked the way he talked.
And oh, the places he had seen!
I don't know where he had not been—

On every road, in every town,
All through the country, up and down.
"Young codger, shun the track," he said.
And put his hand upon my head.
I noticed, then, that his old eyes
Were very blue and very wise.
"Ay, once I was a little lad,"
He said, and seemed to grow quite sad.

I sometimes think: When I'm a man,
I'll get a good black billy-can
And hang some corks around my hat,
And lead a jolly life like that.

**THE
POSTMAN**

I'd like to be a postman, and walk along the street,
  Calling out, "Good Morning, Sir," to gentlemen I meet;
Ringing every door-bell all along my beat,
In my cap and uniform so very nice and neat.
Perhaps I'd have a parasol in case of rain or heat;
  But I wouldn't be a postman if . . .
    The walking hurt my feet.
      Would you?

HIST!

Hist! ...... Hark!
The night is very dark,
And we've to go a mile or so
Across the Possum Park.
Step ...... light,
Keeping to the right;
If we delay, and lose our way,
We'll be out half the night.
The clouds are low and gloomy. Oh!
It's just begun to mist!
We haven't any overcoats
And—Hist! ...... Hist!

(Mo ...... poke!)
Who was that that spoke?
This is not a fitting spot
To make a silly joke.
Dear ...... me!
A mopoke in a tree!
It jarred me so, I didn't know
Whatever it could be.
But come along; creep along;
Soon we shall be missed.
They'll get a scare and wonder where
We—Hush! ...... Hist!

Ssh! ...... Soft!
I've told you oft and oft
We should not stray so far away
Without a moon aloft.
Oo! ...... Scat!
Goodness! What was that?
Upon my word, it's quite absurd,
It's only just a cat.
But come along; haste along;
Soon we'll have to rush,
Or we'll be late, and find the gate
Is—Hist! ...... Hush!

(*Kok!* ...... *Korrock!*)
Oh! I've had a shock!
I hope and trust it's only just
A frog behind a rock.
Shoo! .... Shoo!

We've had enough of you;
Scaring folk just for a joke
Is not the thing to do.
But come along, slip along—
Isn't it a lark
Just to roam so far from home
On—Hist! . . . . . . Hark!

Look! . . . . . . See!
Shining through the tree,
The window-light is glowing bright
To welcome you and me.
Shout! . . . . . . Shout!
There's someone round about,
And through the door I see some more
And supper all laid out.

Now, run! Run! Run! . . .
Oh, we've had such splendid fun—
Through the park in the dark,
As brave as anyone.
Laughed, we did, and chaffed, we did,
And whistled all the way,
And we're home again! Home again!
Hip . . . . . . Hooray!

THE TRAVELLER

As I rode in to Burrumbeet,
I met a man with funny feet;
And, when I paused to ask him why
His feet were strange, he rolled his eye
And said the rain would spoil the wheat;
So I rode on to Burrumbeet.

As I rode in to Beetaloo,
I met a man whose nose was blue;
And when I asked him how he got
A nose like that, he answered, "What
Do bullocks mean when they say 'Moo'?"
So I rode on to Beetaloo.

As I rode in to Ballarat,
I met a man who wore no hat;
And, when I said he might take cold,
He cried, "The hills are quite as old
As yonder plains, but not so flat."
So I rode on to Ballarat.

As I rode in to Gundagai,
I met a man and passed him by
Without a nod, without a word.
He turned, and said he'd never heard
Or seen a man so wise as I.
But I rode on to Gundagai.

As I rode homeward, full of doubt,
I met a stranger riding out:
A foolish man he seemed to me;
But, "Nay, I am yourself," said he,
"Just as you were when you rode out."
So I rode homeward, free of doubt.

1.

2.

3.

4.

5.

THE TRIANTI- WONTI- GONGO- LOPE

There's a very funny insect that you do not often spy,
And it isn't quite a spider, and it isn't quite a fly;
It is something like a beetle, and a little like a bee,
But nothing like a woolly grub that climbs upon a tree.
Its name is quite a hard one, but you'll learn it soon, I hope.
So, try:
  Tri-
    Tri-anti-wonti-
      Triantiwontigongolope.

It lives on weeds and wattle-gum, and has a funny face;
Its appetitie is hearty, and its manners a disgrace.
When first you come upon it, it will give you quite a scare,
But when you look for it again you find it isn't there.
And unless you call it softly it will stay away and mope.
So, try:
  Tri-
    Tri-anti-wonti-
      Triantiwontigongolope.

It trembles if you tickle it or tread upon its toes;
It is not an early riser, but it has a snubbish nose
If you sneer at it, or scold it, it will scuttle off in shame,
But it purrs and purrs quite proudly if you call it by its name,
And offer it some sandwiches of sealing-wax and soap.
So, try:
  Tri-
    Tri-anti-wonti-
      Triantiwontigongolope.

But of course you haven't seen it; and I truthfully confess
That I haven't seen it either, and I don't know its address.
For there isn't such an insect, though there really might have been
If the trees and grass were purple, and the sky was bottle-green.
It's just a little joke of mine, which you'll forgive, I hope.
Oh, try!
  Try!
    Tri-anti-wonti-
      Triantiwontigongolope.

THE CIRCUS

Hey, there! Hoop-la! the circus is in town!
Have you seen the elephant? Have you seen the clown?
Have you seen the dappled horse gallop round the ring?
Have you seen the acrobats on the dizzy swing?
Have you seen the tumbling men tumble up and down?
Hoop-la! Hoop-la! the circus is in town!

Hey, there! Hoop-la! Here's the circus troupe!
Here's the educated dog jumping through the hoop.
See the lady Blondin with the parasol and fan,
The lad upon the ladder and the india-rubber man.
See the joyful juggler and the boy who loops the loop.
Hey! Hey! Hey! Hey! Here's the circus troupe!

A CHANGE OF AIR

Now, a man in Oodnadatta
He grew fat, and he grew fatter,
    Though he hardly had a thing to eat for dinner;
While a man in Booboorowie
Often sat and wondered how he
    Could prevent himself from growing any thinner.

So the man from Oodnadatta
    He came down to Booboorowie,
Where he rapidly grew flatter;
    And the folk will tell you how he
Urged the man in Booboorowie
    To go up to Oodnadatta—
Where he lived awhile, and now he
    Is considerably fatter.

GOING TO SCHOOL

Did you see them pass today, Billy, Kate and Robin,
All astride upon the back of old grey Dobbin?
Jigging, jogging off to school, down the dusty track—
What must Dobbin think of it—three upon his back?
Robin at the bridle-rein, in the middle Kate,
Billy holding on behind, his legs out straight.

Now they're coming back from school, jig, jog, jig.
See them at the corner where the gums grow big;
Dobbin flicking off the flies and blinking at the sun—
Having three upon his back he thinks is splendid fun:
Robin at the bridle-rein, in the middle Kate,
Little Billy up behind, his legs out straight.

1.

2.

BACKBLOCK BALLADS
AND LATER VERSES

THE AUSTRA — LAISE

Fellers of Australier,
 Blokes an' coves an' coots,
Shift yer _____ carcases,
 Move yer_____ boots.
Gird yer_____ loins up,
Get yer _____ gun,
Set the _____ enermy
 An' watch the _____ run.

Chorus   Get a _____ move on,
 Have some _____ sense.
Learn the _____ art of
 Self de- _____ -fence.

Have some _____ brains be-
 Neath yer _____ lids.
An' swing a _____ sabre
 Fer the missus an' the kids.
Chuck supportin' _____ posts,
 An' strikin' _____ lights,
Support a _____ fam'ly an'
 Strike fer yer _____ rights.

Chorus   Get a _____ move, etc.

Joy is _____ fleetin',
 Life is _____ short.
Wot's the use uv wastin' it
 All on _____ sport?
Hitch yer _____ tip-dray
 To a _____ star.
Let yer _____ watchword be
 "Australi-_____ -ar!"

Chorus   Get a _____ move, etc.

'Ow's the _____ nation
 Goin' to ixpand
'Lest us_____ blokes an' coves
 Lend a _____ 'and?

'Eave yer _____ apathy
　　Down a _____ chasm;
'Ump yer _____ burden with
　　Enthusi-_____ -asm.

Chorus　Get a _____ move, etc.

W'en the _____ trouble
　　Hits yer native land
Take a _____ rifle
　　In yer _____ 'and.
Keep yer _____ upper lip
　　Stiff as stiff kin be,
An' speed a _____ bullet for
　　Pos- _____ -terity.

Chorus　Get a _____ move, etc.

W'en the _____ bugle
　　Sounds "Ad- _____ -vance"
Don't be like a flock uv sheep
　　In a _____ trance.
Biff the _____ foeman
　　Where it don't agree.
Spifler- _____ -cate him
　　To Eternity.

Chorus　Get a _____ move, etc.

Fellers of Australier,
　　Cobbers, chaps an' mates,
Hear the _____ enermy
　　Kickin' at the gates!
Blow the _____ bugle,
　　Beat the _____ drum,
Upper-cut and out the cow
　　To kingdom-_____ -come!

Chorus　Get a _____ move on,
　　Have some _____ sense
Learn the _____ art of
　　Self de-_____ -fence!

AN OLD MASTER

We were cartin' laths and palin's from the slopes of Mount St
        Leonard,
    With our axles near the road-bed and the mud as stiff as glue;
And our bullocks weren't precisely what you'd call conditioned
        nicely,
    And meself and Messmate Mitchell had our doubts of gettin'
        through.

It had rained a tidy skyful in the week before we started,
    But our tucker-bag depended on the sellin' of our load;
So we punched 'em on by inches, liftin' 'em across the pinches,
    Till we struck the final section of the worst part of the road.

We were just congratulatin' one another on the goin',
    When we blundered in a pot-hole right within the sight of goal,
Where the bush-track joins the metal. Mitchell, as he saw her
        settle,
    Justified his reputation at the peril of his soul.

We were 'n a glue-pot, certain—red and stiff and most tenacious;
    Over naves and over axles—waggon sittin' on the road.
"'Struth," says, I, "they'll never lift her. Take a shot from Hell to
        shift her.
    Nothin' left but to unyoke 'em and sling off the blessed load."

Now, beside our scene of trouble stood a little one-roomed humpy,
    Home of an enfeebled party by the name of Dad McGee.
Daddy was, I pause to mention, livin' on an old-age pension
    Since he gave up bullock-punchin' at the age of eighty-three.

Startled by our exclamations, Daddy hobbled from the shanty,
    Gazin' where the stranded waggon looked like some half-
        foundered ship.
When the state o' things he spotted, "Looks," he says, "like you
        was potted,"
    And he toddles up to Mitchell. "Here," says he, "gimme that
        whip."
Well! I've heard of transformations; heard of fellers sort of changin'
    In the face of sudden danger or some great emergency;
Heard the like in song and story and in bush traditions hoary,
    But I nearly dropped me bundle as I looked at Dad McGee.

While we gazed he seemed to toughen; as his fingers gripped the
        handle
    His old form grew straight and supple, and a light leapt in his eye;

And he stepped around the waggon, not with footsteps weak and
    laggin',
  But with firm, determined bearin', as he flung the whip on high.

Now he swung the leaders over, while the whip-lash snarled and
    volleyed;
  And they answered like one bullock, strainin' to each crack and
    clout;
But he kept his cursin' under till old Brindle made a blunder;
  Then I thought all Hell had hit me, *and the master opened out*

And the language! Oh, the language! Seemed to me I must be
    dreamin';
  While the wondrous words and phrases only genius could produce
Roared and rumbled, fast and faster, in the throat of that Old
    Master—
  Oaths and curses tipped with lightning, cracklin' flames of fierce
    abuse.

Then we knew the man before us was a Master of our callin';
  One of those great lords of language gone for ever from Outback;
Heroes of an ancient order; men who punched across the border;
  Vanished giants of the sixties; puncher-princes of the track.

Now we heard the timbers strainin', heard the waggon's loud
    complainin',
  And the master cried triumphant, as he swung 'em into line,
As they put their shoulders to it, lifted her, and pulled her through
    it:
  "That's the way we useter do it in the days o' sixty-nine!"

Near the foot of Mount St Leonard lives an old, enfeebled party
  Who retired from bullock-punchin' at the age of eighty-three.
If you seek him folk will mention, merely, that he draws the
    pension;
  But to us he looms a Master—Prince of Punchers, Dad McGee!

" P A W "

Haw!
Ai've just obteened a pension for mai Paw.
And you *should* hev seen the people that were theah.
  Re-ally, it was surpraising!
  Maind, Ai am not criticaising,
But it was *embarrassing*, Ai do *decleah*.
Ai met the Snobson-Smythes and Toady-Browns, and many moah
Belonging to ouah set; and wondahed what *they* came theah foah.

And, of course, Ai didn't say a *word* of Paw.
Ai rather think *they've* nevah *heard* of Paw.
  But Ai thought it well to mention
  That Ai came to get the pension
For an agéd person who had worked for Maw.
The Snobson-Smythes said, "*Fancy!* That is just why *we* came dahn."
But Ai've heard they hev a mothah hidden somewheah out of tahn.

Haw!
Ai *do* deserve some gratitude from Paw.
To think what Ai've *gone thro'* foah him to-day!
  Mixing with the lowah classes—
  And Ai never saw such masses
Of disreputable creatuahs, Ai *must* say.
Impostors, Ai've no doubt, if most of them were but unmasked.
And then, the most *humiliating* questions Ai was asked!

Yes, he forced me to admit it was foah Paw.
Asked me, brutally, if it was foah *mai* Paw.
  Some low-bred official fellow,
  Who conversed in quaite a bellow,
And he patronised me laike a high Bashaw.
And his questions, rudely *personal*, Ai hardly could *enduah*.
The Government should teach its people mannahs, Ai am suah!

Haw!
Ai'm *glad* we've got the pension foah Pooah Paw.
His maintenance has been—O, *such* a strain.
  Ouah establishment's extensive
  And *exceedingly* expensive,
As mai husband has remawked taime and again.
It's quaite a *miracle* how Ai contrive to dress at *all*.
He cut me dahn to *twenty guineas* for last Mayoral Ball!

And it's such a boah to hev to *think* of Paw—
To hev a secret skeleton laike Paw.
  Paw, you know, was once a diggah,

And he cuts no social figgah.
And his *mannahs!* O, they touch us on the raw.
Of course, we're *very* fond of him, and all *thet* sort of thing;
But we couldn't hev him—*could* we?—when theah's naice folk
      visiting.

                      Haw!
It's cost us pawnds and *pawnds* to care foah Paw.
And then, it is so hard to keep him dawk.
   Why, no later then last Mond'y,
   Ai was out with Lady Grundy,
When we ran raight *into* him outsaide the Pawk.
Goodness knows! Ai managed, *somehow*, to elude him with a nod,
And Ai said he was a tradesman; but she must hev thought it *odd*.

You can't *picture* the ubiquity of Paw,
And he's really *very* obstinate, is Paw.
   Why, he held to the contention
   That this most convenient pension
Was a thing *he* hadn't any *raight* to draw!
He said *we'd* kept him eighteen months, and ought to keep him yet.
But mai husband soon convinced him that he couldn't count on *thet*.

                      Haw!
He was a pioneah, you know, mai Paw.
But of mai early laife Ai never tell.
   Paw *worked*, as Ai hev stated;
   And he had us educated;
And, later on, *Ai* married rather *well*.
And then, you know, deah Paw became—er—well, embarrassing.
For he *is* so unconventional and—all thet sort of thing.

But the Government has taken ovah Paw.
We are happy now we've aisolated Paw.
   And a bettah era's dawning,
   For mai husband said this mawning
Thet the money saved would buy a motah-caw.
Paw was so good to us when we were young, that, you'll allow,
It's really taime the Government did something foah him now.

WHEAT

"Sowin' things an' growin' things, an' watchin' of 'em grow;
That's the game," my father said, an' father ought to know.
"Settin' things an' gettin' things to grow for folks to eat:
That's the life," my father said, "that's very hard to beat."
For my father was a farmer, as his father was before,
Just sowin' things an' growin' things in far-off days of yore,
In the far-off land of England, till my father found his feet
In the new land, in the land, where he took to growin' wheat,
   Wheat, Wheat, Wheat! Oh, the sound of it is sweet!
   I've been praisin' it an' raisin' it in rain an' wind an' heat
      Since the time I learned to toddle, till it's beatin' in my noddle,
   Is the little song I'm singin' you of Wheat, Wheat, Wheat.

Plantin' things—an' grantin' things is goin' as they should,
An' the weather altogether is behavin' pretty good—
Is a pleasure in a measure for a man that likes the game,
An' my father he would rather raise a crop than make a name.
For my father was a farmer, an' "All fame," he said, "ain't reel;
An' the same it isn't fillin' when you're wantin' for a meal."
So I'm followin' his footsteps, an' a-keepin' of my feet,
While I cater for the nation with my Wheat, Wheat, Wheat.
   Wheat, Wheat, Wheat! When the poets all are beat
   By the reason that the season for the verse crop is a cheat,
      Then I comes up bright an' grinnin' with the knowledge that I'm
         winnin',
   With the rhythm of my harvester an' Wheat, Wheat, Wheat.

Readin' things an' heedin' things that clever fellers give,
An' ponderin' an' wonderin' why we was meant to live—
Muddlin' through an' fuddlin' through philosophy an' such
Is a game I never took to, an' it doesn't matter much.
For my father was a farmer, as I might 'a' said before,
An' the sum of his philosophy was, "Grow a little more.
For growin' things," my father said, "it makes life sort o' sweet
An' your conscience never swats you if your game is growin'
      wheat."
   Wheat, Wheat, Wheat! Oh, the people have to eat!
   An' you're servin', an' deservin' of a velvet-cushion seat
      In the cocky-farmer's heaven when you come to throw a seven;
   An' your password at the portal will be, "Wheat, Wheat, Wheat."

In the city, more's the pity, thousands live an' thousands die
Never carin', never sparin' pains that fruits may multiply;
Breathin', livin', never givin'; greedy but to have an' take,
Dyin' with no day behind 'em lived for fellow-mortals' sake.

Now my father was a farmer, an' he used to sit and laugh
At the "fools o' life", he called 'em, livin' on the other half.
Dyin' lonely, missin' only that one joy that makes life sweet—
Just the joy of useful labour, such as comes of growin' wheat.
   Wheat, Wheat, Wheat! Let the foolish scheme an' cheat;
   But I'd rather, like my father, when my span o' life's complete.
     Feel I'd lived by helpin' others; earned the right to call 'em brothers
   Who had gained while I was gainin' from God's earth His gift of wheat.

When the settin' sun is gettin' low above the western hills,
When the creepin' shadows deepen, and a peace the whole land fills,
Then I often sort o' soften with a feelin' like content,
An' I feel like thankin' Heaven for a day in labour spent.
For my father was a farmer, an' he used to sit an' smile,
Realizin' he was wealthy in what makes a life worth while.
Smilin', he has told me often, "After all the toil an' heat,
Lad, he's paid in more than silver who has grown one field of wheat."
   Wheat, Wheat, Wheat! When it comes my turn to meet
   Death the Reaper, an' the Keeper of the Judgement Book I greet,
     Then I'll face 'em sort o' calmer with the solace of the farmer
   That he's fed a million brothers with his Wheat, Wheat, Wheat.

A GUIDE FOR POITS

(Compiled by The Sentimental Bloke.)

I ain't no verse-'og. When I busts in song
　An' fills the air wiv choonful melerdy,
I likes fer uvver coves to come along
　An' biff the lyre in company wiv me.

So, when I sees some peb beguile an hour
　Be joinin' in the chorus o' me song,
I never sees no use in turnin' sour;
　Fer singin' days wiv no one larsts too long.

I'd like to see the Rocks an' Little Lon
　Grow centres for the art uv weavin' rhyme,
Wiv dinky 'arps fer blokes to plunk upon,
　An' spruikin' poits workin' overtime.

I'd love to listen to each choonful lay
　Uv soulful coots who scorn to write fer gain;
To see True Art bloom down in Chowder Bay,
　An' Culcher jump the joint in Spadger's Lane.

Gawstruth! Fer us life's got no joy to spare,
　We're short uv bird-songs, "soarin' clear an' pure."
A bloke is 'ardly orf the bottle there
　Before 'e's in the jug—a bird fer sure.

So 'oo am I to say no blokes shall sing
　Jist 'ow an' where an' when sich blokes may choose?
She's got no lines to show, nor yet no ring.
　Lor' bli'me! I ain't *married* to me Muse!

An', square an' all, to show there's no offence,
　To show that in me 'eart true friendship lies,
I gives free gratis, an' wivout ixpense,
　A few igzamples, jist to put 'em wise.

First, choose some swingin' metre, sich as this,
　That Omar used—per Fitz—to boost the wine.
An' 'ere's a point true artists shouldn't miss:
　Sling in a bit o' slang to ev'ry line.

An' when yer full o' them alternate rhymes—
As all the true push poits is at times—
Jist ring the changes, as I'm doin' now:
An' find ixcuse to say: "The bloomin' cow!"

Or, comin' back to Omar's style again,
It's easy fer to pen a sweet refrain

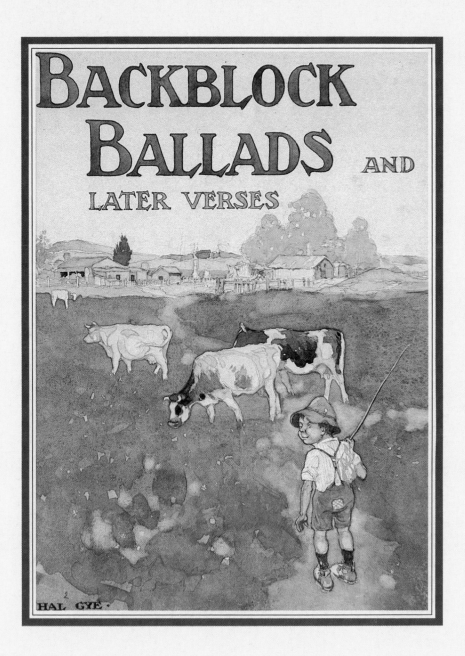

Backblock Ballads, cover illustration

Wiv this 'ere jist a dead-'ead sort o' line,
An' this one rhymin' wiv the former twain.

An' though this style me soul 'as often vext,
  Wiv care an' pains the knack is easy cort:
This line's rhymed wiv the first, an' then the next
  Is cut orf short.
An' if yeh want to round it orf orl neat
Jist add a-couplet 'ere of equil feet.

An' 'ere's a style I've very often done:
  You swing of orf 'ere, an' find a second rhyme,
Then hitch the third line to the leadin' one.
    An' make the fourth lap wiv the second chime,
    An' then you sort o' come another time,
An' jist end up the same as you begun.

It's orl dead easy when yeh know the way,
An' 'ave the time to practise it—But, say,
    Although it sort o' takes the eye, no doubt
(An', mind yeh, I'm not sayin' but it may)—
    Wivout a stock uv rhymes to see you out
This style o' rhymin's like to turn yeh grey.

The triplets comes much 'arder than the twins;
But I 'ave 'ad to bear 'em fer me sins.
    'Ere, fer a single line, yeh change the style,
Switch orf an' rhyme the same as you begins;
    An' then yeh comes back at it wiv a smile,
    Pertendin' it's dead easy orl the while.

Them sawed-orf lines 'as often stood me friends;
Fer you kin cut 'em up to serve yer ends.
    An' frequent I 'ave slung the dotin' throng
      This sort o' song.
To ring su'prises on the eye an' ear
Is 'arf the game. It seems to kind o' queer
    The dull monotony. Yeh make a miss,
      An' then do this.

Aw, 'Struth! it's pretty; but you take my tip,
It gives a bloke the everlastin' pip
    'Oo tries to live upon the game and gets . . .
    Corns on 'is brain an' melancholy debts!

Wiv sweat an' tears, wiv misery an' sighs,
  Yeh wring yer soul-case fer one drop of bliss

To give the cold, 'ard world; an' it replies,
  "Prompt payment will erblige. Please settle this."

The rarest treasures of yer 'eart yeh spend
On callous, thankless coots; an' in the end
It comes to this: if you can't find a muse
'Oo takes in washin', wot's the flamin' use?

'URRY!

Now, *Ma-til-der!* Ain't cher dressed yet? I declare, the girl ain't up!
Last as ushul. Move yerself, you sleepy'-ead!
Are you goin' to lie there lazin',
W'ile I—Nell, put down that basin;
Go an' see if Bill has got the poddies fed;
Tell 'im not to move that clucky—ho, yer up, me lady, eh?
That's wot comes from gallivantin' lat ut night.
Why, the sun is nearly—see now,
Don't chu *dare* talk back at me now!
Set the table, Nell! Where's Nell? Put out that light!

Now then, 'urry, goodness, 'urry! *Mary,* tell the men to come.
Oh there, drat the girl! MA-TIL-DER! *where's the jam?*
You fergot it? Well, uv all ther . . .
Mary! 'Ear me tell you call ther . . .
Lord! there's Baldy TANGLED IN THE BARB'-WIRE—SAM!
Now, then, take 'er steady, clumsy, or she'll cut herself—LEAVE
      OFF!
Do you want the cow to—*There!* I never did!
Well, you mighter took 'er steady.
Sit up, Dad, yer late already.
Did ju put the tea in, Mary? Where's the lid?

Oh, do 'urry! Where's them buckets? *Nell,* 'as Bill brought in the
      cows?
Where's that boy? Ain't finished eatin' yet, uv course;
Eat all day if 'e wus let to.
Mary, where'd yer father get to?
Gone! Wot! *Call 'im back!* DAD! Wot about that 'orse?
No, indeed, it ain't my business; you kin see the man yerself.
No, I *won't!* I'm sure I've quite enough to do.
If 'e calls ter-day about it,
'E kin either go without it,
Or elst walk acrost the paddick out to you.

Are the cows in, *B-i-ll?* Oh, there they are. Well, nearly time
      they—Nell,
Feed the calves, an' pack the — *Yes, indeed ju will!*
Get the sepy-rater ready.
Woa, there, Baldy—steady, *steady.*
Bail up. *Stop-er! Hi, Matilder!* MARY! BILL!
Well, uv all th' . . . *Now* you've done it.
Wait till Dad comes 'ome to-night;
When 'e sees the mess you've—*Don't stand starin' there!*
Go an' get the cart an' neddy;

An' the cream cans—are they ready?
Where's the ... There! Fergot the fowls, I *do* declare!

Chuck!—*Chook!*—CHOOK! Why, there's that white un lost
        another chick to-day!
Nell, 'ow many did I count?—*Oh, stop that row!*
Wot's 'e doin'? Oh, you daisy!
Do you mean to tell me, lazy,
Thet you 'aven't fed the pigs until jus' now?
Oh, *do 'urry!* There's the men ull soon be knockin' off fer lunch.
An' we 'aven't got the ... Reach that bacon down.
Get the billies, Nell, an'—*Mary,*
Go an' fetch the ... Wot? *'Ow dare 'e!*
Bill, yer NOT *to wear yer best 'at inter town!*

'Ave you washed the things, Matilder? Oh, do 'urry, girl, yer late!
Seems to me you trouble more—TAKE CARE!—*You dunce!*
Now you've broke it! Well I never!
Ain't chu mighty smart an' clever;
Try'n to carry arf a dozen things at once.
No *back answers now!* You hussy! Don't chu *dare* talk back at me
Or I'll ... Nelly, did ju give them eggs to Bill?
Wot? CHU NEVER? Well I ... Mary,
Bring them dishes frum the dairy;
No, not them, the ... Lord, the sun's be'ind the hill!

'Ave you cleaned the sepy-rater, Nell? Well, get along to bed.
No; you can't go 'crost to Thompson's place to-night;
You wus there las' Chusday—See, miss,
Don't chu toss your head at *me,* miss!
I won't 'ave it. Mary, *'urry* with that light!
Now then, get yer Dad the paper. Set down, Dad—ju must be tired.
'Ere, Matilder, put that almanick away!
Where's them stockin's I wus darnin'?
Bill an' Mary, stop yer yarnin'!
Now then, Dad. Heigh-ho! Me fust sit down ter-day.

HOPEFUL HAWKINS

Hawkins wasn't in the swim at all in Dingo Flat,
    And to bait him was our chiefest form of bliss;
But, in justice, be it said that he had a business head.
    (That's why I'm standing here and telling this.)

He was trav'ling for a company, insuring people's lives;
    And stayed about a month in Dingo Flat;
But his biz was rather dull, and we took him for a gull,
    An amazing simple-minded one at that.

He was mad, he was, on mining and around about the town
    Prospected every reef. But worse than that—
He'd talk for half a day, in a most annoying way,
    On "The mineral resources of the Flat."

He swore that somewhere nigh us was a rich gold-bearing reef,
    If a fellow only had the luck to strike it;
And he only used to laugh when the boys began to chaff,
    And seemed, in fact, to rather sort of like it.

Well, we stood him for a month until he wellnigh drove us mad.
    And as jeering couldn't penetrate his hide
We fixed a little scheme for to dissipate his dream,
    And sicken him of mining till he died.

We got a likely-looking bit of quartz and faked it up
    With dabs of golden paint; then called him in.
Oh, he went clean off his head; it was gold for sure, he said,
    And if we'd sell our claim he'd raise the tin.

But we weren't taking any—not at least till later on;
    For we reckoned that we'd string him on a while.
When he wanted information of the reef's exact location
    We would meet him with a knowing sort of smile.

At last we dropped a hint that set him pegging out a claim,
    And we saw that we were coming in for sport;
For the next account we heard was when Hawkins passed the word
    He was fetching up an expert to report.

When we heard that expert's verdict we were blown clean out of
        time,
    And absorbed the fact that we had fallen in.
The gold, he said, would run 'bout four ounces to the ton;
    With traces, too, of copper, zinc and tin.

Old Hawkins he was jubilant, and up at Peter's store
    A lovely lot of specimens was showing;

And we gazed at them and groaned, for the truth had to be owned:
  We had put him on a pile without our knowing.

We couldn't let the thing slip through our fingers, so to speak.
  There were thousands in the mine without a doubt.
So me and Baker Brothers, and half a dozen others,
  We formed a syndicate to buy him out.

Well, he said he'd not the money to develop such a claim,
  And he'd sell it if we made a decent bid.
So we made pretence at dealing, and it almost seemed like stealing
  When he parted, for five hundred lovely quid.

* * * *

We haven't seen the vendor in the Flat for nigh a week,
  And we're wishing, on the whole, he'd never come.
The confounded mine's a duffer; for that simple-minded buffer
  He had salted it. The "expert" was a chum.

Hawkins wasn't reckoned much at all in Dingo Flat.
  We'd a notion that his headpiece was amiss.
But we wish to have it stated, he was rather underrated.
  (That's why I'm standing here and telling this.)

THE
SILENT
MEMBER

He lived in Mundaloo, and Bill McClosky was his name,
But folks that knew him well had little knowledge of that same;
For he some'ow lost his surname, and he had so much to say—
He was called "The Silent Member" in a mild, sarcastic way.

He could talk on any subject—from the weather and the crops
To astronomy and Euclid, and he never minded stops;
And the lack of a companion didn't lay him on the shelf,
For he'd stand before a looking-glass and argue with himself.

He would talk for hours on lit'rature, or calves, or art, or wheat;
There was not a bally subject you could say had got him beat;
And when strangers brought up topics that they reckoned he
    would baulk,
He'd remark, "I never heard of that." But all the same—he'd talk.

He'd talk at christ'nings by the yard; at weddings by the mile;
And he used to pride himself upon his choice of words and style.
In a funeral procession his remarks would never end
On the qualities and virtues of the dear departed friend.

We got quite used to hearing him, and no one seemed to care—
In fact, no happ'ning seemed complete unless his voice was there.
For close on thirty year he talked, and none could talk him down,
Until one day an agent for insurance struck the town.

Well, we knew The Silent Member, and we knew what he could do,
And it wasn't very long before we knew the agent, too,
As a crack long-distance talker that was pretty hard to catch;
So we called a hasty meeting and decided on a match.

Of course, we didn't tell them we were putting up the game;
But we fixed it up between us, and made bets upon the same.
We named a time-keep and a referee to see it through;
Then strolled around, just casual, and introduced the two.

The agent got first off the mark, while our man stood and grinned;
He talked for just one solid hour, then stopped to get his wind.
"Yes; but—" sez Bill; that's all he said; he couldn't say no more;
The agent go right in again, and fairly held the floor.

On policies, and bonuses, and premiums, and all that,
He talked and talked until we thought he had our man out flat.
"I think—" Bill got in edgeways, but that there insurance chap
Just filled himself with atmosphere; and took the second lap.

I saw our man was getting dazed, and sort of hypnotized,
And they oughter pulled the agent up right there, as I advised.

209

"See here—" Bill started, husky; but the agent came again,
And talked right on for four hours good—from six o'clock to ten.

Then Bill began to crumple up, and weaken at the knees,
When all at once he ups and shouts, "Here, give a bloke a breeze!
Just take a pull for half a tick and let me have the floor,
And I'll take out a policy." The agent said no more.

The Silent Member swallowed hard, then coughed and cleared his
     throat,
But not a single word would come—no; not a blessed note.
His face looked something dreadful—such a look of pained dismay;
Then he gave us one pathetic glance, and turned, and walked away.

He's hardly spoken since that day—not more than "Yes" or "No".
We miss his voice a good bit, too; the town seems rather slow.
He was called "The Silent Member" just sarcastic, I'll allow;
But since that agent handled him it sort o' fits him now.

THE
PHILISTINE

Smith is a very stupid man;
  He lives next door to me;
He has no settled scheme or plan
  Of domesticity.
He does not own a gramophone,
  Nor rush for morning trains;
His garden paths are overgrown,
  He seldom entertains.

In all our staid suburban street
  He strikes the one false note.
He goes about in slippered feet,
  And seldom wears a coat.
I don't know how he earns his bread;
  'Tis said he paints or writes;
And frequently, I've heard it said,
  He works quite late at nights.

She's quite a pretty girl, his wife.
  Our women-folk declare
It is a shame she spoiled her life
  By wedding such a bear.
And yet she seems quite satisfied
  With this peculiar man;
And says, with rather foolish pride,
  He is Bohemian.

He will not join our tennis club,
  Nor come to may'ral balls,
Nor meet the neighbours in a rub
  At bridge, nor pay them calls.
He just delights to scoff and sneer,
  And feigns to be amused
At everything we hold most dear—
  What wonder he's abused?

Although he's ostracized a deal
  He never makes a fuss;
I sometimes think he seems to feel
  He ostracizes *us!*
But that, of course, is quite absurd;
  And, risking the disgrace,
I sometimes say a kindly word
  When I pass by his place.

But still, although one likes to keep
  One's self a bit select,
And not be, so to speak, too cheap,
  I'm broad in that respect.
So oft, on sultry summer eves,
  I waive all diffidence,
And chat across the wilted leaves
  That garb our garden fence.

But, oh, his talk is so absurd!
  His notions are so crude.
Such drivel I have seldom heard;
  His mode of speech is rude.
He mentions "stomach" in a bark
  You'd hear across the street.
He lacks those little ways that mark
  A gentleman discreet.

Good books he seldom seems to read;
  In Art all taste he lacks.
To Slopham's works he pays no heed;
  He scorns my almanacks—
Framed almanacks! It's simply rot
  To hear the fellow prate
About Velasquez, Villon, Scott,
  And such folk out of date.

He lacks all soul for music, too;
  He hates the gramophone;
And when we play some dance-tune new
  I've often heard him groan.
He says our music gives him sad,
  Sad thoughts of slaughtered things.
I think Smith is a little mad;
  Nice thoughts to me it brings.

Now, I have quite a kindly heart;
  Good works I do not stint;
Last week I spoke to Smith apart,
  And dropped a gentle hint.
He will be snubbed, I told him flat,
  By neighbours round about,
Unless he wears a better hat
  On Sundays, when he's out.

Last Sunday morn he passed my place
  About the hour of four;
A smile serene was on his face,
  And rakishly he wore
A most dilapidated hat
  Upon his shameless head.
"This ought to keep 'em off the mat,"
  He yelled. *I cut him dead.*

THE BRIDGE
ACROSS
THE CRICK

Joseph Jones and Peter Dawking
    Strove in an election fight;
And you'd think, to hear them talking,
    Each upheld the people's right.
Each declared he stood for Progress and against his country's foes
When he sought their votes at Wombat, where the Muddy River
        flows.

Peter Dawking, scorning party,
    As an Independent ran;
Joseph Jones, loud, blatant, hearty,
    Was a solid party man.
But the electors up at Wombat vowed to him alone they'd stick
Who would give his sacred promise for the "bridge across the crick".

Bland, unfaithful politicians
    Long had said this bridge should be.
Some soared on to high positions,
    Some sank to obscurity;
Still the bridge had been denied it by its unrelenting foes—
By the foes of patient Wombat, where the Muddy River flows.

Up at Wombat Peter Dawking
    Held a meeting in the hall,
And he'd spent an hour in talking
    On the far-flung Empire's Call,
When a local greybeard, rising, smote him with this verbal brick:
"Are or are yeh not in favour of the bridge across the crick?"

Peter just ignored the question,
    Proudly patriotic man;
Understand a mean suggestion
    Men like Peter never can,
Or that free enlightened voters look on all Great Things as rot,
While a Burning Local Question fires each local patriot.

Joseph Jones, serene and smiling,
    Took all Wombat to his heart.
"Ah," he said, his "blood was b'iling"—
    He declared it "made him smart"
To reflect how they'd been swindled; and he cried in ringing tones
"Gentlemen, your bridge is certain if you cast your votes for Jones!"

Joseph Jones and Peter Dawking
    Strove in an election fight,
And, when they had finished talking,

On the great election night
They stood level in the voting, and the hope of friends and foes
Hung upon the box from Wombat, where the Muddy River flows.

Then the Wombat votes were counted;
   Jones, two hundred; Dawking, three!
Joseph, proud and smiling, mounted
   On a public balcony,
And his friends were shrill with triumph, for that contest, shrewdly
     run,
In the House gave Jones's Party a majority of one.

Jones's Party—note the sequel—
   Rules that country of the Free,
And the fight, so nearly equal,
   Swayed the whole land's destiny.
And the Big Things of the Nation are delayed till Hope grows sick—
Offered up as sacrifices to "the bridge across the crick".

Dawking now is sadly fearing
   For the crowd's intelligence.
Joseph, skilled in engineering,
   Full of pomp and sly pretence,
Still holds out the pleasing promise of that bridge whene'er he goes
Up to Wombat, patient Wombat, where the Muddy River flows.

A SONG
OF RAIN

Because a little vagrant wind veered south from China Sea;
Or else, because a sun-spot stirred; and yet again, maybe
Because some idle god in play breathed on an errant cloud,
The heads of twice two million folk in gratitude are bowed.

Patter, patter . . . Boolcoomatta,
Adelaide and Oodnadatta,
Pepegoona, parched and dry
Laugh beneath a dripping sky.
Riverina's thirsting plain
Knows the benison of rain.
Ararat and Arkaroola
Render thanks with Tantanoola
For the blessings they are gaining,
And it's raining—raining—raining!

Because a heav'n-sent monsoon the mists before it drove;
Because things happened in the moon; or else, because High Jove,
Unbending, played at waterman to please a laughing boy,
The hearts through all a continent are raised in grateful joy

Weeps the sky at Wipipee
Far Farina's folk are dippy
With sheer joy, while Ballarat
Shouts and flings aloft its hat.
Thirsty Thackaringa yells;
Taltabooka gladly tells
Of a season wet and windy;
Men rejoice on Murrindindie;
Kalioota's ceased complaining;
For it's raining—raining—raining!

Because a poor bush parson prayed an altruistic prayer,
Rich with unselfish fellow-love that Heaven counted rare;
And yet, mayhap, because one night a meteor was hurled
Across the everlasting blue, the luck was with our world.

On the wilds of Winininnie
Cattle low and horses whinny,
Frolicking with sheer delight.
From Beltana to The Bight,
In the Mallee's sun-scorched towns,
In the sheds on Darling Downs,
In the huts at Yudnapinna,
Tents on Tidnacoordininna,
To the sky all heads are craning—
For it's raining—raining—raining!

Because some strange, cyclonic thing has happened—God knows
        where—
Men dream again of easy days, of cash to spend and spare.
The ring fair Clara coveted, Belinda's furs are nigh,
As clerklings watch their increments fall shining from the sky.

Rolls the thunder at Eudunda;
Leongatha, Boort, Kapunda
Send a joyous message down;
Sorrows, flooded, sink and drown.
Ninkerloo and Nerim South
Hail the breaking of the drouth;
From Toolangi's wooded mountains
Sounds the song of plashing fountains;
Sovereign Summer's might is waning;
It is raining—raining—raining!

Because the breeze blew sou'-by-east across the China Sea;
Or else, because the thing was willed through all eternity
By gods that rule the rushing stars, or gods long aeons dead,
The earth is made to smile again, and living things are fed.

Mile on mile from Mallacoota
Runs the news, and far Baroota
Speeds it over hill and plain,
Till the slogan of the rain
Rolls afar to Yankalilla;
Wallaroo and Wirrawilla
Shout it o'er the leagues between,
Telling of the dawning green.
Frogs at Cocoroc are croaking,
Booboorowie soil is soaking,
Oodla Wirra, Orroroo
Breathe relief and hope anew.
Wycheproof and Wollongong
Catch the burden of the song
That is rolling, rolling ever
O'er the plains of Never Never,
Sounding in each mountain rill,
Echoing from hill to hill . . .
In the lonely, silent places
Men lift up their glad, wet faces,
And their thanks ask no explaining —
It is raining—raining—raining!

HYMN OF FUTILITY

Lord, Thou hast given unto us a land.
　In Thy beneficence Thou has ordained
That we should hold a country great and grand,
　Such as no race of old has ever gained.
A favoured people, basking in Thy smile:
　So dost Thou leave us to work out our fate;
But, Lord, be patient yet a little while.
　The shade is pleasing and our task is great.

Lo, Thou hast said: "This land I give to you
　To be the cradle of a mighty race,
Who shall take up the White Man's task anew,
　And all the nations of the world outpace.
No heritage for cowards or for slaves,
　Here is a mission for the brave, the strong.
Then see ye to it, lest dishonoured graves
　Bear witness that he tarried overlong."

Lo, Thou hast said: "When ye have toiled and tilled,
　When ye have borne the heat, and wisely sown,
And every corner of the vineyard filled
　With goodly growth, the land shall be your own.
Then shall your sons and your sons' sons rejoice.
　Then shall the race speak with a conqueror's mouth;
And all the world shall hearken to its voice,
　And heed the great White Nation of the South."

And Thou hast said: 'This, striving, shall ye do.
　Be diligent to tend and guard the soil.
If this great heritage I trust to you
　Be worth the purchase of a meed of toil,
Then shall ye not, at call of game or mart,
　Forgo the labour of a single day.
They spurn the gift who treasure but a part.
　Guard ye the whole, lest all be cast away."

* * * *

Great cities have we builded here, O Lord;
　And corn and kine full plenty for our need
We have; and doth the wondrous land afford
　Treasure beyond the wildest dreams of greed.
Even this tiny portion of Thy gift,
　One corner of our mightly continent,
Doth please us well. A voice in prayer we lift:
　"Lord, give us peace! For we are well content."

Backblock Ballads, title page

Lord, give us peace; for Thou has sent a sign:
    Smoke of a raider's ships athwart the sky!
Nay, suffer us to hold this gift of Thine!
    The burden, Lord! The burden—by and by!
The sun is hot, Lord, and the way is long!
    'Tis pleasant in this corner Thou has blest.
Leave us to tarry here with wine and song.
    Our little corner, Lord! Guard Thou the rest!

But yesterday our fathers hither came,
    Rovers and strangers on a foreign strand.
Must we, for their neglect, bear all the blame?
    Nay, Master, *we have come to love our land!*
But see, the task Thou givest us is great;
    The load is heavy and the way is long!
Hold Thou our enemy without the gate;
    When we have rested then shall we be strong.

Lord, Thou hast spoken ... And, with hands to ears,
    We would shut out the thunder of Thy voice
That in the nightwatch wakes our sudden fears—
    "The day is here, and yours must be the choice.
Will ye be slaves and shun the task of men?
    Will ye be weak who may be brave and strong?"
We wave our banners boastfully, and then,
    Weakly we answer, "Lord, the way is long!"

"Time tarries not, but here ye tarry yet,
    The futile masters of a continent,
Guard ye the gift I gave? Do ye forget?"
    And still we answer, "Lord, we are content.
Fat have we grown upon this goodly soil,
    A little while be patient, Lord, and wait.
To-morrow and to-morrow will we toil.
    The shade is pleasing, Lord! Our task is great!"

But ever through the clamour of the mart,
    And ever on the playground through the cheers:
"He spurns the gift who guardeth but a part"—
    So doth the warning fall on heedless ears.
"Guard ye the treasure if the gift be meet"—
    (Loudly we call the odds, we cheer the play.)
"For he who fears the burden and the heat
    Shall glean the harvest of a squandered day."

THE SINGING
GARDEN

GREEN WALLS

I love all gum-trees well. But, best of all,
  I love the tough old warriors that tower
About these lawns, to make a great green wall
  And guard, like sentries, this exotic bower
  Of shrub and fern and flower.
These are my land's own sons, lean, straight and tall,
Where crimson parrots and grey gang-gangs call
  Thro' many a sunlit hour.

My friends, these grave old veterans, scarred and stern,
  Changeless throughout the changing seasons they.
But at their knees their tall sons lift and yearn—
  Slim spars and saplings—prone to sport and sway
  Like carefree boys at play;
Waxing in beauty when their young locks turn
To crimson, and, like beacon fires burn
  To deck Spring's holiday.

I think of Anzacs when the dusk comes down
  Upon the gums—of Anzacs tough and tall.
Guarding this gateway, Diggers strong and brown.
  And when, thro' Winter's thunderings, sounds their call,
  Like Anzacs, too, they fall . . .
Their ranks grow thin upon the hill's high crown:
My sentinels! But, where those ramparts frown,
  Their stout sons mend the wall.

THE LYRETAIL

Far in the forest depths I dwell,
  The master mimic of them all,
To pour from out my secret dell
  Echo of many a bushland call,
That over all the forest spills;
  Echo of many a birdland note,
When out about the timbered hills
Sounds all that borrowed lore that fills
  My magic throat.

I am the artist. Songs to me
  From all this gay green land are sped;
And when the wondrous canopy
  Of my great, fronded tail is spread—
A glorious veil, at even's hush—
  Above my head, I do my part;
Then wren and robin, finch and thrush—
All are re-echoed in a rush
  Of perfect art.

Here by my regal throne of state,
  To serve me for a swift retreat,
The little runways radiate;
  And when the tread of alien feet
Draws near I vanish: ever prone
  To quick alarm when aught offends
That secret ritual of the throne.
My songs are for my mate alone,
  And favoured friends.

I am the artist. None may find,
  In all the world, a match for me:
Rare feathered loveliness combined
  With such enchanting minstrelsy.
In a land vocal with gay song
  I choose whate'er I may require;
I wait, I listen all day long,
Then to the music of a throng
  I tune my lyre.

THE
INDIAN
MYNA

Gimme the town an' its clamour an' clutter;
   I ain't very fond of the bush;
For my cobbers are coves of the gardens and gutter—
   A tough metropolitan push.
I ain't never too keen on the countryfield life;
It's the hustle an' bustle for me an' me wife.

So I swagger an' strut an' I cuss an' I swagger;
   I'm wise to the city's hard way.
A bit of a bloke an' a bit of a bragger;
   I've always got plenty to say.
Learned thro' knockin' about since my people came out
From the land at the back of Bombay.

When out in the bush I am never a ranger;
   There never ain't nothin' to see.
Besides, them bush birds got no time for a stranger;
   So town an' the traffic for me.
I sleep in the gardens an' loaf in the street,
An' sling off all day at the fellers I meet.

An' I swagger an' scold an' strut an' I swagger,
   An' pick up me fun where I can,
Or tell off me wife, who's a bit of a nagger,
   Or scrap with the sparrers for scran.
A bonzer at bluffin', I give you my word,
For, between you an' me, I'm a pretty tough bird.

THE PALLID CUCKOO

Dolefully and drearily
  Come I with the spring;
Wearily and eerily
  My threnody I sing.
Hear my drear, discordant note
  Sobbing, sobbing in my throat,
  Weaving, wailing thro' the wattles
  Where the builders are a-wing.

Outcast and ostracized,
  Miserable me!
By the feathered world despised,
  Chased from tree to tree.
Nought to do the summer thro',
  My woeful weird a dree;
  Singing, "Pity, ah, pity,
  Miserable me!"

I'm the menace and the warning,
  Loafing, labour-shy.
In the harmony of morning
  Out of tune am I—
Out of tune and out of work,
Meanly 'mid the leaves I lurk,
  Fretfully to sing my sorrow,
    Furtively to spy.

Outcast and desolate,
  Miserable me!
Earning ever scorn and hate
  For my treachery.
Shiftless drone, I grieve alone,
  To a mournful key
  Singing, "Sorrow, ah, sorrow!
  Miserable me!"

HEAT
WAVE

Day after day, week after burning week,
   A ruthless sun has sucked the forest dry.
Morn after anxious morn men's glances seek
   The hills, hard-etched against a harder sky.
    Gay blossoms droop and die.
Menace is here, as day draws to its peak,
And, 'mid the listless gums along the creek,
   Hot little breezes sigh.

To-day the threat took shape; the birds were dumb.
   Once more, as sullen, savage morning broke,
The silence told that trembling fear had come,
   To bird and beast and all the forest folk.
    One little wisp of smoke
Far in the south behind the listless gum
Grew to a purple pall. Like some far drum,
   A distant muttering broke.

Red noon beheld red death come shouting o'er
   These once green slopes—a leaping, living thing.
Touched by its breath, tree after tall tree wore
   A fiery crown, as tho' to mock a king —
    A ghastly blossoming
Of sudden flame that died and was no more.
And, where a proud old giant towered of yore,
   Stood now a blackened thing.

Fierce raved the conquering flame, as demons rave,
   Earth shook to thunders of the falling slain.
Brambles and bushes, once so gay and brave,
   Shrank back, and writhed, and shrieked and shrieked again
   Like sentient things in pain.
Gone from the forest all that kind spring gave ...
And now, at laggard last, too late to save,
   Comes soft, ironic rain.

**THE
SILVER-EYE**

Down among the strawberries,
   Up among the plums,
Cheeping in the cherry-tree
   When early autumn comes,
In our silver spectacles
   And sober olive suits.
We're very, very innocent;
   We wouldn't touch your fruits.

Well, maybe just a speckled one,
   A windfall here and there.
But raid your precious strawberries?
   Oh on, we wouldn't dare.
Behold our bland astonishment,
   The charge is quite absurd!
It must have been a parrot
   Or some other kind of bird.

It must have been a satin bird;
   It must have been a crow.
It couldn't possibly be us;
   We are so meek, you know,
With our silver spectacles.
   The accusation's vile!
How can you deem us guilty
   When we're whistling all the while?

Well, if you've caught us in the act
   There's no more to be said.
The plums are blue and succulent,
   The strawberries are red.
And who'd refuse a dainty dish
   When early autumn comes?
Oh, write a rhyme about us, man,
   And pay for all your plums.

THE GROUND THRUSH

I'm a business man; and I can't spare time
   For this fluting and fussing and frilling.
The song of my cousin may be sublime,
   But I never have found it filling.
So I run and I dig and I dig and I run,
And I'm at it soon as the day's begun,
And I never knock off till the light is done
   Over the garden and lawn and tilling.

I'm a business man on my business bent,
   And I've never an hour of leisure.
I have little regard for sentiment,
   And I fritter no time in pleasure.
But I dig and I run and I run and I dig;
And you never see me at my ease on a twig,
Prinking and posing in holiday rig
   Or trilling a tuneful measure.

I'm a business man, and I've much to do;
   So the day's work must be speeded.
For time is fleeting and worms are few—
   I've never had all I needed.
So I run and I dig and I dig and I run
From sun to shadow, from shadow to sun,
I'm a business man, and the world I shun;
   So I live and I die unheeded.

**THE
YELLOW
ROBIN**

I'm the friendliest of them all,
    When winter comes;
Daily at your door I call
    Begging crumbs.
Clinging sideways to a stake,
Eloquent appeal I make.
"Spare a scrap for pity's sake!
    This cold air numbs."

I will follow as you dig
    And search the dirt.
Worms or bettles, small or big,
    Are my dessert;
And, should you seem gently kind,
From your hand I do not mind
Taking anything you find;
    But I'm a flirt.

For when spring comes to the land
    You are forgot.
I have great affairs on hand
    As days wax hot.
Should I pass you, I pretend
To ignore my winter's friend;
Intimacy's at an end;
    I know you not.

Yet, when winter comes once more,
    And summer ends,
You will find me at your door
    To make amends;
Clinging sideways to a stake,
Eloquent appeal I'll make:
"Spare a scrap for pity's sake!
    Aw, let's be friends!"

DUSK

Now is the healing, quiet hour that fills
  This gay, green world with peace and grateful rest.
Where lately over opalescent hills
  The blood of slain Day reddened all the west,
  Now comes at Night's behest,
A glow that over all the forest spills,
As with the gold of promised daffodils.
  Of all hours this is best.

It is the time for thoughts of holy things,
  Of half-forgotten friends and one's own folk.
O'er all, the garden-scented sweetness clings.
  To mingle with the wood fire's drifting smoke.
  A bull-frog's startled croak
Sounds from the gully where the last bird sings
His laggard vesper hymn, with folded wings;
  And Night spreads forth her cloak.

Keeping their vigil where the great range yearns,
  Like rigid sentries stand the wise old gums.
On blundering wings a night-moth wheels and turns
  And lumbers on, mingling its drowsy hums
  With that far roll of drums,
Where the swift creek goes tumbling midst the ferns . . .
Now, as the first star in the zenith burns,
  The dear, soft darkness comes.

JOURNALIST DAYS

(A SELECTION OF POEMS

FROM THE MELBOURNE *HERALD*)

VAGRANT'S REVENGE

I could wish for a house like this (he said)
    For a home, to rest a while . . .
Thanks for the 'baccy, an' meat an' bread;
    'Twill last me another ten mile . . .
But I sicken of miles that end in a camp
    An' a dreamin' of things I miss,
An' board and bed in the dark an' the damp,
An' the aimless life of a lonely tramp.
    I could wish for a house like this.

If I had a house like this (he said)
    An' a trifle of cash at call,
I'd be a king, with a roof o'erhead,
    An' me own hearth-fire an' all.
Why, if I had a house like this—an' yet,
    Ere more than a month was o'er,
I'd maybe weary of stayin' set,
An' likely sell it for what I could get,
    An' take to the roads once more.

I'd paddle abroad on the same old beat
    With a fine, fat purse in me kick,
An' I'd come to a house that denied me meat
    When I'd begged for it, tired and sick.
There I'd plead an' I'd wait for the cold, hard stare,
    An' the prim, superior "No"!
Then I'd tell 'em off from the doorway there,
An' I'd sling 'em a couple o' bob for the fare
    When I'd tole 'em where they could go.

An' I'd tramp to every house (he said)
    Where out of a scanty fare,
Came a morsel o' meat or a bite o' bread—
    Such scraps as the poor may spare.
An' I'd nibble me crust or I'd sup me broth
    At the humble meal they'd spread;
Then I'd slip a bank-note under the cloth,
An' scuttle away to escape the wrath
    When they found what a crook they'd fed.

SHOW THOUGHTS FROM THE BUSH

(With apologies to the shade of Browning)

O to be in Melbourne
  Now the Show is there;
    For whoever goes to Melbourne
  Sees now the broad brood mare
And the lowing bull and the champion sheaf
Of golden grain, nigh past belief,
And the litter of pigs with their fine, fat sow,
  In Melbourne—now!

I hear again the hooves a-rattle,
The barking dogs and the bellowing cattle.
  Hark, where old Blossom o'er the Show stall's ledge
Looks out and dreams of pleasant fields of clover.
  Leaning her dewlap on the door's hard edge—
That's the wise calf, he bellows ten times over
  As if he thought—altho' she stands quite near him—
  His parent couldn't hear him . . .
And, tho' the beards, look rough that lean about,
They have been very carefully combed out.
  So the talk ebbs and flows of crops and seasons,
Costs and world prices and the threat of war
  And war's effect; while men discover reasons
Why this year will be well worth waiting for.
  "Stick to the land," they say, "The land's all right.
  Since twenty-eight it's been a fair tough fight;
But, Lord, the world has got to have its tucker
And clothes to wear." Then Smith, with brows a-pucker,
  Says, "Look; my sow had ought of won that Cup
  After the hours I spent dollin' her up."
Then someone calls, "Come on! The jumpin's started!"
  And there are sights to see, smells on the air,
Old friends I know—it makes a man down-hearted
  Thinking. Heigh-ho! I wish that I was there.

THE HAPPY MAN

Today I met a happy man;
    A joyous light shone in his eye;
I marked the ruffling smiles that ran
    Athwart his face, and wondered why
His recent gloom had given place
    To joy, so strangely he behaved.
He waved a paper in my face
    And cried aloud, "We're saved!
      We're saved!"

"We're saved!" he yelled. "It's in the news!
    Oh, have you seen it, man? It's great!"
"Why, yes," said I. "I did peruse
    My daily sheet. But why this state
Of jubilation? Has the fall
    Of deficits caused you this glee?
It's welcome news; but, after all,
    Your marked excitement puzzles me."

"Times might," said I, "on some day
      hence
    Improve: but we've a way to go."
"Aw, deficits!" said he. "Talk sense!
    We're saved, I tell you! Don't you
      know
That what Australia these weeks past
    Has talked and thought and dreamed of, too,
In doubt, has come about at last?
    The country's saved, I'm telling
      you!"

"You speak of armaments, perchance,"
    Said I. "Has Germany agreed—"
He cast on me one pitying glance
    And waved his sheet. "Man! Can't
      you read?
Or are you off your nut?" he raved.
    "It's here! The news! The very
      best!
I tell you, man, the country's saved!
    They've picked Don Bradman for
      the Test!!"

TWO
VETERANS

Side by side near the road they stand
  Like grave old men grown wise with years,
Veterans twain in this forest land,
Marching together, hand to hand,
  Sober as ancient seers.
Gnarled and bitten and scarred and bent,
Sap run sluggish and youth all spent,
  They lift spare limbs to the heartening sky,
  World-worn and weary, yet loth to
      die.

They had known the bite of the blunt stone axe
  (Wounds like warrior's long healed scars)
When they hid the quarry of hunting blacks,
Ranging the forest with eyes on the tracks
  That led to these lusty spare—
Spars grown old ere the spoilers came
To give this forest to blade and flame;
  Too old to profit that ruthless greed
  Which their likelier kinsmen went to feed.

For eight score summers the winds that blow
  Down thro' the forest have worked their will;
For eight score winters storm and snow,
Frost and fury have bowed them low;
  Yet stand the veterans still,
By the side of the road where the cars run down
With their transient freights to the mushroom town;
  And they lift spare limbs to the deathless sky,
  World-worn and weary, yet loth to die.

OUR
TOWN
AWAKES

Six o'clock. From the railway yard
   The engine toots; careering hard,
  A milk-cart rattles by and stops;
  A magpie calls from the gum-tree tops;
The pub "boots", sweeping out the bar,
Waves to the early service-car,
  While the town's chief toper waits outside,
  Woe-begone and bleary-eyed;
Two cows go lowing down the way;
A rooster crows. It's another day.

Eight o'clock. The tradesmen come—
  Shop-boys whistling, masters glum,
  To stand at doors and stretch and yawn;
  Fronts are swept and blinds are drawn;
The washerwoman, Mrs Dubbs,
Slip-slops off to her taps and tubs,
  Washing clothes for other folk;
  The cheery barber cracks a joke,
But the day's first client fails to laugh—
Fresh from a tiff from his better half.

Nine o'clock. Precise and neat,
  Miss Miggs comes mincing down the street,
  The town's dressmaker, pert and prim,
  Sly eyes, from under her hat's brim,
Gathering gossip by the way:
The same old goings-on today—
  That grocer off for his morning nip;
  The chemist, too, that married rip,
Flirting again with the girl next door.
Miss Miggs gleans twenty tales to store.

Ten o'clock. The town grows brisk;
  Down the main street motors whisk;
  Jinkers, carts and farmers' drays
  Stop at shops and go their ways;
In soleman talk with the town surveyor
Comes Mr Mullinger, our mayor,
  Pausing at doors for a friendly chat;
  He bows, he smiles, he lifts his hat . . .
Now a brisker rush and a sudden din:
"That's her!" And the city train comes in.

UNCON- SIDERED TRIFLES

"A piece of turkey gobbler here, a half a chicken there,
Plum-duff an' pies an' things, scraps o' Christmas fare—
Most folks has some oddments they're loth to pitch away
When they are fed an' satisfied," said Ole Pete Parraday.
"An' then, quite accidental like, I happens at the door
When folks is fine an' generous just as the feast is o'er.
'Why, here's a bit o' luck,' they says, delighted. 'Here's ole Pete.
An' jist in time to help us out from wastin' things to eat.'

"Not that I wants for dinner of a Christmas time each year,
The way the neighbours presses me an' fights for me round here.
But I can't play no fav'rites; it's turn an' turn about;
For if I dined with Robertsons when it's the Johnsons' shout
Why, I'd never hear the end of it. But when I've ate me fill
I calls on all the neighbours as a matter of goodwill
Just to wish 'em 'Merry Christmas' an' treat 'em all the same.
An' if they presses things on me, well, how am I to blame?

"I reckon when the holid'ys is pretty nearly thro'
My larder's jist about as full an' jist as varied, too,
As any in the districk—stuff to make yeh lick yer chops.
Not bad for one ole pensioner wot don't spend much in shops.
Fancy sortser tucker, too, soothin' to the taste—
Not that I'm greedy, mind yeh; but I hates to see things waste;
I hates to see things throwed away wot easily might be
Meals from the lap o' luxury for my ole dog an' me.

"Not that I holds with beggin' mind, as you knows very well,
But if you seen my hut this week you'd think the Grand 'Otel
Or else the Caffy Parry was shifted to the scrub,
Half ways a slap-up resterong an' half a toney pub;
With chicken laigs an' turkey wings an' cake, got up reel fine,
An' a bottle, that ain't opened yet, of reel sherry wine!
But I puts it on the table every time I has a meal;
An' it's near as good as drinkin' it, the way it makes me feel."

GLOSSARY

Alley, to toss in the: To give up the ghost.

Also ran, The: On the turf, horses that fail to secure a leading place; hence, obscure persons, nonentities.

Ammer-lock (Hammer-lock): A favourite and effective hold in wrestling.

Ard Case (Hard Case): A shrewd or humorous person.

Aussie: Australia; an Australian.

'Ayseed (Hayseed): A rustic.

Back Chat: Impudent repartee.

Back and Fill: To vacillate; to shuffle.

Back the Barrer: To intervene without invitation.

Bag of Tricks: All one's belongings.

Barmy (Balmy): Foolish; silly.

Barrack: To take sides.

Beak: A magistrate. (Possibly from Anglo-Saxon, Beag—a magistrate

Beano: A feast.

Beans: Coins; money.

Beat: Puzzled; defeated.

Beat, off the: Out of the usual routine.

Beat the band: To amaze.

Beef (to beef it out): To declaim vociferously.

Beller: The lungs.

Biff: To smite.

Bint: Girl.

Bird, to give the: To treat with derision.

Blighty: London.

Bli'me: An oath with the fangs drawn.

Blind: Deception, "bluff".

Blob: A shapeless mass.

Bloke: The head. To lose or do in the block: To become flustered; excited; angry; to lose confidence. To keep the block: To remain calm; dispassionate.

Block, the: A fashionable city walk.

Bloke: A male adult of the genus homo.

Blubber, blub: To weep.

Bob: A shilling.

Bokays: Compliments, flattery.

Boko: The nose.

Bong-tong: Patrician (Fr. bon ton).

Bonzer, boshter, bosker: Adjectives expressing the surperlative of excellence.

Boodle: Money; wealth.

Book: In whist, six tricks.

Book: A bookie, q.v.

Booked: Engaged.

Bookie: A book-maker (turf); one who makes a betting book on sporting events.

Break (to break away, to do a break): To depart in haste.

Breast up to: To accost.

Brisket: The chest.

Brown: A copper coin.

Brums: Tawdry finery (from Brummagem-Birmingham).

Buckley's (Chance): A forlorn hope.

Buck up: Cheer up.

Bump: To meet; to accost aggressively.

Bun, to take the: To take the prize (used ironically).

Bundle, to drop the: To surrender; to give up hope.

Bunk: To sleep in a "bunk" or rough bed. To do a bunk: To depart.

Bunnies, to hawk the: To peddle rabbits.

Bus, to miss the: To neglect opportunities.

Caboose: A small dwelling.

Cat, to whip the: To cry over spilt milk; i.e., to whip the cat that has spilt the milk.

C.B.: Confined to barracks.

Cert: A certainty; a foregone conclusion.

Chap: A "bloke" or "cove".

Chase yourself: Depart; avaunt; "fade away". q.v.

Chat: To address tentatively; to "word", q.v.

Cheque, to pass in one's: To depart this life.

Chew, to chew it over; to chew the rag: To sulk; to nurse a grievance.

Chiack: Vulgar banter; coarse invective.

Chin: To talk; to wag the chin.

Chip: To "chat", q.v. Chip in: To intervene.

Chiv: The face.

Chow: A native of far Cathay.

Chuck up: To relinquish. Chuck off: To chaff; to employ sarcasm.

Chump: A foolish fellow.

Chunk: A lump; a mass.

Clean: Completely; utterly.

Click: A clique; a "push".

Cliner: A young unmarried female.

Clobber: Raiment; vesture.

Cobber: A boon companion.

Collect: To receive one's deserts.

Colour-line: In pugilism, the line drawn by white boxers excluding coloured fighters—for diverse reasons.

Conk: The nose.

Coot: A person of no account (used contemptuously).

Cop: To seize; to secure; also, s., an avocation, a "job".

Cop (or Copper): A police constable.

Copper-top: Red head.

Count, to take the: In pugilism, to remain prostrate for ten counted seconds, and thus lose the fight.

Cove: A "chap" or "bloke". q.v. (Gipsy).

Cow: A thoroughly unworthy, not to say despicable person, place, thing, or circumstance. A fair cow: An utterly obnoxious and otherwise

inexpressible person, place, thing or circumstance.

Crack: To smite. s. A blow.

Crack a boo: To divulge a secret; to betray emotion.

Crack hardy: To suppress emotion; to endure patiently; to keep a secret.

Cray: A crayfish.

Crib: A dwelling.

Croak: To die.

Crook: Unwell; dishonest; spurious; fraudulent. Superlative, Dead Crook.

Crool (cruel) the pitch: To frustrate; to interfere with one's schemes or welfare.

Crust: Sustenance; a livelihood.

Cut it out: Omit; discontinue it.

Dago: A native of Southern Europe.

Dash, to do one's: To reach one's Waterloo.

Date: An appointment.

Dawg (dog): A contemptible person; ostentation. To put on dawg: To behave in an arrogant manner.

Dead: In a superlative degree; very.

Deal: To deal it out; to administer punishment; abuse, &c.

Deal: A "hand" at cards.

Deener: A shilling (Fr. Denier. Denarius, a Roman silver coin).

Derry: An aversion; a feud; a dislike.

Dickin: A term signifying distrust or disbelief.

Dile (dial): The face.

Dilly: Foolish; half-witted.

Ding Dong: Strenuous.

Dinkum: Honest; true. "The Dinkum Oil": The truth.

Dipped: Mentally deficient.

Dirt: Opprobrium; a mean speech or action.

Dirty left: A formidable left fist.

Divvies: Dividends; profits.

Dizzy limit: The utmost; the superlative degree.

Do in: To defeat; to kill; to spend.

Done me luck: Lost my good fortune.

Dot in the eye: To strike in the eye.

Douse: To extinguish (Anglo-Saxon).

Drive a quill: To write with a pen; to work in an office.

Duck, to do a: (See "break").

Duds: Personal apparel (Scotch).

Dud: No good; ineffective; used up.

Dutch: German; any native of Central Europe.

'Eads (Heads): The authorities; inner council.

'Eadin': "Heading browns"; tossing pennies.

'Ead over turkey: Head over heels.

'Ead Serang: The chief; the leader.

'Ell fer leather: In extreme haste.

End up, to get: To rise to one's feet.

Fade away, to: To retire; to withdraw.

Fag: A cigarette.

Fair: Extreme; positive.

Fair thing: A wise proceeding; an obvious duty.

Fake: A swindle; a hoax.

Final, to run one's: To die.

Final kick: Final leave.

Finger: An eccentric or amusing person.

Flam: Nonsense; make-believe.

Float, to: To give up the ghost.

Fluff, a bit of: A young female person.

Fly: A turn; a try.

Foot (me foot): A term expressing ridicule.

Frame: The body.

Frill: Affectation.

Furphy: An idle rumour; a canard.

Galoot: A simpleton.

Game: Occupation; scheme; design.

Gawsave: The National Anthem.

Gazob: A fool; a blunderer.

Get, to do a: To retreat hastily.

Gilt: Money; wealth.

Give, to: In one sense, to care.

Gizzard: The heart.

Glarrsy: The glassy eye; a glance of cold disdain. The Glassey Alley: The favourite; the most admired.

Glim: A light.

Going (while the going is good): While the path is clear.

Gone (fair gone): Overcome, as with emotion.

Goo-goo eyes: Loving glances.

Gorspil-cove: A minister of the Gospel.

Grandstand play: Playing to the gallery.

Griffin, the straight: The truth; secret information.

Grip: Occupation; employment.

Groggy: Unsteady; dazed.

Grouch: To mope; to grumble.

Grub: Food.

Guff: Nonsense.

Guy: A foolish fellow.

Guy, to do a: To retire.

Guyver: Make-believe.

Handies: A fondling of hands between lovers.

Hang out: To reside; to last.

Hang-over: The aftermath of the night before.

Hitch, to: To wed.

Hitched: Entangled in the bonds of holy matrimony.

Hit things up: To behave strenuously; riotously.

Hokey Fly, by the: A mild expletive, without any particular meaning.

Hot: Excessive; extreme.

Hump, the: A fit of depression.

241

Hump, to: To carry as a swag or other burden.

Imshee: Begone; retreat; take yourself off.

Intro: Introduction; knock-down. q.v.

It (to be It): To assume a position of supreme importance.

Jane: A woman.

Jiff: A very brief period.

Job, to: To smite.

Joes: Melancholy thoughts.

John: A policeman.

John 'Op (or Jonop): Policeman.

Joint, to jump the: To assume command: to occupy the " joint", i.e., establishment, situation, place of business.

Jolt, to pass a: To deliver a short, sharp blow.

Josser: A simple fellow.

Jug: A prison.

Keep one down: Take a drink.

Keeps, for: For ever, permanently.

Kersplosh: Splash.

Kick: Leave. Kick about: To loaf or hang about.

Kid, to: To deceive; to persuade by flattery.

Kid stakes: Pretence.

King Pin: The leader; the person of chief importance.

Kip: A small chip used for tossing pennies in the occult game of two-up.

Kipsie: A house; the home.

Knob: The head; one in authority.

Knock-down: A ceremony insisted upon by ladies who decline to be "picked up"; a formal introduction.

Knock-out drops: Drugged or impure liquor.

Knock-out punch: A knock-down blow.

Knut: A fop; a well-dressed idler.

Lark: A practical joke; a sportive jest.

Lash: Violence.

Ledding: Leaden.

Leery: Vulgar; low.

Leeuwin: Cape Leeuwin on the South West coast of Australia.

Lid: The hat. To dip the lid: To raise the hat.

Limit: The end; the full length.

Line up: To approach; to accost.

Lingo: Language.

Lip: Impertinence. To give it lip: To talk vociferously.

Little Bourke: Little Bourke Street, Melbourne, Australia.

Little Lons: Little Lonsdale Street, Melbourne, Australia.

Lob, to: To arrive.

'Loo: Woolloomooloo, a part of Sydney.

Lumme: Love me.

Lurk: A plan of action; a regular occupation.

Mafeesh: Finish; I am finished.

Mag: To scold or talk noisily.

Mallee: A species of Eucalypt; the country where the Mallee grows.

Mash: To woo; to pay court. s. A lover.

Maul: To lay hands upon, either violently or with affection.

Meet, a: An assignation.

Mill: A bout of fisticuffs.

Mix: To mix it; to fight strenuously.

Mizzle: To disappear: to depart suddenly.

Mo.: Abbreviation of "moment".

Moniker: A name; a title; a signature.

Mooch: To saunter about aimlessly.

Moon: To loiter.

Mud, my name is: i.e., I am utterly discredited.

Mug: A fool; also the mouth.

Mug, to: To kiss;

Mug: A simpleton.

Mullock, to poke: To deride; to tease.

Mushy: Sentimental.

Nail: Catch.

Nark: s. A spoil-sport; a churlish fellow.

Nark, to: To annoy; to foil.

Natchril: Natural.

Neck and neck: Side by side.

Neck, to get it in the: To receive severe punishment, i.e., "Where the chicken got the axe."

Nick: Physical condition; good health.

Nipper: A small boy.

Nix: Nothing.

Nod, on the : Without payment.

Nose around, to: To seek out inquisitively.

Nothing (ironically): Literally "something considerable".

Odds, above the: Beyond the average; outside the pale.

Oopizootics: An undiagnosed complaint.

Orfis (office): A warning; a word of advice; a hint.

Oricle (oracle), to work the: To secure desired results.

Orl (orl in): Without limit or restriction.

'Ot Socks: Gaily coloured hose.

Out, to: To render unconscious with a blow.

Out, all: Quite exhausted; fully extended.

Pack, to send to the: To relegate to obscurity.

Pal: A friend; a mate (Gipsy).

Pard: A partner; a mate.

Part: Give; hand over.

Pass (pass 'im one): To deliver a blow.

Pat, on one's: Alone; single-handed.

Peach: A desirable young woman; "fresh as a peach".

Peb (pebble): A flash fellow; a "larrikin".

Phiz: The face.

Pick at: To chaff; to annoy.

Pick up, to: To dispense with the ceremony of a "knock-down" or introduction.

Pilot cove: A clergyman.

Pile it on: To rant; to exaggerate.

Pinch: To steal; to place under arrest.

Pins: Legs.

Pip: A fit of depression.

Pitch a tale: To trump up an excuse; to weave a romance.

Plant: To bury.

Plug: To smite with the fist.

Plug along, to: To proceed doggedly.

Plunk: An exclamation expressing the impact of a blow.

Podgy: Fat; plump.

Point: The region of the jaw; much sought after by pugilists.

Point, to: To seize unfair advantage; to scheme.

Pole, up the: Distraught through anger, fear, &c.; also, disappeared, vanished.

Pot, a: A considerable amount; as a "pot of money".

Pot, the old: The male parent (from "Rhyming Slang", the "old pot and pan"—"old man").

Prad: A horse.

Pug: A pugilist.

Pull my (or your) leg: To deceive or get the best of.

Pull, of: Desist.

Pull, to take a: To desist; to discontinue.

Punch a cow: To conduct a team of oxen.

Punter: The natural prey of a "bookie". q.v.

Push: A company of rowdy fellows gathered together for ungentle purposes.

Push up the daisies, to: To be interred.

Queer the pitch: To frustrate; to fool.

Quid: A sovereign, or pound sterling.

Quod: Prison.

Rabbit, to run the: To convey liquor from a public-house.

Rag, to chew the: To grieve; to brood.

Rag, to sky the: To throw a towel into air in token of surrender (pugilism).

Rain, to keep out the: To avoid danger; to act with caution.

Rat: A street urchin; a wharf loafer.

Rattled: Excited; confused.

Recomember: Remember.

Red 'ot: Extreme; out-and-out.

Registry: The office of a Registrar.

Renege: To fail to follow suit (in playing cards); to quit.

Ribuck: Correct, genuine; an interjection signifying assent.

Rile: To annoy. Riled: Roused to anger.

Ring, the: The arena of a prize-fight.

Ring, the dead: A remarkable likeness.

Ringer: Expert.

Rise, a: An accession of fortune; an improvement.

Rocks: A locality in Sydney.

Rook, to: To "take down".

Rorty: Boisterous; rowdy.

Roust, or rouse: To upbraid with many words.

'Roy: Fitzroy, a suburb of Melbourne; its football team.

Ructions: Growling; argument.

Run against: To meet more or less unexpectedly.

Run 'is final: Died.

Saints: A football team of St Kilda, Victoria.

Sandy blight: Ophthalmia.

Savvy: Commonsense; shrewdness.

Sawing wood: "Bluffing"; biding one's time.

School: A club; a clique of gamblers, or others.

Scoot: To hurry; to scuttle.

Scran: Food.

Scrap: Fight.

Set, to: To attack; to regard with disfavour.

Set, to have: To have marked down for punishment or revenge.

Shick, shickered: Intoxicated.

Shook: Stolen; disturbed.

Shook on: Infatuated.

Shyin', or Shine: Excellent; desirable.

Sight: To tolerate; to permit; also to see; observe.

Sir Garneo: In perfect order; satisfactory.

Skirt, or bit of skirt: A female.

Skite: To boast. Skiter: A boaster.

Sky the wipe: See "Rag".

Slab: A portion; a tall, awkward fellow.

Slam: Making all the tricks (in card-playing).

Slanter: Spurious; unfair.

Slap-up: Admirable; excellent.

Slats: The ribs.

Slick: Smart; deft; quick.

Sling: Discard; throw.

Slope, to: To elope; to leave in haste.

Sloppy: Lachrymose; maudlin.

Slushy: A toiler in a scullery.

Smoodge: To flatter or fawn; to bill and coo.

Smoodger: A sycophant; a courtier.

Snag: A hindrance; formidable opponent.

Snake-'eaded: Annoyed, vindictive.

Snake juice: Strong drink.

Snare: To acquire; to seize; to win.

Snarkey: Angry.

Snide: Inferior; or no account.

Snob: A bootmaker.

Snort: To bear a grudge.

Snouted: Treated with disfavour.

Snuff, or snuff it: To expire.

Sock it into: To administer physical punishment.

Solid: Severe; severely.

So-long: A form of farewell.

Sool: To attack; to urge on.

Soot, leadin': A chief attribute.

Sore, to get: To become aggrieved.

Sore-head: A curmudgeon.

Sour, to turn, or get: To become pessimistic or discontented.

Spank: To chastise maternal-wise.

Spar: A gentle bout at fisticuffs.

Spare me days: A pious ejaculation.

Specs.: Spectacles.

Splash: To expend.

Splice: To join in matrimony.

Spout: To preach or speak at length.

Sprag: To accost truculently.

Spruik: To deliver a speech, as a showman.

Spuds: Potatoes.

Square: Upright, honest.

Square an' all: Of a truth; verily.

Squeak: To give away a secret.

Squiz: A brief glance.

Stand-orf: Retiring; reticent.

Stajum: Stadium, where prize-fights are conducted.

Stiffened: Bought over.

Stiff-in: A corpse.

Stoke: To nourish; to eat.

Stop a pot: To quaff ale.

Stop one: To receive a blow.

Straight, on the: In fair and honest fashion.

Strength of it: The truth of it; the value of it.

Stretch, to do a: To serve a term of imprisonment.

Strike: The innocuous remnant of a hardy curse.

Strike: To discover, to meet.

Strike me!: The innocuous remnant of a hard curse.

Strong, going: Proceeding with vigour.

'Struth: An emaciated oath.

Stuff: Money.

Stunt: A performance; a tale.

Swad, Swaddy: A private soldier.

Swank: Affectation; ostentation.

Swap: To exchange.

Swell: An exalted person.

Swig: A draught of water or other liquid.

Swiv'ly: Afraid, or unable, to look straight.

Tabbie: A female.

Take down: Deceive; get the best of.

Take 'em on: Engage them in battle.

Take it out: To undergo imprisonment in lieu of a fine.

Tart: A young woman (contraction of sweetheart).

Tater: Potato.

Tenner: A ten-pound note.

Throw in the alley: To surrender.

Time, to do: To serve a term in prison.

Time, to have no time for: To regard with impatient disfavour.

Tip: To forecast; to give; to warn.

Tipple: Strong drink; to indulge in strong drink.

Toff: An exalted person.

Togs: Clothes.

Togged: Garbed.

Tom: A girl.

Tony: Stylish.

Took: Arrested; apprehended.

Top, off one's: Out of one's mind.

Top off, to: To knock down; to assault.

Toss in the towel: See "rag".

Tossed out on my neck: Rejected.

Touch: Manner; mode; fashion.

Tough: Unfortunate; hardy; also a "tug". q.v.

Tough luck: Misfortune.

Track with: To woo; to "go walking with".

Treat, a: Excessively; abundantly.

Tucked away: Interred.

Tucker: Food.

Tug: An uncouth fellow; a hardy rogue.

Tumble to, or to take a tumble: To comprehend suddenly.

Turkey, head over: Heels over head.

Turn down: To reject; to dismiss.

'Turn, out of one's: Impertinently; uninvited.

Twig: To observe; to espy.

Umpty: An indefinite numeral.

Umptydoo: Far-fetched; "crook".

Upper-cut: In pugilism, an upward blow.

Uppish: Proud.

Up to us: Our turn; our duty.

Vag, on the: Under the provisions of the Vagrancy Act.

Wade in: Take your fill.

Wallop: To beat, chastise.

Waster: A reprobate; an utterly useless and unworthy person.

Waterworks, turn on the: To shed tears.

Welt: A blow.

Wet, to get: To become incensed; ill-tempered.

Whips: Abundance.

White (white man): A true, sterling fellow.

White-headed boy: A favourite; a pet.

Willin': Strenuous; hearty.

Win, a: Success.

Wise, to get: To comprehend; to unmask deceit.

Wise, to put: To explain; to instruct.

Wolf: To eat.

Word: To accost with fair speech.

Wot price: Behold; how now!

Wowser: A narrow-minded, intolerant person.

Yakker: Hard toil.

Yap: To talk volubly.

Yowling: Wailing; caterwauling.